UNIVERSITY and YOU

strengthen your skills develop your potential

UNIVERSITY and YOU

strengthen your skills develop your potential

Catriona Wilson
and Rebecca Wilson

Routledge
Taylor & Francis Group
LONDON AND NEW YORK

First published in 2025 by Critical Publishing Ltd

Published 2025 by Routledge
4 Park Square, Milton Park, Abingdon, Oxon OX14 4RN
605 Third Avenue, New York, NY 10017

Routledge is an imprint of the Taylor & Francis Group, an informa business

British Library Cataloguing in Publication Data
A CIP record for this book is available from the British Library

ISBN: 9781041057802 (hbk)
ISBN: 9781916925021 (pbk)
ISBN: 9781041057819 (ebk)

Text and cover design by Out of House Limited

DOI: 10.4324/9781041057819

CONTENTS

ACKNOWLEDGEMENTS

We would like to thank our colleagues at the University of St Andrews for their continued support, especially to our Vice-Principal of Education, Professor Clare Peddie. We have been inspired by numerous conversations with colleagues and students over the years that have contributed to the book.

A special thank you to our amazing colleagues at The International Education and Lifelong Learning Institute. Notably, Dr Shruti Narayanswamy for her fantastic input on Chapter 9, to Dr Eilidh Harris for her study skills expertise, especially her ideas on critical reading, and to Dr Lauren Christie who read one of the first complete drafts of the book. We are so appreciative of all of the practitioners and students who shared their insights in the book.

Similarly thank you to Olav Darge, for his highly useful feedback, and to all the anonymous reviewers whose feedback has enhanced the book greatly. Thank you to Nicola Harley and Daisy Pemble for their help with the earliest drafts.

A further thank you goes to our fantastic team of students who designed the graphics: Faith Heffernan, Oscar Hechter, Jon Tarquinio and Aurélie Coop. The book is so much more special due to their contributions. Our beautiful cover is by the talented Aurélie.

Rebecca would like to thank her family, her parents and her sister, Bern, for all their encouragement. In particular, she would like to thank Rob, who has read every proposal and every chapter and been an amazing source of support.

Cat would like to thank her family and friends for their belief and support, from the first page to the last.

Finally, we would like to thank the team at Critical Publishing for believing in the book and helping us to bring it to print. We are very grateful to Julia Morris, Lily Harrison and the wider team.

MEET THE AUTHORS

Catriona Wilson's favourite memory of studying at university is being in charge of doing the shopping for the Psychology Society lunches, and sharing sandwiches with lots of inspirational psychologists. Now she is Co-director of The International Education and Lifelong Learning Institute at the University of St Andrews. Catriona is a Fellow of CIPD and has a Master's in organisational psychology. She has 20 years of experience in skills development and is passionate about improving the student experience. She recently led the introduction of the graduate attributes framework at the University of St Andrews. Catriona is a champion of developing a holistic approach to skills development that integrates academic and professional skills, enabling students to achieve their potential during their studies and beyond.

Rebecca Wilson's favourite memory of studying at university is revising with classmates at the side of the campus lake on a surprisingly sunny day in Birmingham. Now Rebecca has over ten years' experience of pioneering skills development in both Scotland and East Africa. She is a Head of Student Development at the University of St Andrews and holds a PhD in international relations. She has practical experience of lecturing and tutoring students and specialises in the transition of students into university, including expertise in mentoring, study skills and the award-winning 'Transitions Toolkit'. Rebecca is a strong advocate for equality and inclusivity in education. She excels in motivating others, helping them to reach their potential and understand previously inaccessible topics.
For more information, visit www.universityandyou.com

INTRODUCTION

When working with new university students who are about to begin their studies, we ask some fundamental questions. We want to know:

- why they want to come to university;
- what they did before coming to university;
- what they have enjoyed and disliked about studying up until now;
- what they think learning at university level will be like.

We also ask how confident people feel about beginning university. On a 10-point scale, where 0 is not at all confident and 10 is extremely confident, the average response is 6.

Where would you be on the scale?

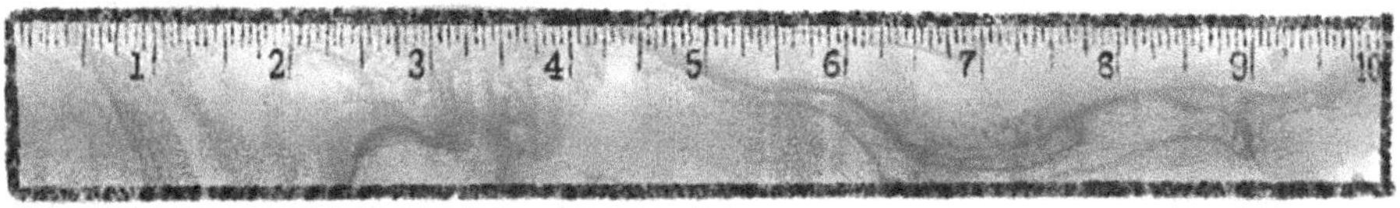

Don't worry if your answer is below 6 – it's completely normal to be nervous about making the transition to university.

Students tell us that they are excited about coming to university and that they really want to study and explore their chosen subject in more detail. They also want to meet new people and become more employable in the future. However, students are also aware that there might be challenges that they will have to navigate – some are unique to them, but others are common to many. In this book we explore some of these common challenges with you and help equip you with the knowledge and skills to meet them.

Challenges we explore with you in this book include the following:

- feeling confident enough to get the most out of university (Chapter 1);
- coping well with change (Chapter 2);
- succeeding in tough times (Chapter 3);

- understanding what university teaching is like and how you can best learn at this level (Chapter 4);
- focusing on what to spend your time on and which skills to develop (Chapter 5);
- organising yourself to stay motivated, responding to setbacks and managing your time and energy (Chapter 6);
- thinking like a university student (Chapter 7);
- understanding all the benefits diversity brings to a university community (Chapter 8);
- communicating well with lots of different people and making connections with others to help you in the future (Chapter 9);
- feeling part of a group and making change happen (Chapter 10);
- setting yourself up for success at interviews and with job or further study applications (Chapter 11);
- continuing to use this book to help you into the future (Chapter 12).

So, whether you read this book from cover to cover or dip into the sections that are most relevant to you, you should find the answers to help you thrive at university and beyond. The book is interactive; in every chapter there are activities for you to work through and features for you to explore. The more you engage with these, the more you will get out of the book overall. There are five types of activities.

	1. **Goal setting** – these activities allow you to set targets and provide something to work towards.
	2. **Reflection** – these activities allow you to look inwardly and think about your approach in different situations.
	3. **Personal development** – these activities help you to grow your skills.
	4. **Test your knowledge** – these activities help you to embed knowledge.
	5. **Research** – these activities help you to explore and learn.

Before we start the main body of the book, we would like to say well done! It's likely that you are currently attending university, about to attend or are in the process of applying. Whether you are finishing school and most of your peers are doing the same, or you are returning to education later in life, or something different, well done for taking on this challenge and investing in yourself!

A small congratulations is also needed for reading this book, whether borrowed, gifted or bought. Taking the time to read it shows the initiative you'll need to be successful in your studies. You have actively decided to use your time to research how to get the most out of university by reflecting on what type of student you would like to be.

You are embarking on an experience that might well alter the course of your life. No, not reading this book (although if it does let us know), but by becoming a student at university. You will have opportunities to stretch yourself, meet many new people, learn lots of new things and make connections. Those connections might be in relation to things you realise about yourself, or connections with the new people you meet, or connections between the things you learn.

This book aims to help you prepare for being a successful student and perform to your full potential. It will help you be open to the skills you already have and those you will develop during your university experience. We are going to do this by splitting the book into three parts.

Part 1 meets you where you are right now and helps you think about who you are as a person, where you fit in this changing world and to realise the importance of being prepared to deal with change. Part 2 looks ahead to where you are going and asks: how will you get there? The 'getting there' involves developing a range of skills that will help you in your studies and beyond. These skills fall under the categories of self-leadership, research mindset, diversity, connectivity and being a good member of the communities you are part of, along with developing your self-awareness and understanding how you learn best. Finally, Part 3 helps you think about the transition you will make after university, when you need to be able to articulate your skills and be ready for your next chapter.

This book goes beyond traditional study skills books, as mastering study techniques is only one part of the picture for being successful at university. It's important to also look at how you approach university, thinking about your mindset, resilience, how you navigate change and the fundamental skills you will need to undertake this approach.

In this book we also like to be realistic about the university experience. There will likely be parts of university you really enjoy and parts that you definitely don't. Your experience of university is yours alone and we can't predict what your journey will feel like to you. Your past experiences, your character, your abilities, your attitude and the circumstances of your life will all affect what you can put into and get out of your university experience.

Everyone will experience university in different ways. Our experiences at university included loneliness, homesickness, failure, imposter syndrome and fixed mindsets, but also freedom, exploration, a love of learning, self-growth, great friendships and achievements. These are just our experiences, of course. Yours will be different.

You might be joining university with much more life experience than either of us did. You might have the skills and confidence. You might already have a very clear sense of who you are. We think you will still find challenges though. In a sense, university is meant to be challenging and you should feel challenged at points. No challenge equals no growth. The best we can do is give you a set of tools, resources and insights that we have noticed others in your position have found helpful in their university journeys. You won't need all of the tools but you'll need to know which tool to choose when, and how to use it. Some of the tools are manual – you need to put a bit of effort in – but it is worth it.

We hope the approach and skills we share in this book will help you to thrive at university. One of the most exciting but scariest things about higher education, we think, is that success is largely within your control. Yes, some of you will have more challenges or privileges than others but with some hard work and the right approach, everyone can thrive.

Thank you for sharing a small part of your university experience with us, and spending time to think about how you can get the most out of your studies.

OVERVIEW OF BOOK

Throughout the chapters you will find key terms in bold, with a definition in the glossary at the end of the book.

Part 1 of this book asks the question: Where are you now? It explores your motivations and approach to studying in a changing environment.

Chapter 1, *You as you are: becoming the student you want to be*, gives you the opportunity to reflect on your existing skills and think about your confidence, motivations and ambitions for studying. In this chapter you will have the opportunity to complete activities that help you reflect on your strengths and aspirations, as well as what success means to you and what skills you are proud of.

Chapter 2, *You as you change*, begins to explore the transitions you are undertaking, with a focus on comfort zones and tracking your progress. You are asked to think about change you've already experienced and your coping strategies, alongside practising reflection.

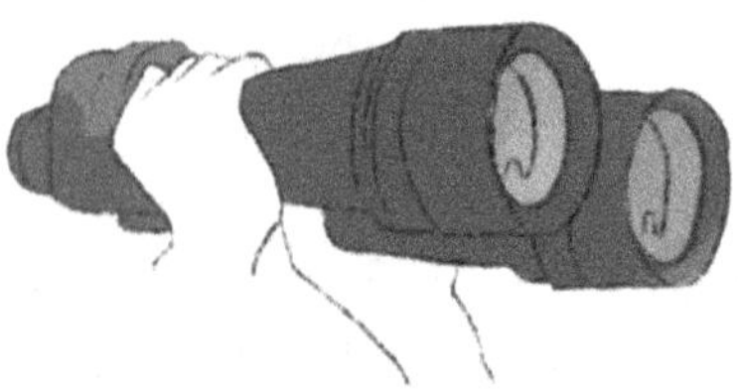

Chapter 3, *You in a changing world*, builds upon Chapter 2 but explores external changes and how you will navigate them. It looks at flexibility and resilience in a changing world and how to rise to the challenges you will face. In this chapter you are invited to think about challenges you enjoy and what resilience means to you.

Part 2 of the book asks the question, 'where are you going, and how will you get there?'. Chapter 4, *You as a student: how to build a learner*, looks at the fundamentals of studying by using cognitive science to outline the best approaches to learning and how to become an autonomous learner. You are asked to reflect on what it is to be a student, think about the difference between active and passive learning, and develop an action plan for receiving feedback.

Chapter 5, *Your skills and attributes*, looks at the importance of developing a broad range of skills while at university, and gives you tools you can use for goal setting, prioritisation and planning, as well as introducing you to a set of five skills categories containing 20 graduate attributes. You are asked to complete activities to help you develop your own list of prioritised goals and to analyse your current skill levels across the attributes. These attributes and categories will be unpacked in the remaining chapters in Part 2.

Chapter 6, *Your self-leadership*, focuses on who you are: what is it that motivates you? How do you manage your time and energy? What is your preferred style of leadership? The chapter also examines how you can be effective in teams and groups where you are not in a leadership position. Your activities for this chapter include identifying your key values, categorising how you spend your time, learning a technique for developing resilience, action planning how you best manage your time and energy, and identifying your leadership style.

Chapter 7, *Your research mindset*, looks at the foundations of effective research skills, such as note-taking and essay writing, as well as how to develop a research mindset, exploring meta cognition and critical thinking. You can enhance your learning in this chapter by reflecting on your note-taking technique and analysing question types and an academic article.

Chapter 8, *You and diverse universities*, looks at the diversity within higher education. It explores the problematic and exclusionary histories of universities, before moving on to highlight how you can thrive in this now diverse setting and appreciate cultural differences. The activities in this chapter include reflecting on what diversity means to you and what 'privilege' you bring to university, reflecting on allyship and teamwork and analysing negotiations and their outcomes.

Chapter 9, *Your connectivity*, acknowledges that you are studying in a changing world which is increasingly interconnected. The chapter examines the importance of developing global networks and practising clear communication when writing or presenting, as well as how you can best influence and negotiate. You are invited to develop some networking questions you can use and to reflect on your barriers to effective communication.

Chapter 10, *You, agency and community*, explores the different communities you enter as a student. This includes thinking of yourself as someone who can affect change and acting with ethical awareness and integrity, particularly regarding your academic conduct. The associated activities in this chapter ask you to identify the communities you are part of and the inspirational changes agents within them, to think about what it means to be part of your academic discipline and to analyse academic writing.

Part 3 of this book concentrates on how you can articulate your strengths and the skills you develop while at university. Chapter 11, *Connecting and articulating your skills*, hones in on how you can connect your skills and the strengths this creates in you, as well as the connection between skills and the activities that develop them. Following on from this, the chapter outlines when you might have to talk about your skills and suggests some tips and techniques to help with this. You are asked to identify your strongest skills combinations, create a map of your activities and skills, and practise the 'STAR' technique for articulating your skills, as well as to think about ways that you can develop particular attributes.

The final chapter of this book asks the question *What do you do now?* and lays out a number of practical steps you can take to make the most of your learning. To help with this you are invited to identify your own first steps to get your skills development plan started, to think about what additional resources and support you will need, and to research the student and career support in place for you at your university. To round things off, you are asked to write down one take-away message from each of the preceding 11 chapters to make sure you have got the most out of this book and are well on the way to developing the skills, behaviours and mindset necessary for success in university and beyond.

PART 1

Where are you now?

CHAPTER 1

YOU AS YOU ARE: BECOMING THE STUDENT YOU WANT TO BE

CHALLENGES WE EXPLORE IN THIS CHAPTER

In this chapter we explore three questions:

1. why you decided to come to university;
2. why you want to be a student and, most importantly;
3. how you can become the student you want to be.

We begin by looking at what motivates you as a student and, in particular, what drives you to study and be engaged. Building on this, we then ask you to consider your ambitions and think about what you would like to achieve while at university and how the belief in yourself will impact your university experience. The final sections of this chapter look at how to develop your **skills** in order to grow your confidence and pursue your ambitions. We then take a step back and ask: what is a skill? This chapter concludes by encouraging you to think about how you can approach your university experience holistically, developing skills not only in your **curricular** or academic subjects, but in your **co-curricular** and **extra-curricular** activities too, setting you up to strengthen your skills and develop your potential in the best possible way.

INTENDED LEARNING OUTCOMES

By the end of this chapter, you should be able to:

- reflect on your motivations for being at university;
- explore your ambitions for being a student;

→

- understand what (self) confidence is and identify strategies to develop your confidence;
- gain awareness of why reflecting on your skills is important;
- identify development opportunities outside of your academic environment.

1.1 EXPLORING YOUR MOTIVATIONS FOR APPLYING TO UNIVERSITY

You may have spent hours (or days) thinking about this question, or it may not have even crossed your mind: why did you decide to go to university?

There could be many reasons why you have decided to study at university. It may be that you have a particular career path in mind and your course is the first step in getting your dream job. You may have a great passion for a certain subject that you want to study in depth and see where it takes you. You may want to study something that gives you lots of career options, or you may not be sure what to do next in your life and attending university feels like a natural next step. Maybe you came to university to experience a university lifestyle and grow your social network, and experience living somewhere new. It's likely that there are multiple reasons why you decided to study at university, and it's likely these **motivations** will shift during your years of study.

STUDENT INSIGHT

Adèle Abada, mathematics and physics, second year

The main attraction of university is the freedom it allows. While it can be intimidating to be lost in a crowd of students it is also the best place to learn how to work and be on your own.

University makes room for choice, courses, extracurriculars, friends … I found it appealing because it is big enough for everyone to fit in in their own way.

I wanted to study at university for the opportunity to study subjects at a high level from not only professors but researchers and the possibility to partake in research early on in my studies. I believed it would offer me professional and academic opportunities I couldn't have found outside a university.

The motivations to both apply and commit to university can be divided into **intrinsic motivations** and **extrinsic motivations.**

- Intrinsic motivation: Students are motivated by the inherent pleasure or satisfaction of the experience. Students are often identified as being intrinsically motivated if they are motivated by the passion for their subject. For example, a student completing a history degree may have chosen it simply because they love history, and that is all the motivation they need to complete their course.
- Extrinsic motivation: Students are motivated by the external incentives of the activity. Students are often identified as extrinsically motivated if they want a specific outcome for their course. For example, a student completing an accounting degree may have chosen it in order to get a well-paid job after university.

However, this dichotomy over-simplifies what motivation is and, crucially, what it means to each individual student. Thinking about whether you are primarily motivated by intrinsic or extrinsic factors is an interesting starting point, but our decisions are never this straightforward. Thinking about the decision to go to university and study a specific subject, you were likely motivated by many factors, some intrinsic and some extrinsic.

Recently, a third category has been added to the discussion around motivation: 'academic motivation', which the researchers Locke and Schattke (2019) argue is the desire 'to do well' in your studies. This is distinct from intrinsic motivation as you can dislike your subject, or not be passionate about it, but still want to succeed and vice versa.

Try to visualise your motivations in the form of a pie chart. What percentage of the pie would be intrinsic, extrinsic and academic? It's likely this split will change throughout your degree, and it's worth noting that each of you will have a unique set of motivations. An 'excellent student' is not someone who is only driven by their love of their subject; they are motivated and engaged regardless of where the motivation comes from.

Perhaps a more useful question to determine your motivation is: what makes you get out of bed in the morning? What excites you most about being at university? Or, a somewhat odd question: if you could win an award in anything, what would it be? This does not need to be a real award; it could be world's greatest doctor/engineer/writer/entrepreneur. It could be a prize for the greatest new discovery or invention, or for producing the most creative piece of artwork.

ACTIVITY 1.1

Award

- You can add your award to the medal below:

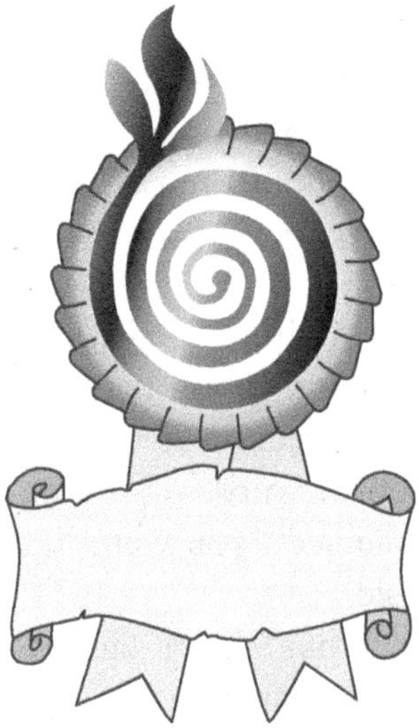

Think about how your university journey is going to help you achieve this award (luckily you are the one and only judge). If your award is for the 'greatest engineer' and you're on an engineering degree, this is quite straightforward. If your award is for most creative artwork, it might be that you are aware your degree is developing your creativity skills and adding to your awareness of different types of art throughout history. If you can't find a way to tie your medal to your degree, later in this chapter we will discuss holistic skills, which will help you to think more widely about the skills you will develop in your degree and how these can help you to achieve your award. University is a brilliant experience, but it is also challenging and a lot of hard work. Holding on to your motivations and aiming for your imaginary medal will help you keep focused and driven, especially during challenging times.

When you find this drive, you can use this to think of macro and micro motivations. Macro motivations are larger goals that push decisions such as what optional modules to take, what internships to apply for or what extra-curricular activities to engage with. You will also have micro motivations that will link to your macro motivations, but will help you focus day to day. For example, your macro motivations may have led you to write an application to apply for an internship at a local radio station; your micro motivations may be to have your CV checked to fulfil this.

You can use your macro motivations to help stay focused throughout the day. The American motivational speaker and author Mel Robbins argues that '*motivation is garbage*' and that in order to achieve your goals, self-discipline is required instead. Robbins highlights that it's unlikely that you will want to wake up early to undertake your activity, and instead you have to make yourself do it (Robbins, 2017, p 131). While this book does not take such a strong stance on motivation, there is a lot of truth in the idea that waiting for motivation to come is not always effective. Applying this thinking to university, while you may not always *feel* like doing the course reading, if you wait until you feel like it, you may never do it. Instead, you need to actively structure the task into your day. When reflecting on your motivations, it can be useful to think about your ambitions for your time at university, as we will do now.

1.2 PURSUING YOUR AMBITIONS: WHAT ARE YOUR STUDIES LEADING TO?

Imagine you were delivering a speech at your graduation. Before this speech, your Vice-Chancellor (the leader of the university) introduces you and your outstanding achievements as a student. What would you want them to say? Would they note your excellent academic accomplishments? Your wide social group? Your ability to successfully manage multiple commitments and still excel in your studies? Or will they speak about you leading the ultimate frisbee team to sporting victory? Use the speech bubble in Activity 1.2 to outline what you would want to be remembered or celebrated for once you finish university:

ACTIVITY 1.2

Graduating achievements

- Write these outcomes down and put them somewhere you will see daily, possibly on your desk, the back of your door or on your mirror. This will be a powerful motivator and will help you to shape your goals, which we explore further in Chapter 5.

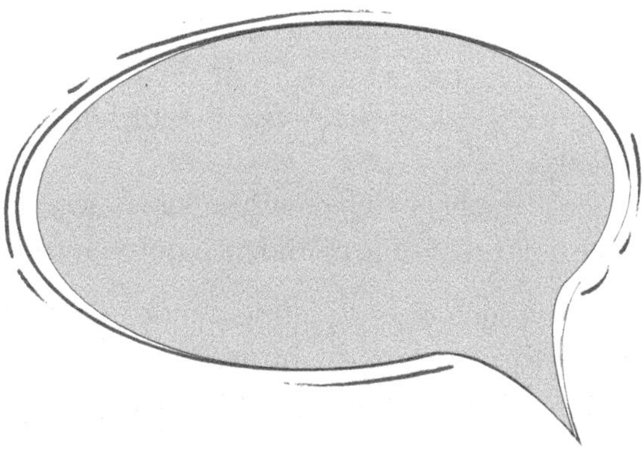

The purpose of this activity is to highlight your **values** and ambitions, and to get you really thinking about what's important to you and to your identity. By placing a focus on what you would like to achieve during your degree on a long-term basis, you can start to reflect on what your ambitions are. Exploring these ambitions will be useful in choosing what to focus on at university, from choosing modules to co-curricular and extra-curricular activities. If you found this activity useful, you may also wish to create your dream CV, listing the accomplishments that you would like to achieve by the end of your degree, or even in the next five to ten years.

If you're still figuring out what your ambitions are, that's completely fine. Think about what you are most excited about: what activities do you most enjoy and what makes you 'feel alive'? You can also think about the activities you don't enjoy or that you find challenging. For example, you may hate being meticulous and find attention to detail quite frustrating. These motivations and challenges will be affected by many aspects of your life, including **neurodiversity**, previous experience and your personality. You can learn what you find motivating and enjoyable or challenging by reflecting on your skills development and confidence. This is something that is explored in the remainder of the chapter.

1.3 BUILDING CONFIDENCE AND DEALING WITH IMPOSTER SYNDROME

We all know a 'confident' person; they are the ones who answer the questions in class, suggest ideas at work, perhaps wear what my mum would call 'bold' outfits. Maybe you have even been called confident or strive to be like this person.

Often when we see people as confident, we think that this is all encompassing, that they must be confident in every activity they undertake. However, confidence comes and goes, and is contextual according to the task, the situation and even the day. In addition, someone who displays confidence is not always confident, and often someone who's really underconfident can overcompensate and appear more confident than they actually are.

We can understand confidence as belief in something or someone. When we talk about confidence, this could be your confidence in your car reliably taking you to class or your confidence in the staff who work at the local café to produce a tasty lunch. In this book, when we speak about developing or building confidence, we are interested in **self-confidence**.

Therefore, if confidence is the belief in something or someone then *self-confidence* is a belief in yourself. We can break self-confidence down into three parts:

1. belief in your own ability, such as completing a task or an activity;
2. predicting your own performance in the future;
3. reflecting on your actions after you have completed a task.

Part 1, believing in your own abilities, can be seen as how you engage in the present. For example, whether you have the confidence to complete an immediate task such as writing a lab report.

Part 2 looks at predicting your performance in the future; this may be longer term or involve bigger tasks, such as your ability to complete an entire module or even your degree.

Part 3, which is one we often neglect when thinking about confidence, is having a realistic overview of your previous actions and how you completed them. For example, if you are lacking confidence, you may say it was just a fluke or luck rather than reflecting on your own hard work and appreciating how this led to your success. In comparison, if you are **overconfident**, you may not be able to reflect on how your lack of hard work led to a challenging situation and instead blame only external factors.

Of course, when reflecting on past successes or failures, there will always be many external and internal influencing factors – things we could have changed or done differently or that were outside our sphere of control (examined in Chapter 2). What is important with self-belief is to be able to acknowledge the things that you could have done differently or did well, in order to change or replicate these in the future.

One area of confidence you may have heard of is **imposter syndrome**, where you lack so much confidence you feel like a fraud. Many university students will face imposter syndrome during their degree, so it's important to unpack this issue. Valerie Young (2011), the leading expert on the topic, has identified five categories within imposter syndrome.

1. Perfectionist: setting unattainable goals for themselves and then faces self-doubt when they are unable to achieve the goal.
2. Superwoman/man/person: feeling insecure in comparison to their perceived superior peers; they consistently overwork, seeking validation.
3. Natural genius: believing they are naturally gifted, they give themselves not only unattainable goals but expect themselves to master a subject or new challenge immediately.
4. Soloist: feeling that asking for help will reveal their fraudulence.
5. Expert: fearing they will be seen as incompetent, or even stupid, they base their success on how much they know.

You may relate to one or many of these categories. It's most likely there will be times when your peers know more than you, but imposter syndrome is more than this. Imposter syndrome is the feeling you don't belong at university or that you are going to get 'caught' for knowing so little. This can impact anyone regardless of gender identity, previous experience or the grades you receive. The next section of this chapter further unpacks confidence before looking at strategies on how to improve your self-belief and tackle imposter syndrome.

LACKING SELF-CONFIDENCE

A lack of self-confidence or self-belief can be very frustrating for your university studies and for life in general. There are four main challenges you may face if you are lacking in self-confidence:

1. doubt;
2. procrastination;
3. lack of commitment;
4. over commitment.

Unsurprisingly, doubt is one of the biggest challenges you'll face when lacking self-confidence: a feeling of uncertainty about everything you do. In your university studies, this is often manifested as doubt in your ability to understand the material, complete a project or even make new friends.

Procrastination affects almost everyone and is a topic that we will continue to look at throughout this book, especially in Chapter 6. When we are not feeling confident, when we think we are not good enough to complete a task (such as writing an essay), we put it off and procrastinate, hoping that in the future we will feel more confident.

Our final two challenges are a lack of commitment and over commitment. For many people, a lack of commitment would not be surprising when thinking of someone who lacks self-confidence. It might be that you don't sign up to be captain of your sports team or group leader of a project for your course because you don't believe you have the ability to do so. This can become a self-fulfilling prophecy, as when you don't think you have the skills or ability to do something, you don't try to do it and, therefore, you never have the opportunity to build your confidence in this area. In contrast to this, some students will overcompensate for their low self-confidence and try to commit to lots of different activities. But over-committing to things means you won't have the time or the energy to complete your tasks to a standard that you are happy with. Consequently, you can feel like you are not achieving what you would like to, which can be demoralising rather than confidence building.

A final challenge you may face if lacking self-confidence is your sense of identity. Each of you reading this book has your own unique identity and sense of self, influenced by many factors. It is therefore important to consider **intersectionality** when building confidence. Here, we are not stating that someone's identity should impact their student experience, but we know that characteristics such as race, ethnicity, class, gender identity, disability, neurodiversity and many other factors do affect their experience (Bhopal, 2020). Your identity can impact your sense of belonging within your subject area and university (which we explore in more detail in Chapter 8).

OVERCONFIDENCE

What might not be obvious is that it can be problematic to be overconfident! Of course, a good level of self-belief is essential to complete your work, succeed at university and generally be happy in day-to-day life. Low confidence makes it difficult to work effectively and have a joyful university experience, but so too does **overconfidence**.

Overconfidence is overestimating your abilities. We need a certain amount of confidence in order to try something for the first time (whether this is joining a sports team or answering a question in class). However, when we become overconfident, we can become ignorant and naïve. A primary example is thinking that you understand the text or the formulas explained in a lecture to a greater extent than you actually do. As a consequence, it's likely that your exam or assignment will not go as hoped or you will need to spend more time than you initially planned to try to understand the principles. Active learning techniques can help with this, which we discuss in Chapter 4.

There are three challenges which can emerge from being overconfident at university:

1. not seeking help;
2. unrealistic expectations;
3. poor judgement and planning.

First, and something you won't necessarily automatically associate with being overconfident, is not seeking help. If you have blind faith that you can write the perfect piece of coursework, you may not seek help. Therefore, you might not only get a lower grade than you had hoped, but you will also risk further learning. It is likely that your university will have a team of dedicated specialists to help you develop your writing skills or direct you to an excellent textbook or a reliable YouTube video on the subject matter, and we would strongly encourage you to engage with them for your own development.

A second outcome of being overconfident is having unrealistic expectations and the 'illusions of grandeur' that come with this. Having unrealistic expectations can lead to a misunderstanding of the break-down of steps you need to complete a task or master a skill. When you have unrealistic expectations, your university experience can be challenging. You may over-commit to activities, believing that you have the ability to take on many different tasks, projects and activities, but quite often that isn't the case. Equally, it may be that you're overly ambitious about completing that first essay and do not understand the different steps that go into essay writing, including editing and proofreading.

One challenge that comes from overconfidence is poor judgement and planning. For example, you may not allow enough time to complete a task, or if you think you have the knowledge required to complete the task already, you may not plan to get adequate resources such as library books in order to complete it.

As we have discovered, a person is neither confident, underconfident or overconfident; it really swings between tasks and days. It's good to reflect on your confidence: being able to judge your confidence is a skill which you can develop with time and practice. For example, knowing how long it takes you to complete a piece of reading or coursework, or minutes of a meeting, will be invaluable for your **time management** and success at university.

COMPARING YOURSELF TO OTHERS

One of the most common things we hear students say throughout their university journey is that they feel less prepared or capable than their peers. There seems to be a phenomenon among students that everyone else is on top of their work and thriving at university, when in reality they are not. This problem is escalated by social media where it is very easy to compare your entire life with a single snippet from someone else's. Everyone is on their own path; comparing your university journey to someone else's is not helpful. Especially when you have different experiences, challenges and neurodiverse approaches. You may have heard the famous phrase from Theodore Roosevelt that '*comparison is the thief of joy*'.

Comparing ourselves to others can subtract from our own success, which is a difficult issue to overcome. We would encourage you to come up with your own definition of success, rather than comparing yourself to what other people have achieved and how you are matching up to their standards. For example, your definition of success may be to get all of your assessed work in on time and to join a sports team in your first **semester**. When you begin comparing yourself to others, you can reflect back on your own goals and think that they are your priorities for now. If other people are finding success in one of your priorities, try and be inspired by this, thinking about how you can learn from their successes.

ACTIVITY 1.3

Priorities and evidence of success

- Fill in the table to describe what success might look like for you.

Example:

Priority	Evidence of success
Be actively involved in a student society or club	Join new society and attend 90% of meetings in first semester

Priority	Evidence of success

PERFECTIONISM

If you are struggling with low self-belief, imposter syndrome or comparing yourself to others, you may be struggling with **perfectionism**: the feeling that your work, or sadly sometimes you, will never be good enough, as you are aiming for everything to be exact. This can be incredibly unmotivating as you constantly try to achieve an unachievable goal. Even if you do manage to achieve an overambitious goal and are struggling with perfectionism, the bar that you are trying to reach will constantly move, meaning that you will never be satisfied. This can end up becoming a negative cycle as you set unrealistic goals which you cannot obtain, and so your confidence drops.

Unfortunately, showing perfectionism towards part of your studies is quite common. This is especially prevalent among students who worked very hard in college, school or in the workplace to gain their place at university. In addition, the burden of student debt that you are accruing while at university can result in increased pressure on yourself to 'make the most of it', or there may be external pressures such as from family members or sponsors who are paying for your degree. Therefore, it is important to explore your aims, questioning whether they are realistic or if you're engaging in perfectionism.

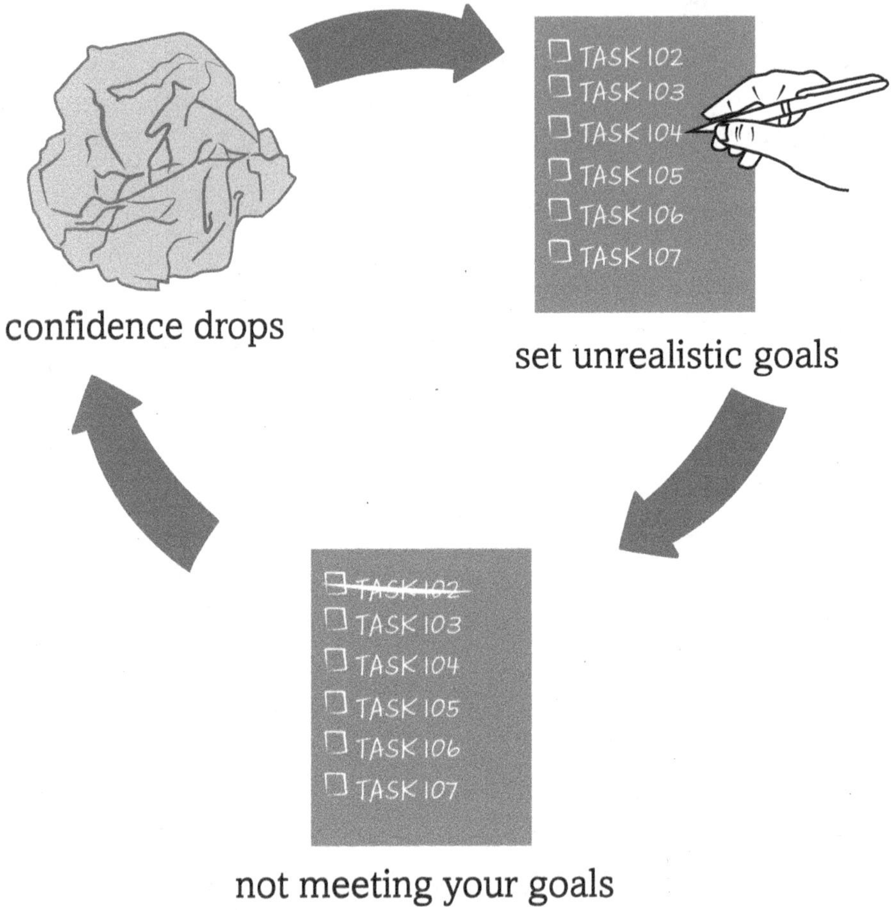

FIGURE 1.1: A negative goal-setting cycle

Perfectionism can also be a form of procrastination or a reason why you are engaging in procrastinating tendencies. This often takes the form of engaging in the **mindset** that a piece of work will never be to the desired standard so '*why should I even try?*' We explore procrastination in more detail in Chapter 6.

Perfectionism is difficult to overcome. If you feel this is having an impact on your well-being (as we explore in Chapter 2), make sure you seek support at your university. One way to lessen the effects of perfectionism is to aim for excellent rather than perfect. Something can be excellent, created to an extremely high standard, but there are still things that you would like to change or do differently next time. Just because something isn't perfect doesn't mean that it doesn't do the job; in order to get a first-class degree, which is an exceptional qualification, you have to get 70 per cent, not 100 per cent. We are not suggesting that everyone should aim to obtain a first-class degree (there are thousands of examples of people who did not gain a first-class degree and went on to be very successful), but rather highlighting that a first-class degree does not require perfection. To conclude in more academic terms, Voltaire (a French philosopher), once said '*don't let the perfect be the enemy of the good*'; in other words, don't let perfectionism become a barrier to achieving something great.

Perfectionism is about looking at your goals and deciding if they are realistic for you. Sometimes we have to prioritise and understand that it's better to get a lot of things done to a high standard rather than one or two things done to a perfect standard. If you fear that you are engaging in perfectionism, one helpful exercise is to reflect and ask yourself, if a friend had told you these standards would you think they were reasonable? We are far harsher on ourselves than on others and can often be our own worst critics.

DEVELOPING YOUR CONFIDENCE

Unfortunately, there is no magic answer to the question of how to develop your confidence, but there are several steps you can take to ensure that your confidence reaches (and is maintained at) a good level, neither lacking self-belief nor overestimating your skill levels, while continuing to develop.

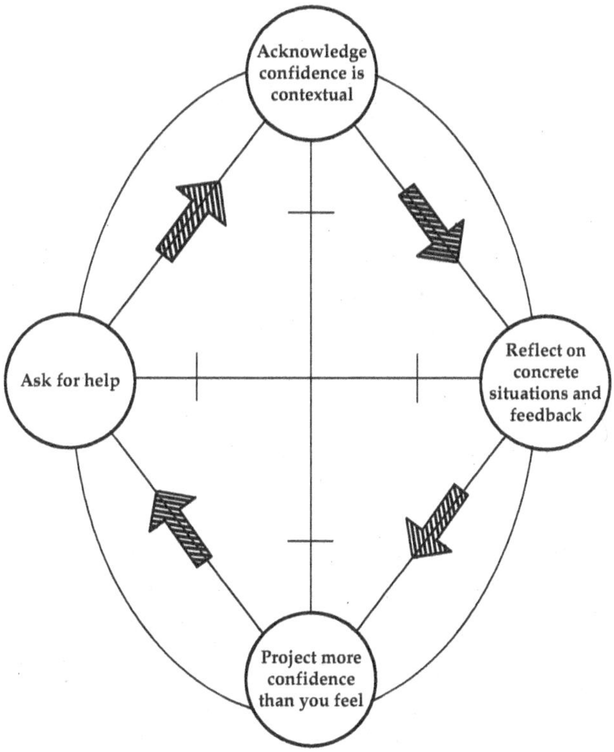

FIGURE 1.2: Developing your confidence

ACKNOWLEDGE THAT CONFIDENCE IS CONTEXTUAL

One of the fundamental ways to develop your confidence is to acknowledge that confidence is contextual and ever-changing. This removes the pressure of thinking that you have to become a super-confident person in all areas of your life: confidence is a belief, not an identity.

You can start by thinking about how you can develop your confidence in a specific area. By setting goals that are contextual, you can make the situation far more manageable than by trying to change your entire approach. For example, instead of thinking '*I wish I was more confident*', you can break this down into a specific goal: '*I wish I was more confident at delivering presentations*' or '*I wish I was better at delivering academic presentations on maths in class*'. You can see that this has gone from a huge and overwhelming challenge to quite a specific goal that you could then devise an action plan for (as we explore in Chapter 5). Beyond this, the thought that confidence is something that comes and goes means that you have the power to do something about it and develop this area.

REFLECT ON CONCRETE SITUATIONS AND FEEDBACK

Building upon this, you can reflect on concrete situations and feedback in order to develop your self-confidence. When you lack self-belief, it becomes very easy to catastrophise, causing you to become overly critical regarding your predicted performance or **reflection** on events, often deciding that the worst possible outcome will or did happen. Realistically, this is unlikely to happen. Of course, there will be presentations that don't go to plan, awkward conversations with new flatmates and exams that did not go as hoped. However, you will not be the first or last person that this happened to, and one situation does not define who you are as a person. Luckily, we normally get a chance to re-sit an exam or speak again with the new person next door.

Therefore, when trying to build your self-confidence, your own interpretation of events can be quite often skewed by unrealistic expectations or catastrophised reflections. Instead, it can be helpful to focus on tangible outcomes and, if possible, feedback from an event. For example, rather than deciding that all of your answers in class are awful, think about the response your lecturer and peers gave to you. It's likely that a lot of the questions asked in your classes are open to interpretation, rather than being a yes or no answer. Even if you give a wrong answer, you are still contributing to the class by opening up topics for debate or by helping another student who got the answer wrong to understand it too (you won't be the only one with the wrong answer!). You can also look at feedback you may already have; one of the primary resources you can refer back to is your assessed coursework. When considering your feedback, don't simply focus upon the areas for improvement – also take note of all the great things that you did! Reflect on how you produced the piece of work to this standard; a great way to do this is to use a feedback tool, as outlined in Chapter 4.

PROJECT MORE CONFIDENCE THAN YOU FEEL (WHEN APPROPRIATE)

The next step in developing your confidence is trying to project more confidence than you feel. This will not work in all situations but sometimes acting confident, even if you don't feel it, is one of the best ways to develop confidence. Public speaking is an excellent example: maybe you've joined a society and you'd really like to get more involved, but you're too nervous to share your ideas. If you pretend that you are confident, appearing to speak calmly, the likelihood is that eventually you will stop needing to pretend to be confident as you actually will be. The idea of 'fake it until you make it' does have some truth to it!

Part of Rebecca's job is to deliver lectures on a range of topics such as critical thinking and research skills. When first delivering these lectures, she can vividly remember feeling very nervous, despite having expertise in the area. However, she knew if she stood up in front of a class worried, and started speaking really quickly, she would deliver a poor lecture. Rebecca also believed that this would become a self-fulfilling prophecy: if she was nervous (and therefore the lecture did not go well), she would have grounds to be anxious in the future, and this could become a vicious circle.

It sounds strange, but she just pretended to be confident. Rebecca thought about great lectures that she had seen and tried to emulate this behaviour. She aimed to speak clearly and have relaxed body language. After a while, she could stop pretending to be confident because she slowly gained confidence with practice. Of course, there are times when she still gets nervous, such as presenting new materials or to particularly big classes, but her 'pretend' confidence developed into the real thing.

ASK FOR HELP

Our final tip is simple: ask for help. One of the best things about being at university is the extensive support system that you have access to. If you are really struggling with your confidence, then you may be able to access counselling or **coaching**. If you are looking to build confidence in certain areas, you could ask your lecturers for feedback in this area, such as how to improve your essay writing skills. Moreover, there might be a workshop, a book in the library or a trustworthy video on YouTube you could access.

PRACTITIONER INSIGHT

Dr Joseph Bowen, lecturer in moral and political philosophy, University of Leeds

Sometimes you forget how well you've done to get to where you are. You do well at school, working towards getting into university, and suddenly you find yourself surrounded by a bunch of other people who've done really well to get into university. They ask great questions in classes. They found the reading really easy. They seem to have it together. They seem not to be worried.

This will keep happening as you progress. When I started my masters, suddenly everyone around me was brilliant. I started my PhD, suddenly everyone around me was again brilliant. But at each stage, I had done really well to get to where I'd got. Sometimes I needed to stop and remind myself that – remember that I had done well to get to where I was, and stop beating myself up by thinking about how others were doing.

1.4 REFLECTING ON YOUR EXISTING SKILLS AND HOW YOU GAINED THEM

In this book, we focus a lot on **skills** and how you can develop them to make the most of your time at university. Skills are fundamental to success in all areas of your life, from knowing how to make the perfect omelette to undertaking critical analysis of an academic article.

A skill can be understood as an ability or the knowledge required to undertake a task. A fundamental aspect of a skill is that it can be learnt; it is not a natural talent (ie one that you either do or do not have), but an area that, with practice, you can develop. No one is born with the ability to make the perfect omelette: while some people may find it harder than others and face different challenges, we all have the opportunity to practise this until we become experts.

The concept that a skill is something that can be learnt is fundamental to this book. Among other things, we will outline how to develop your skills holistically and provide different directions and tools for you to be able to do this. However, if you take the mindset that you cannot develop certain skills, that it is pre-determined that you are either good or bad at something, you will find the process far more difficult (a **growth mindset** is extremely important; we explore this in detail in Chapter 2). So, we invite you to undertake your skills development with an open mind so that you can develop all of the areas we will speak about, even if you do not currently feel comfortable in this area.

We can categorise essential skills for your success at university into overlapping areas – academic, professional and digital skills being the most prominent. While the boundaries between these categories are somewhat blurred, we can understand them as the following.

Academic skills: Skills essential to success in your university studies. For example:

- critical thinking;
- reading;
- writing;
- time management;
- analysis.

Professional skills: Skills essential to endeavours relating to your career, such as internships and graduate jobs, but also skills key to co- and extra-curricular activities. For example:

- communication;
- project management;
- time management;
- presentation skills;
- team working.

Digital skills: Also known as technological skills, these are skills that are essential in using technology or computers. For example:

- using online learning platforms or virtual learning environments (VLEs);
- proficiency using Microsoft Office and presentation software;
- being able to work using good cybersecurity practices;
- an awareness of Artificial Intelligence (AI) and how to navigate it in your studies and life.

You can already see a lot of crossover between these three categories. For example, you will need digital skills to undertake many academic and professional skills. Time management could be placed in all three categories. There is also crossover with other skills, such as presentation skills, which could be included in both academic and professional skills.

In addition to these are general life skills; these again include time management and self-organisation, as well as practical skills such as budget management, knowing how to cook and knowing how to use a washing machine (if you are in halls of residence, mastering the finicky and temperamental shared machines can be especially difficult!). You shouldn't underestimate the profound impact these life skills will have on navigating your degree. You can have excellent understanding of your topic and excellent critical reading skills, but if you are spending your time struggling to look after yourself, these will not matter.

Once you begin the process of identifying the different skills you will need to succeed at university, you can develop them and reflect on your current confidence and competence in these areas, highlighting what you would like to improve. Your ability to reflect upon the status of your skills is fundamental to skills development. We are often surprised at students' lack of ability to reflect on their skills, how they developed them and what they would like to do next. We would highly recommend getting used to this reflective practice early on in your university journey, as being able to evidence your skills will be really useful when it comes to applying for society positions, internships and jobs. The ability to identify the skills that you have developed, and give examples of how you have developed them and when you used them, will stand you in good stead for life at university and beyond, and therefore is central to this book.

Having said this, the personal progression and satisfaction you feel when you are able to reflect upon and recognise your skills is also very important. It allows you to see the progression that your time and practice has led to and highlights areas of expertise that you may wish to develop or improve in. It is all vital to your own motivation, especially in higher education. As there is a great shift in autonomy, you are responsible not only for your own work but also for your own sense of achievement and skills development.

Therefore, it is important to take the time to think about what your skills are, how you got these skills and how you will develop them. It is important to consider how you can develop your skills holistically. By this we mean that you can develop your communication skills by taking part in a student society that has regular meetings, but this will also help to develop your communication skills that you use in class, for your part-time job or if you undertake an internship. Seeing skills as singular and context specific is often a limiting approach to learning. In Chapter 5, we look in detail at how to set goals and map your skills development.

ACTIVITY 1.4

Identifying skills

- Fill in the table below to list three skills that you are proud of. These can be generic skills, such as communication, or they can be small practical skills, such as making that perfect omelette or finding the perfect setting on the communal washing machine (we hope they are less complicated than when we last lived in a halls of residence).

Skill 1	
Skill 2	
Skill 3	

- How did it feel to not only think of your ability in various skills, but then choose ones you were proud of?

1.5 THINKING BEYOND YOUR STUDIES: DEVELOPING THROUGH CURRICULAR, CO-CURRICULAR AND EXTRA-CURRICULAR OPPORTUNITIES

You may have already come across the terms curricular, co-curricular and extra-curricular. These are three different areas where you'll have the opportunity to develop skills, learn new things and create enjoyable and fun memories while studying.

- Curricular: an area that is directly linked to your studies. This is most likely something that is assessed or that will be part of your core modules or classes.
- Co-curricular: something that is linked to your studies that, for example, you may not be assessed on. This may include essay writing workshops which will help with your studies or a skills award, where you attend workshops run by the university.
- Extra-curricular: activities which take place through the university but are not academic. Examples include sports clubs, societies such as theatre, model UN or more niche groups of interest.

One of the most special things about attending university is the opportunity to engage in a multitude of different activities and meet like-minded people alongside your studies. Whether you are continuing a sport you have played since you were young, or learning a brand-new activity such as debating, co- and extra-curricular activities are often integral parts of a university experience.

We are of course aware that students' individual circumstances will place limitations on how much they can engage with these co- and extra-curricular activities, especially those who study remotely or do not live near their campus, those who have caring responsibilities, or those who have to undertake many hours of paid employment to support their studies. Despite these circumstances, you can still apply a holistic approach to part of your university experience. For example, you are likely to have excellent time and project management skills by co-ordinating different personal responsibilities, such as family commitments, and if you have a part-time job you will still develop strong communication skills.

CHAPTER SUMMARY

In this chapter, we looked at why you want to be a student and what type of student you want to be. For some of you, this may have been an easy activity; it may be that you have planned why, where and how you're going to study for years. But for many of you, this won't be true. You might still be figuring out why you're even at university, possibly questioning whether your course was the best option and how you're going to choose from the multiple different decisions you face between modules, societies and how to spend your time. These are not easy questions to answer, and whether you've planned out the next three to four years, or you're still figuring it out, this chapter has hopefully helped you to start thinking about the student you want to be and how you can get there.

The chapter started by looking at motivations and ambitions, thinking about what drives your ambition. We then spent a lot of time looking at confidence and the factors that may limit these ambitions. By exploring confidence as contextual, you can start to develop strategies to improve your self-belief as a university student. To conclude the chapter, we looked at how you're going to put this new confidence into practice to pursue your ambitions. To do this, we first looked at what we mean by skills, highlighting the fact that we take a holistic approach to university study. While, of course, you're at university to study, co-curricular and extra-curricular activities are also a fundamental part of your university journey.

TOP TIPS AND NEXT STEPS

- Understanding your motivations and ambitions will help you make the most of your university journey.
- Remember that self-confidence is contextual and can be developed. A person is neither confident nor lacking in confidence. It depends on the situation and task!
- Using Figure 1.2, create an action plan for how you will develop your confidence.
- Think holistically about your skills development and approach to university – studies are important but so are other projects, commitments and co-/extra-curricular activities.

CHAPTER 2

YOU AS YOU CHANGE

CHALLENGES WE EXPLORE IN THIS CHAPTER

In this chapter, we look at change. This is a huge topic, so we will specifically look at how to *navigate* change. The challenge many students face is how to cope with change well. We can help you prepare for this by looking at the normality of change, and how it's common in our day-to-day life, from car journeys to breakfasts. We will then think about our **comfort zones**, how to engage with our **challenge zone** and how to avoid the **danger zone**! To further help you tackle change well, we'll show you how to switch on your growth mindset and what you can do to coach yourself through change, look after your well-being and track your progress.

One of the biggest things to remember when dealing with transitions, whether it is starting university, entering final year or even graduating, is that change takes time to get used to! Hopefully, this chapter will act as an indispensable guide to help you navigate change.

INTENDED LEARNING OUTCOMES

By the end of this chapter, you should be able to:

- reflect on transitions you have already undertaken;
- explore strategies for navigating transitions, specifically looking at your mindset and how coaching techniques can help you with this navigation;
- identify techniques for keeping track of your progress.

2.1 WAYS YOU'VE CHANGED ALREADY AND WHAT PROMPTED THE CHANGE

It is likely that you have already navigated multiple changes, from starting new schools and jobs to perhaps moving to a new place. Most notably, you'll have embarked (or will be about to) on one of the biggest changes of your life so far: starting university. Alongside this are other substantial changes you may undertake (or already have, such as moving country or having children). You will have had smaller, but no less significant, changes too, from starting a new school year to fitting into a new position at work or starting a new sport or hobby. We encounter changes every day; however, we often don't realise or see these things as a change, such as roadworks redirecting our journey or trying a new cereal for breakfast. Some of these changes you will have made consciously, such as choosing a new cereal, while others will have been out of your control, such as your journey being rerouted due to roadworks.

ACTIVITY 2.1

Change I have already undertaken

What is important to consider here is that change is part of our daily lives; it's both big and small, and happens whether we choose to consciously undertake it or whether it just happens to us and is beyond our control. Use this activity to think about three changes you have undertaken. We have given you an example to start.

A change I have undertaken is:

- starting college to study history, English and drama during my A levels at college.
-
-
-

How you navigate change will be one of the biggest indicators of your success, and that's why it's such a central theme of this book. Whether you have prompted the change, for example by applying to university, or it happened unexpectedly, such as learning a **referencing** system you were previously unaware of, your approach to these changes will have a substantial impact on your university experience.

Of course, change is often a mixture of things we choose and things that are outside of our control. In this chapter we focus on how to respond and thrive during these changes. Therefore, the remainder of this chapter will provide some practical support to navigate change, in order for you to have the best experience possible at university.

2.2 HOW TO NAVIGATE TRANSITIONS

A useful way to navigate transitions is to think about a comfort zone, a challenge zone and a danger zone.

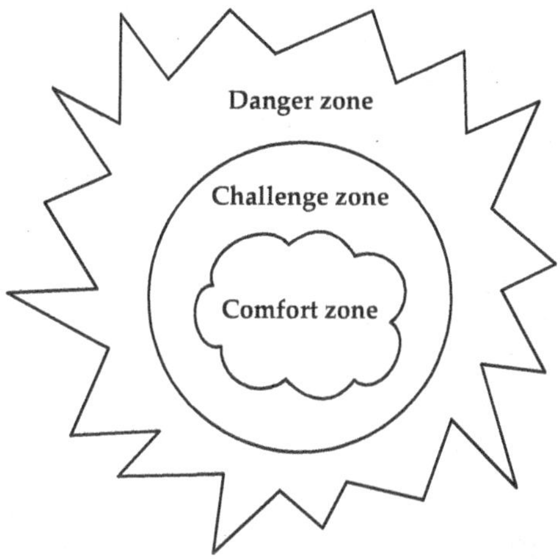

FIGURE 2.1: Transition zones

'Comfort zone' is a term you're probably already familiar with. This zone includes activities that you feel comfortable doing, such as reading books by Chaucer, and may include spending time with people that you already know, such as playing hockey with your team. Each comfort zone is individual to each person. Something that might be in one person's comfort zone may be in another person's challenge zone (reading Chaucer would definitely not be in your comfort zone!). These are based on your experiences and interests.

You may have also heard the expression *'life begins outside your comfort zone'*. We think there is a lot of truth in this expression: when we challenge ourselves to explore new possibilities, we learn new things, have new experiences and meet new people. It would be impossible to be a student without leaving your comfort zone, and this is especially true when you start university. Eventually, things that are in your challenge zone when you start university will migrate into your comfort zone. Some things may migrate quickly, for example understanding your university's online learning platform, while others may take longer, such as building up the confidence to speak in tutorials.

It is important to recognise that there are two zones outside your comfort zone: the challenge zone, which is where you have great experiences and learn new things, and beyond this the danger zone. This is when the activity, or more likely multiple activities, is so far out of your comfort zone that it becomes overwhelming. Here, you are not in a position to learn, and being in this zone for too long can be detrimental to your well-being.

There is not a clear list of activities which automatically put you in the danger zone. We are sure you can think of a couple of things that truly scare you which would be in there. For Rebecca, as a dyslexic person who has struggled with spelling her whole life, the idea of a spelling bee would definitely be in the danger zone.

It could be, though, that something which would in other circumstances only slightly challenge you can put you in the danger zone if there are other things going on! To understand this, we can look at the idea of stacking in Figure 2.2. Starting at zero, just at the edge of your comfort zone, you accrue activities and situations that challenge you until you get to five, where you stray into the danger zone.

It may be that, normally, you wouldn't be that fazed by a difficult text or reading, but after an overwhelming day, this pushes you into the danger zone: you become overwhelmed and are unable to engage with that reading. It's normally cumulative experiences of a series of events rather than a single activity (although this does happen) which pushes you into this danger zone.

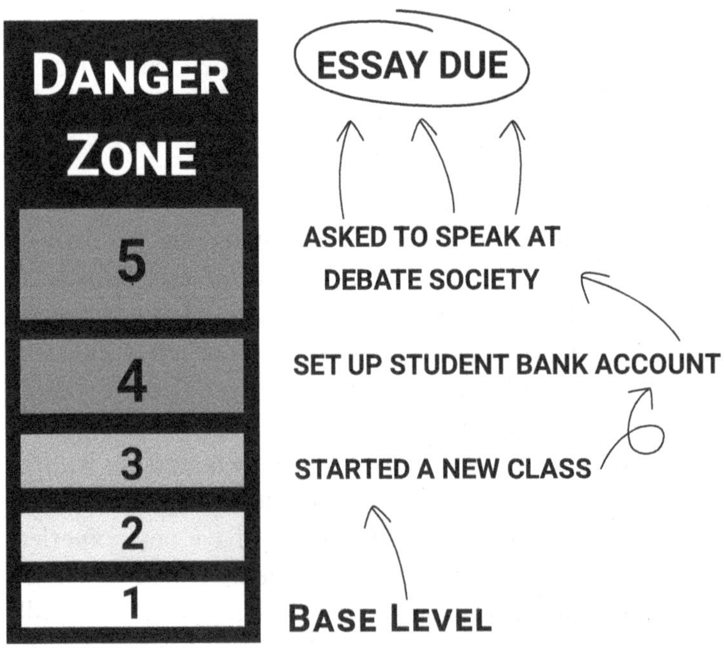

FIGURE 2.2: Stacking to your danger zone

It is very important to remember that this is contextual to the day or week you are having and depends on the individual person. Some things that terrify some people don't faze others. Rebecca has friends who would enjoy taking part in a spelling bee, but would be terrified to attend a ballet class, which she loves. So, although it's tricky, try not to judge yourself based on what other people are comfortable with because we all have different strengths.

Sometimes you can navigate upcoming activities to try and avoid entering the danger zone. In the example above, it may have been that this student became aware that they were near their danger zone and decided to leave the reading until later in the week. They might have engaged in an activity they found restorative instead, such as going for a walk or speaking with a friend. Other times we don't have this option: perhaps the reading was needed for a class which was in a few hours, or we are put in an unexpected situation that we have to deal with.

When you feel like you are far out of your comfort zone, reflecting on the situation is important in any circumstance. When we are in our own danger zone, we can feel so overwhelmed that often we don't have the coping mechanisms to handle the situation. But acknowledging that you are feeling this way and just being aware of this can help a great deal. Then you can try to calmly plan your next steps.

For example, you may have realised that your assignment is due tomorrow, rather than next week as you initially thought. It can be easy to become overwhelmed, decide you'll never get it finished in time, and then snap at your new roommate when they used your milk (even if you don't normally mind). In this situation, you could take five minutes to calm down, perhaps listen to your favourite song, and then make a to-do list of everything you would need to do to finish the assignment. By calmly reflecting on the situation and then navigating the next steps, you have been able to overcome the obstacle. It is useful to think of activities that you find calming ahead of time.

ACTIVITY 2.2

Coping mechanisms

When we are feeling stressed, it can be difficult to think about strategies to deal with the situation in the moment. These should have a positive impact on your short- and long-term well-being, such as going on a walk, rather than be detrimental such as alcohol or recreational drugs. Use the activity below to think of coping mechanisms for when you are feeling overwhelmed.

- What helps you feel calm when you are getting overwhelmed? Write your thoughts in the box below.

This is much easier said than done, but like most things in this book practice will make it significantly easier. Envisioning your danger zone can be helpful, as well as knowing something you can do quickly if you are getting overwhelmed. The most famous one is slowly counting to ten or taking deep breaths. But other people's solutions include doing 20 star jumps, envisioning their happy place or singing.

If you feel like you are consistently in or on the edge of your danger zone, then it would be very beneficial to seek help. Your university will have a team which can support you (whether this is well-being advisers, coaches or counsellors). Seeking help means that you will get the most out of your university experience. There are also some great online resources from mental health charities such as Mind.

Reflecting on your comfort, challenge and danger zones can be difficult to navigate if you have a long-term mental health condition and, therefore, this analogy might not work for you. Again, it may be more helpful to speak to your university support team or your GP for guidance in this area.

This chapter has so far focused a lot on danger zones. But now we want to focus on the magic 'challenge zone': this is where both your learning and unforgettable experiences will happen. In order to engage with this challenge zone, you need to think about your mindset, as how you approach university is just as important as the actions you actually undertake.

MINDSET

How you approach learning (and university in general) will be determined by your mindset: we can understand a mindset as an established group of assumptions, attitudes or beliefs that influence individuals or groups to adopt behaviours.

Carol Dweck's (2017) highly influential theory highlights that we can have two specific mindsets: fixed and growth.

A **fixed mindset** is the notion that your success or failure is pre-determined. Here, failure is seen as a lack of ability. This mindset suggests that talents, or intelligence, are fixed traits that you either do or do not possess. Therefore, this can become a self-fulfilling prophecy, as if you do not think you have the ability to undertake a task, or ever will, you are unlikely to try.

In comparison, a **growth mindset** is the belief that, with hard work and effort, abilities can be developed. Engaging in a growth mindset is very beneficial for your learning, as not only are you more likely to achieve your desired goal, but you can actually change the way your brain is learning. When we challenge ourselves, we make new connections in the brain, thereby strengthening it.

ACTIVITY 2.3

Fixed or growth mindset

- Challenge yourself to decide whether the belief in the examples outlined below is an example of a fixed or a growth mindset.

Situation, belief and outlook	Fixed or growth
Situation: You had tried hard on this assignment but did not receive the grade you wanted. Belief: What was the point in working hard? Outlook: Next time you won't try.	
Situation: A classmate is offered a highly competitive internship for the summer. Belief: You feel pleased for them. Outlook: You ask for any advice in writing applications.	
Situation: You didn't make the first hockey team. Belief: You can still compete on the second team. Outlook: If you keep working hard you may make the first team in the future.	

→

Situation, belief and outlook	Fixed or growth
Situation: A friend is appointed editor of the university newspaper. Belief: You feel that you will never have that level of success. Outlook: You become very jealous of your friend and, possibly, even stop writing for the paper.	

The correct answers are fixed, growth, growth, fixed.

A simple way to understand a growth mindset is the word 'yet'. Instead of thinking '*I cannot understand this theory or formula*', you can add the word 'yet' to the end of the sentence. '*I cannot comprehend this reading, yet*'. '*I cannot hike this distance, yet*'. By adding the word 'yet', you reframe the situation to something you will be able to do or achieve in the future. But you must put in time and effort to get there. This means motivating yourself to leave your comfort zone.

It's also worth noting that you do not have either a fixed or growth mindset, but your mindset can change according to the task or challenge. For example, '*I have a growth mindset about cooking, as I enjoy finding new challenging recipes to try. In comparison, I have a fixed mindset with regard to parallel parking, as I have decided I am unable to park in this way, I don't try, and I am out of practice. This then becomes a self-fulfilling prophecy!*'

There are several things you can do to develop your growth mindset at university.

- Welcome feedback and engage with it (don't simply look at the grade).
- Embrace new challenges. This may be as minor as engaging with the additional reading that you find challenging or as significant as enrolling onto that module that you think looks very interesting, but is outside of your comfort zone.
- Be open to failure and realise that it may take you a while to master some areas (from learning to use strange washing machines to academic reading).

It is important to note that while your mindset will have a large impact on your success at university, there are many other aspects that will have an impact too; structural **inequalities**, neurodivergence, previous experience and so many other aspects will unfairly impact how difficult university will be for you.. Here, your mindset can help you navigate the challenges you face.

PRACTITIONER INSIGHT

Dr Rachel Pennington, clinical psychologist

Thinking back to starting my undergraduate degree makes me smile. I was terrified. It's only with hindsight that I can see all the small transitions I made and how I changed as a person. The shift into adulthood is hard, it's messy and everyone else seems to know what they're doing but you don't. Spoiler alert: everyone is winging it.

Change is never easy; it takes us into the unknown, which for me personally is not a place I like to be. Learning to sit with the unknown is only something I've managed to master as I've got older, and even now if change is sprung upon me I can be caught off guard.

If I could give first-year me any advice I would say, be scared and do it anyway. I like to be good at things and so avoid situations I fear I'll fail. That failure word is key; it's an unhelpful thought, just a thought, not a fact. It's okay to get things wrong and to try again, and again, and again.

2.3 MAINTAINING YOUR WELL-BEING

In this chapter, we have looked at leaving your comfort zone and engaging in a growth mindset. Both of these are vital in helping you successfully navigate university. Fundamental to this success, and the multiple changes you will experience at university, is maintaining your well-being.

ACTIVITY 2.4

The definition of well-being

- How would you define well-being? Complete a copy of the table below to guide your answer.

What is the definition of well-being?	
What do you think are important factors in maintaining your well-being?	

We can understand well-being as a positive approach to university and your life, rather than a lack of mental or physical health illness, such as stress.

Let's look at two issues that students often struggle with which have implications for maintaining well-being:

1. overthinking;
2. avoidance and absenteeism.

OVERTHINKING

Rebecca has a young dog; he's a cocker spaniel called Hobbes. Like many dogs, Hobbes does not like the vacuum cleaner, yet as he sheds fur all over the house, cleaning is an inevitable and necessary chore. When Hobbes sees the vacuum cleaner, he will bark and moan (if you have a dog yourself, then you may well have encountered this behaviour). What is unusual about Hobbes is that he comes and seeks out the vacuum cleaner. This is of course frustrating for both Rebecca and Hobbes; Rebecca does not want her dog to be upset, but when he is following her around he is also getting in the way and sheds more hair in the places that she is trying to clean. Rebecca previously tried telling Hobbes to simply '*ignore the vacuum*' or '*leave the vacuum alone*'. However, when this inevitably failed, she tried a different approach. Rather than telling Hobbes to ignore the vacuum cleaner she tried to distract him instead, giving him his favourite chew, and he happily sat in the garden eating it while Rebecca cleaned in peace.

You may be curious as to why we are sharing this story of a dog following round a vacuum cleaner. Sometimes things happen in our lives that are out of our control and can cause us to be unsettled. Typically, our response is to ruminate about the situation, overthinking and coming back to it at times when we are meant to be focusing on other tasks. It would be better to avoid thinking about the situation entirely; however, this is unlikely to work.

Of course, when something unexpectedly, and sometimes unpleasantly, happens you have the right to feel frustrated and upset. However, it is not helpful to continually focus on the topic, as it will not change the outcome. Here, you can think of Hobbes following round the vacuum cleaner and getting in its way; the vacuum cleaner (the situation) was always going to happen, regardless of whether Hobbes (the subject) wanted it to happen or not. Therefore, trying not to think about the situation is akin to telling Hobbes to '*ignore the vacuum*', which is extremely unhelpful.

When trying to stop overthinking, it is far more effective to direct your thoughts onto something else, much like it was easier for Hobbes not to be concerned about the vacuum cleaner when he had a chew to distract him (although we are not suggesting you use a chew to distract yourself!). This does not mean you cannot focus on the topic; many experts instead advise us to designate a short amount of time (for example, 10–20 minutes) to worry and think about the situation (NHS, 2024). Outside of this designated time, when your train of thought goes back to the topic, you have to find a way to distract yourself. You could think of different topics, such as trying to remember times tables or a name of a country for every letter of the alphabet. This is often enough to derail this overthinking loop and, ultimately, allows you to get back to the task you are trying to focus on. You may also wish to develop your mindfulness skills; there are many great apps and books on this topic.

Being aware of overthinking is also helpful in overcoming it. When you find yourself ruminating, you can reflect upon it. This analogy mainly works for situations that are out of your control, for example waiting to hear about an internship you applied for or for your exam results. It can be easy to overthink these topics; however, the analogy is not as helpful if, for example, you have a fast-approaching exam that you feel unprepared for. Of course, here you don't want to overthink or be so nervous about the exam that you struggle to prepare, but a small amount of nerves can be useful in increasing your productivity. It's about finding a balance to ensure that you are not overthinking the topic while being productive in your revision and preparation for the exam.

AVOIDANCE AND ABSENTEEISM

Our next section will explore avoidance and absenteeism; these are well-being issues where students do not engage with their studies.

Plan on Monday: this project will take around ten hours to finish and is due in a week. So, if I work on it for a couple of hours a day, then it should be finished by Friday, and I can have the weekend off.

Actual progress: do nothing on the project all week and then spend all of Sunday working on the project, feeling frustrated with self and the quality of the work.

Unfortunately, despite great effort, this will happen to all of us at some point. Sometimes we can have the best intention to complete a project, but something happens beyond our control that prevents this; for example, we might become ill in that particular week. When things happen that are out of our control, hopefully we have allowed extra (contingency) time in our schedule to accommodate for this. If not, that is when exceptions can be made such as extensions to assessment deadlines (although you should not count on obtaining these). However, sometimes we are fully in control of the situation and choose, for whatever reason, not to complete the task until we absolutely have to or not at all.

In Chapter 5, we explore some great time management techniques to help you keep on top of your work and schedule your week. In this section, however, we will focus on when things are not going to plan, or when you don't have a plan at all.

As we discussed earlier in this chapter, one of the most difficult parts of the transition to university is becoming an **autonomous** learner and managing your own time. The ability to hold yourself accountable for your own learning and development is an extremely important aspect of this. A common issue that can occur, especially with new university students, is avoiding completing assessed work, attending class or doing these to an unsatisfactory level. This is when avoidance and absenteeism can become a problem, for example not completing your essay or, more commonly, attending class but not really 'being there'. By this, we mean that you are physically in the room, but you are not paying attention. A group of students Rebecca recently delivered a workshop to were very shocked to hear her say that if they didn't listen in class, that was their responsibility and not hers! Of course, Rebecca goes to great efforts to make sure all her classes are accessible and engaging, including plenty of interactive activities. In addition, she will allow and encourage students to ask questions throughout the class so that if they don't understand something, they have the opportunity to change this. However, if a student chooses to spend their time in the class on their phone rather than engaging with the activities and listening, this is the student's responsibility and decision to do so. They are the ones who won't get the information from the class.

As with all well-being topics, there is a balance here. It is unlikely that you're going to be fully focused for every single one of your classes over the course of the year, especially if you're having a hard week or something else is happening in your life. In addition, it may be that you miss a reading for class one week. Therefore, having a system to help you compensate for these situations will be extremely beneficial to you; you can do this by looking at the schedules we outline later in this chapter and in Chapter 5.

When you find yourself being avoidant or absent, the first thing to do is to reflect on the situation: was it a one off because you're having a bad day, or is there an overarching issue? One of the main reasons we often see students being avoidant or absent is because they are feeling overwhelmed, especially if they feel like there is too much work or they're not confident in completing the work. If you feel like you're in this situation, speaking to the student service team at your university will be the most helpful step forward.

MANAGING YOUR WELL-BEING

All of the examples that we have given to help maintain your well-being consider occasional bumps in the road. It's highly likely that during your degree you will face an unexpected issue; however, it's important to reflect on how you would respond to these things. It's normal to experience some stress in day-to-day life, but being continually stressed for a long period of time obviously becomes problematic. Similarly, at some point in your degree, you're likely to be nervous or anxious about something, for example giving a presentation in class or an upcoming exam.

We are not mental health professionals and, therefore, cannot offer specific advice on how to deal with mental health conditions, but the important thing is to know when you feel like you'll need a little bit more help. Your university will offer a whole host of mental health and other services that we highly recommend you use if you feel that you cannot manage or maintain your well-being. We also recommend you find out about these services and how to access them *before* you need them.

2.4 COACHING YOURSELF THROUGH CHANGE

One of the largest problems when going through change is the lack of control we often feel. This is a normal reaction, as being autonomous and wanting to be in control is a fundamental feature of human behaviour (Pink, 2010, p 73). It is easy to resist change that we didn't choose, rejecting it rather than looking for what autonomy we do have. You may have heard the saying '*you can't control the situation, but you can control how you deal with it*'.

The amount of control we have in each situation can be vastly different; for example, you may remember that when the UK first entered into lockdown due to Covid-19, this had a huge impact on people's autonomy. In the first lockdown, people were not allowed to socialise indoors, had to undertake work and schooling from home (unless they were a key worker), and were only allowed to leave their house for a small selection of reasons, including buying food. Outdoor exercise was only permitted once per day. This was an extremely traumatic and stressful change. In order to aid a change like this, people could focus on the autonomy they did have during the lockdown; this may have included which meals the person could eat, which music to listen to, or which work to undertake from their home. Although these seem small in comparison to the loss of autonomy, people were perhaps able to navigate the lockdown change better by focusing on what they could control.

We can use this to think about an academic setting: for example, a common issue is that students feel as if they are lacking autonomy due to upcoming fixed assignment deadlines or a large number of upcoming exams. This can be especially stressful if the student feels that they could have managed their time more efficiently or could have been more organised at the start of the semester. You have little autonomy over this upcoming change, as the exams will happen whether you are ready for them or not.

Here, you can decide whether to act or not to act: you have the first piece of autonomy back. Secondly, you can decide how you respond to the situation. One conscious decision you can make is to create an extensive to-do list on all the topics you would like to revise before the exam and a list of the upcoming deadlines and assessments. You could choose to implement a revision timetable to help reach these goals.

By seeing your response to the challenge as a choice, you regain autonomy, and this can help as you navigate the change.

COACHING

One of the best ways to see this choice and gain autonomy is through coaching. Coaching aims to help individuals improve their confidence, become better problem-solvers and navigate transitions well. There are some great coaching charities and organisations which offer coaching to university students, and it may be that your university even offers a coaching service to you.

However, you don't need a coach to engage in coaching. You can use the techniques yourself! One of the most effective models which can help your problem-solving skills and boost your confidence is called the OSCAR model. This was created as a coaching technique by Karen Whittleworth and Andrew Gilbert in 2002, and has been adapted and used across the world. OSCAR is an acronym.

O – Outcome
S – Situation
C – Choices
A – Action
R – Review

In order to use the OSCAR model, you need to think of a challenge you would like to overcome.

OUTCOME

To begin our questions, you can think of your end goal: what you want the outcome of the change to be. Try to be as specific as possible here and choose something you can say whether you have achieved it or not (using the goals overview in Chapter 5 may be useful here).

SITUATION

....

You then need to think about the current situation in order to implement change. What exactly is going on? Who is involved? How long has the situation been going on for? Try to look at the situation from all angles and create the fullest understanding of it that you can.

CHOICES

....

The next step is choices. Here you think of the options you can consider to navigate the change. If you are struggling to think of options for actions, you can reduce this down to the most fundamental choice: do something different or stay the same.

There are likely several options of how you can navigate change, so once you have decided that you are going to approach the situation differently, you can reflect back on the consequences of each suggestion. We would advise you to mindmap multiple options (perhaps give yourself 30 minutes to an hour to undertake this task, as you could spend all day doing this; it is even more effective if you can do this with a friend). Then reflect on two or three of your choices.

By looking at the pros and cons of each option, you can plan to move forward. You may wish to implement some changes straight away or decide that another option is not the right decision for you at this point. You may wish to come back to a different option after a period of trying a new strategy and some reflection.

ACTION

....

Once you have thought through the choices, you can make an action plan. This is important, as often we think through the best options and want to make change but don't actually implement change. This is the hardest bit!

REVIEW

....

The final part is to review your actions and reflect back to see if you met your intended outcome. It may be that you have achieved this goal, which is great, or you may have to adjust your timelines or action points to achieve it.

It is important to actually review the situation and not just hope for the best! One of the easiest ways to help make this happen is to put a note in your diary or calendar. Perhaps this could be for a few minutes once a week to reflect on how you are doing with your goals.

IMPLEMENTING OSCAR

Now when you are approaching change or a challenge, you can use the OSCAR model to think about your options and turn them into an action plan. To help, you may wish to use some of the following questions for each letter:

O – Outcomc

- What would you like to achieve?
- What would you like this situation to look like in one month or one year?
- How will you know that you have achieved this outcome?

S – Situation

- How would you summarise your current situation in one sentence?
- Why do you want to change this situation?
- What impact is this situation having on yourself/others/your studies?

C – Choices

- If there were no consequences, how would you approach this situation?
- What would you like to do differently or keep the same?
- What advice would you give to someone else who was also facing this challenge?

A – Action

- What are the next steps in achieving your goals?
- How likely are you to undertake these goals (on a scale of 1 to 10)?
- What challenges do you fear in achieving your goals?

R – Review

- What steps have you taken so far?
- What is left to be done?
- Has anything stopped your progress? If so, is there anything you can do to change this?

STUDENT INSIGHT

Joanna Magnuson, biochemistry, third year

As a student, you will fail – whether it's not passing a course or not getting accepted to an internship, whether it is failing in an objective sense or not meeting the standards you've set yourself. I don't think I've met a student that hasn't felt like they have failed at some point in their university career. But what sets people apart is the way they deal with failure. If you let it overwhelm you and beat yourself up over it, it can tear you down. But if you reframe it as an opportunity for learning, as a chance to evaluate your mistakes and improve in the future, it is the most powerful way to grow. Failure is fundamentally a part of success. It's important to remember that failure does not define you; instead use it as motivation to get up, try again and use it as a stepping stone to reach your goals.

2.5 HOW TO KEEP TRACK OF YOUR PROGRESS

Keeping track of your own progress is important at university, as in the workplace you have a manager and in school or college you will have teachers to highlight your successes and challenges, but at university this will be your responsibility. Figuring out what you have done well, and where you need to develop, is one of the most difficult skills to master in becoming an autonomous learner at university.

Of course, this means celebrating the big things, such as assessments and sports competitions. But it's important to celebrate the small successes too! This could include finishing that challenging reading, completing the lab report you didn't want to write or, even if you struggle with it, making it to every class on time that week.

There are many benefits of keeping track of your progress, such as those listed below:

- having a written account of all the great things that you have done;
- understanding how long it will take to complete certain tasks;
- gaining an awareness of your strengths and weaknesses;
- helping you reach your goals.

We think the most important benefit of keeping track of your progress is that it helps with your motivation. It can be easy to feel a bit disheartened when you focus only on deadlines. It can feel a bit like as soon as you have reached and completed one deadline, you have another one right around the corner. If you do this, you ignore all the great work that you have already done!

You can track your progress in a number of ways; you could have weekly times in your diary when you set yourself goals for the week and then reflect on whether you met your previous week's goals. Or you could use project management software, such as Trello or create a page using an organisational tool such as on a Notion dashboard. One of the best ways is to use a habit tracker or reward chart. This is a great way to maintain your motivation and track your progress.

A reward chart is a visual representation of your success that allows you to monitor your achievements and create new goals. Recently, we have seen this effective tool used by both PhD students completing their final draft of their thesis and competitive long-distance runners preparing for a 100k race. The system works very simply through a calendar or planner; this could be a digital one on your phone/tablet or computer or a physical copy on your wall. Whatever system you use, it will be most effective if you regularly see it, so you can have a reminder of your goals and your successes.

A reward chart works very simply: you have a goal each day (see Figure 2.3). For a PhD student, this may be to write 1000 words on their thesis; for a long-distance runner this may be to train for two hours a day. To make it most effective you will need to include rest days, so a great system to implement is to use a working week as your target, with rest periods at the weekend. You can also change your measure of success throughout the academic year; for example, you may have a revision target specifically during exam periods or a target to complete your lab diary during the semester.

A good method for implementing your reward chart is to have a to-do list as your measure of success. Your to-do list (or any measure of success) must be achievable. One of the quickest ways to fail at establishing a reward chart is to set goals that are so unrealistic you are continuously struggling to complete them, which means that on days when you are able to achieve these goals, you have to make too many sacrifices to make it a possibility. On every day that you meet your goal (or complete your to-do list) you mark this on your reward chart. This could be as simple as putting a tick on that date or using a colourful sticker! This is then a great motivation tool in itself, where you can track your progress on achieving your goals and see your success. It can also provide motivation on a smaller scale, knowing that if you complete that small task, you will get another tick or sticker on your chart. Some students we have worked with like to assign a reward if they regularly achieve their goals.

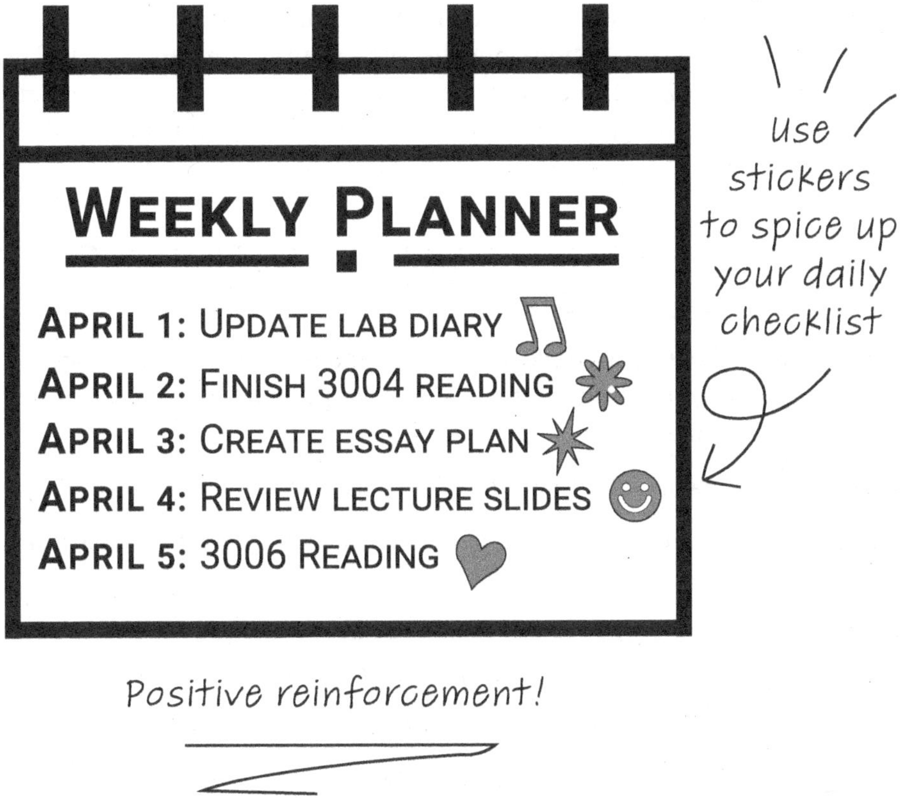

FIGURE 2.3: Examples of success chart

CHAPTER SUMMARY

In this chapter, we explored how you can navigate change successfully, from huge transitions, like starting at university, to smaller ones, such as joining a new sports team. We encouraged you to enter into your challenge zone, going beyond your comfort zone in order to undertake new experiences while limiting becoming overwhelmed in your danger zone. In order to thrive in this challenge zone, we thought about mindset and why (and how) you should aim for a growth mindset. This means ensuring you consider time and effort as essential measures of success and trying to stop limiting beliefs. This led us to think about well-being, which is paramount not only for managing change but for a happy life. Furthermore, we shared some thoughts on common well-being issues students face: overthinking and avoidance and absenteeism.

The final sections of the chapter considered some practical actions you can undertake to help navigate change and be successful at university. This included thinking about coaching techniques and how you could use these to help create an action plan for change. Finally, we explored a method to keep track of all the great progress you will make!

TOP TIPS AND NEXT STEPS

- Actively think about your comfort, challenge and danger zones. Motivate yourself to be in your challenge zone while trying to limit how much you are in your danger zone.
- Reflect on your own well-being and decide what success means to you.
- Reflect – think of a time when you have been in your comfort, challenge and danger zones.
- Think of a short action you can undertake to help you if you enter into your danger zone (for example, counting to ten, breathing exercises etc).
- Use the OSCAR model to help think about an upcoming challenge.
- Create a success chart to keep track of your progress; you can link this to your daily to-do list.

CHAPTER 3
YOU IN A CHANGING WORLD

CHALLENGES WE EXPLORE IN THIS CHAPTER

This chapter looks at the external opportunities and challenges which can impact your university experience. While promoting an awareness of a changing world, this chapter primarily focuses on the tools you can engage with to navigate these changes.

We start with a brief overview of how the world is changing, before moving on to explore the importance of **flexibility**. We then look at **resilience** and rising to challenges before concluding this chapter by examining the importance of **transferable skills** in our changing world. The aim of this chapter is to help you reflect on changes happening all around you and give you the confidence to thrive under these conditions.

INTENDED LEARNING OUTCOMES

By the end of this chapter, you should be able to:

- appreciate the relevance of a changing world to your university studies;
- reflect on the changing world and see the importance of flexibility;
- recognise the value in accepting certain challenges and changes;
- understand the importance of resilience and how to develop your own resilience;
- gain an awareness of the importance of transferable skills in a changing world.

3.1 HOW THE WORLD IS CHANGING

Can you think of three substantial changes that have taken place in the world in the last year? What about in the last decade?

Whether you are 16 or 60, you will have experienced a vast number of changes in your lifetime. The world, and our society, is changing at an accelerated rate: change that previous generations would have seen over a decade take place in only a few months now.

It has become almost clichéd to hear that we are preparing for jobs that do not even exist. Yet, when we think of our own experiences, this is very true. When Rebecca finished her A levels in 2009, Facebook was still in its infancy and other social media platforms such as TikTok, Snapchat and Instagram didn't yet exist. It would have been an odd concept to consider that entire careers would be built around social media.

On a more personal level, her own job did not exist when she was leaving school. As universities have evolved, there has been an increase in student support and learning roles and, therefore, new jobs such as her own have been created. This is significant because, had Rebecca focused on choosing a degree (and gaining experience throughout her degree) based on a specific career path, this would have limited her options. That is not to say that you cannot be motivated and guided throughout your studies with an ideal job in mind, but we want you to think about the ever-evolving nature of different roles within employment. Even some of the oldest and most traditional jobs such as teaching, accountancy, engineering and medical roles have had unprecedented changes in the last decade. This means we must be **adaptable** to these unanticipated changes.

We can identify this shift far beyond employment though: technology is developing at a fast pace, with huge implications for the way we live our lives, travel and communicate. We have seen huge change resulting from the Covid-19 pandemic and its aftermath, which fundamentally changed our day-to-day behaviours, systems, governments, corporations and even values (Beylier and Molinari, 2022, p 1). This change has highlighted the interlinked nature of the world and how global we have become, not only in the spread of the pandemic but the impact of travel limitations.

One of the most fundamental changes is the climate emergency, which has begun to, and will increasingly, dominate decisions on what our world looks like. Eco-anxiety and climate anxiety is especially felt by young people: A recent study surveyed 10,000 young people (aged 16–25) in ten countries, and 75 per cent of respondents shared that the future is frightening (Hickman et al, 2021, p 863).

YOU IN A CHANGING WORLD

The climate emergency is only one element of the global environmental shift, with interlinking problems of freshwater shortages, elimination of species with mass biodiversity loss and devastation in the world's oceans. These environmental issues exploit existing social injustices, and we must acknowledge the multifaceted inequalities and discrimination that exist at the intersections of race, gender, sexuality, nationality, class, (dis)ability, education, and various other social and economic identities, which perpetuate the struggles many individuals and communities face. This is taking place within a fourth industrial revolution, with a digital transformation of our world, including generative AI.

Even being aware of these constant changes can be difficult, with many individuals facing eco-anxiety and concerns for social justice. These large questions can hang over our study and life decisions. In this unknown and ever-changing world, there is an even greater need to become change-makers.

These global changes will have an impact on your degree at a micro and macro scale, affecting your daily experience of being a student, but also what the purpose of a university is. Universities have changed a lot since they first started (which is explored in more detail in Chapter 8), and even 100 years ago the vast majority of the population was excluded from studying. This significant change has impacted the function of universities too, as now they welcome a diverse range of students and are expected to contribute to wider society. This includes the research they undertake and the policies they create, in addition to the education they provide for their students. Historically, you 'read' a specific subject, and this became the primary focus of your degree; you would be a specialist in economics or physics, for example. While this specialism is a fundamental part of your learning, a university degree now includes not only subject-specific knowledge, but also incorporates cross-discipline experiences and skills (which are at the heart of this book). Increasingly, universities are expected to share their values and provide opportunities for their students, so they not only become graduates but global change-makers who have an awareness of the wider world.

It would be easy to question why we have briefly highlighted the changing nature of the world at the start of this chapter. While this short overview does not even begin to provide a snapshot of the world, it is important to reflect on the external challenges and opportunities that exist outside your degree. You will neither study nor live your life in a vacuum. Some of these changes you may be very aware of; perhaps you chose your degree subject as you wanted to battle climate change, and we are sure you are already aware of the impact a pandemic can have on how you learn. What is vital is that you actively use tools to help you navigate these changes. If you are resistant to change or simply ignore it, you can become frustrated and down-heartened. However, you can think about the FAR framework (F – flexibility, A – accepting challenges, R – resilience) (shown in Figure 3.1) to navigate this changing world.

FIGURE 3.1: The FAR framework

3.2 THE IMPORTANCE OF FLEXIBILITY IN A CHANGING WORLD

Throughout these global changes, you need to exhibit flexibility in order to navigate the unforeseen directions that your life, and crucially your degree, may take. That's why the first letter in our acronym is F, for flexibility. To start thinking about this strategy, you need to first understand what flexibility is.

ACTIVITY 3.1

Defining flexibility

- What do you think the definition of flexibility is? Add it to the box below.

Flexibility can be understood as the ability to modify plans in order to meet a goal or overcome change. You can think of flexibility as being **adaptable** and changing your actions, especially when faced with an obstacle. This could be an actual obstacle; for example, if the path you were following on your hike was flooded you would need to find an alternative route. It could be academic, such as not having access to an online journal article you need to complete an assignment.

A useful way to understand flexibility is to think about earthquake-proof buildings. It would be easy to presume that buildings were made earthquake-proof by building them as rigid and strong as possible to oppose the shaking. You may be surprised to learn that the opposite is true; buildings are designed to move and flex with the shaking, as opposing the movement causes the most damage. The buildings also have strong foundations. You can apply this idea to flexibility. It is often tempting to be rigid to change and try to resist it, especially if the change is unexpected or causes you to question your knowledge and abilities.

Let's say our metaphorical earthquake is that university maths classes are much harder than a student expected. Perhaps they always found studying maths easy at school and college, and always got the best grades in their class. After the first couple of weeks of university classes, though, they are struggling. The course is proceeding at a faster pace than they are used to, and they have to undertake a lot of additional work outside of class, which they aren't used to either. It would be tempting for the student to try and be rigid and resist this change, to think that their methods for studying at school were effective and doing the same now will have the same results, hoping for the best.

From an outside perspective, you can probably see that resisting this change is likely to make things worse, not better. This student is likely to get further behind in their work and therefore not enjoy their studies as much as they'd hoped. What advice would you give the student?

We would advise them that, unfortunately, this is a common issue we have seen many students face and also that they need to be flexible and make a plan based on their current situation. They could think about the main issue they are having – perhaps it's the large workload they are facing or generally adapting to university life? We would also encourage them to accept the challenge, which we will explore now.

3.3 ACCEPTING THE CHALLENGE

The second letter in our acronym is A for **accepting** the challenge. Here, you not only want to be aware that challenges exist but rise to them and, if possible, even enjoy some of them.

Challenges are fundamental to life and something that you will face during your student experience. Some challenges are inevitable, such as writing your first essay or report, while others may be less predictable, for example trying to understand the complicated laundry system in halls of residence!

It is very useful to think about reframing challenges as something positive. While we appreciate that some challenges will not be positive, in many cases there will be at least one positive element. People often collect challenges: for example, in Scotland there is a hobby called 'Munro bagging'. This is where individuals spend their free time trying to climb all 282 of the highest mountains in Scotland, called the Munros. This challenge requires planning, training on how to read a map and hike safely, and the vast amount of energy required to traverse the mountain. There are multiple benefits to climbing these mountains, including the beautiful landscape; however, a big part of the appeal of climbing them is that they are challenging. Furthermore, it's a challenge for individuals to see how many they can climb. If the mountains were easy, or they were not classified as mountains, it would be less appealing.

You might be thinking that not everyone (us included) is a 'Munro bagger' and that only people with certain personality traits will undertake these challenges. Yet, you can think of multiple other challenges that you like to participate in, such as completing a park run, cooking soufflés or solving difficult puzzles.

ACTIVITY 3.2

Enjoying challenges

- Use the space below to think of three challenges that you enjoy undertaking.

1.
2.
3.

Our brains like to be challenged; that's why in Chapter 2 we encouraged you to enter the 'challenge zone'. Your academic work will be challenging; how challenging it is will depend on your previous experience and learning approach. You can, obviously, no longer control your previous experiences but you can change your approach by thinking about how you organise your time and by aiming to become an autonomous learner. We look at this in detail in Chapter 5. You should, though, try to embrace this challenge; your degree is designed to push you in order to gain new knowledge and eventually expertise in this area. There have been studies that show that when you work harder and engage in deeper learning, you are more likely to retain the information and, surprisingly, even enjoy the task a little bit more (Dehaene, 2020, p 242).

You can think about being 'in the zone', that great feeling when you skilfully navigate a tricky problem, and you are fully focused on that problem. It may be your academic reading that you have previously been struggling with or even a computer game that you need to concentrate on. So try to lean into the challenge!

Of course, taking on challenges, like completing degrees or climbing mountains, is difficult. It's important to take regular breaks and not push yourself so far that you leave your challenge zone and enter your danger zone (as we explored in Chapter 2).

When accepting your challenges, it's important to understand what you are taking on. If you can try to break down the challenge, then you will reveal the best way to succeed! For example, perhaps you are finding your academic studies challenging. This is quite a broad challenge and it's likely that there is something more specific you are finding particularly challenging within this area. You can ask yourself these four questions to break down the challenge.

1. What about this challenge most excites me?
2. When do I feel most overwhelmed?
3. Can I describe the challenge in one sentence?
4. What am I most nervous about?

You can use these questions to start breaking down your big challenge (it may be useful to think about these questions with a friend). Finding your studies challenging could be a result of a combination of any of the following factors or others.

- You are feeling homesick, and this is distracting you.
- The content of the module is unfamiliar to you, and you are struggling to grasp basic concepts.
- You are not used to the amount of independent work you are having to undertake.
- You are learning new ways of assessment, and this is overwhelming.

There may be other circumstances that are making this challenge harder; for example, you may have a specific learning difference, an unexpected family issue or you might be learning in your second language. However, knowing your challenge is the first way to overcome it, and embracing it will only be of benefit to you.

Once you understand the challenge, you can find the right support to overcome it. If we return to the analogy of climbing a mountain, the hiker must understand the route they are taking, make sure they have the correct equipment, check the weather conditions and know who to contact if things don't go to plan. When you undertake your challenge, you need to have the right support in place to overcome it. A big part of this is engaging your resilience, as we explore next.

PRACTITIONER INSIGHT

Dr Sean Talamas, managing partner, Proof Leadership Group and associate editor of the *Journal of Character and Leadership*

Hey there! As you step into university, you're entering a landscape filled with new experiences and inevitable changes. It's exciting, sure, but let's be real – it can also be a bit overwhelming. Embracing this change positively is key to making the most out of your university journey.

Change is not just about new challenges; it's about the opportunities these challenges bring for growth and learning. Stuck on a tough assignment? That's your cue to get creative and maybe find a new study buddy. Feel lost in the sea of clubs and activities? This is your moment to explore and perhaps stumble upon a passion you never knew you had.

It's normal to feel a bit stressed amid all this change. Stress isn't always a bad thing though – it can actually enhance your creativity, work quality and ability to navigate new situations.

Remember, every new experience at university is shaping you into a more capable and versatile individual. Approach each change with a spirit of adventure, and you'll find that university isn't just about learning from books, but about growing through experiences. Here's to making every moment count!

3.4 HONING THE RESILIENCE WITHIN YOU

The final letter in our acronym is R for resilience. This is vital in overcoming changes, but resilience can be difficult to define.

ACTIVITY 3.3

Defining resilience

• How would you interpret resilience? Write your own definition.

Resilience is how you cope with challenges and bounce back from adversity. Being resilient means that you are able to navigate changes, particularly challenging ones, and continue to move forward. While resilience can be tiring, it's essential for dealing with the changes of the world around you.

One of the best ways to build your resilience is to reflect on a change that you have previously experienced and think about how this was made worse or better by the actions you took. This could be something small, such as your favourite chocolate bar being discontinued, to something substantial, such as getting a new teacher or manager. Here you can think about how your approach helped or hindered navigating this change.

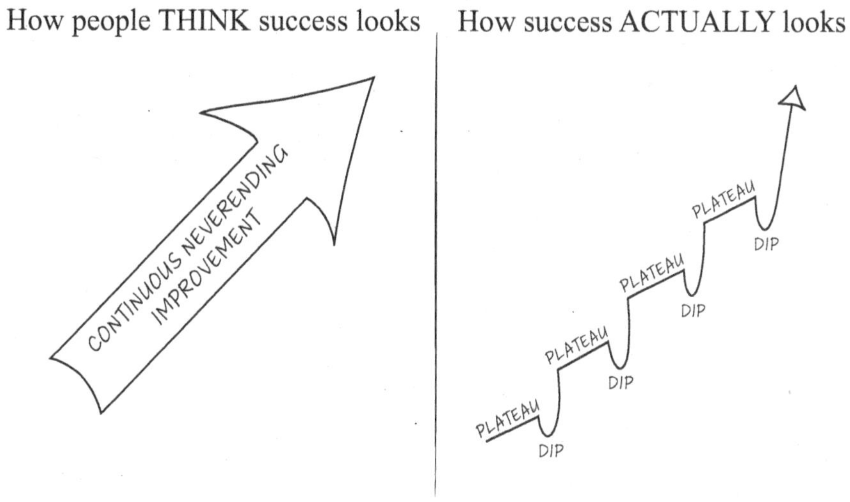

FIGURE 3.2: What success looks like

It is possible that you have seen the image in Figure 3.2 previously. This is very true for what success looks and feels like when you are a university student. It could be easy to think that you have an end goal, perhaps to get a certain grade on all your assignments or to complete all the assigned reading each week. It is unlikely, though, that your journey to this goal will fall upon an ever-rising curve; instead, there will be many expected and unexpected challenges to face before reaching your goal.

These may include anything from not being able to find the text you need to the most extreme disruption you have seen in decades: a pandemic that forces your learning to move online! While it's far more likely that you will need to prepare for not finding adequate resources than for another pandemic, being resilient will have a big impact on how you overcome all challenges, big or small, personal or global.

It is likely that during the disruption experienced over the past years, you will have greatly strengthened your resilience skills. A useful framework to think about resilience is the ABC model (Ellis, 1991).

FIGURE 3.3: Adversity, Belief, Consequence

This model is very effective at challenging negative thoughts, highlighting that these can be usual and that there are logical steps to challenge them. The three-step process challenges these unhelpful, often limiting beliefs, and encourages us to implement change.

1. Adversity highlights an event or situation that's challenging.
2. Belief is our response to this event.
3. Consequence is the outcome of our belief.

It's important to note that consequence can be impacted by our attitude toward the situation. This is useful as you often can't control the situation, but you can control your response to it. You can use this model to build your resilience. Take a look at the difference in responses in the following two examples, despite the adverse event being the same.

Situation A

- Adversity: I am demoted to the second football team from the first team.
- Belief: I am not good enough at football, so what's the point in trying?
- Consequence: I leave the football team, which I enjoy greatly, as well as losing out on the opportunity to meet and socialise with other players.

In comparison, situation B

- Adversity: I am demoted to the second football team from the first team.
- Belief: I understand that I don't have enough time to train compared to most first-team players. I have other commitments that are more important to me. If I stay on the second team I will still get to play football and meet new people, while keeping my other commitments.
- Consequence: I greatly enjoy my new team and even became second-team captain.

Although this seems like an idealised example, you can see that your attitude to an event has a big impact on the consequence. Being resilient in the face of adversity means that you can often navigate situations with more positive outcomes. Of course, you are human and you may not always react in a way that you are proud of, but this doesn't mean you can't use the ABC model to help you overcome change.

You can use this in an academic example too: imagine that you completed your first university assignment, and you did not receive the grade you were hoping for. The feedback you were given was that although you understood the basic concepts, you had not completed enough further research to attain a higher grade. This small stumbling block could result in the following thought process.

- Adversity: I had tried hard on this assignment but didn't receive the grade I wanted.
- Belief: What was the point in working hard? Next time I won't try.
- Consequence: I don't complete future work to a standard I am pleased with.

Reflecting on your growth mindset (as we explored in Chapter 2), you can challenge this thinking.

- Adversity: I had tried hard on this assignment but didn't receive the grade I wanted.
- Belief: I need to continue to work hard and use constructive feedback to improve my writing and research skills.
- Consequence: I spoke to my lecturer and improved my research skills, and I was much happier with my next assignment.

ACTIVITY 3.4

Resilient thinking

- Use the activity box below to reflect on a time you were resilient (or not so much) and think about how your belief affected the consequence.

Adversity	
Belief	
Consequence	

Once you have an understanding of your A, B, Cs, you can add a fourth letter, D, to the model. D stands for 'disputing the unhelpful beliefs' and you can read a bit more about the kinds of unhelpful beliefs we hold in Chapter 6. When you recognise what your belief is, you can then ask yourself some useful questions.

- Is my belief helpful?
- Is my belief realistic?
- Would a good scientist agree with my logic?
- Would I talk to my friend in this way?

If the answer to any of these questions is no, you can push back on your belief and try to replace it with a more helpful, realistic, logical and kind one.

Along with many topics in this book, simply noting or being mindful of your resilience can be useful. You should be proud when picking yourself up and moving on in the face of adversity. By trying to engage an optimistic mindset, meaning that you are hopeful that the next change will be easier to navigate, then you will improve your resilience skills. For example, if you really struggled with your first report or essay, you would be optimistic that by using the feedback you received on this assignment, your next one will be easier to complete.

Being optimistic is hard work. It's easier to throw in the towel and claim that you'll never be able to write a good report, make new friends, learn how to cook eggs or whatever task you are trying to undertake. Being resilient also takes a lot of energy, and even us telling you to 'try to be optimistic' can seem burdensome. If you can engage this optimistic mindset, though, you are more likely to be able to complete the task and enjoy the experience. Without this resilience, there is a strong possibility that you will enter into a self-fulfilling prophecy (as we explored in Chapter 2), where you decide that you are unable to undertake a task and then don't try to overcome the obstacles.

However, we know that it's not always possible to engage this optimistic mindset. If you are struggling to maintain your resilience, or you're facing many challenges in parallel to your university work, seeking support at your university or from your GP can be a useful step in maintaining your well-being.

3.5 THE IMPORTANCE OF TRANSFERRABLE SKILLS IN A CHANGING WORLD

Throughout this chapter, we have highlighted that the world is shifting – from the climate crisis to advancements in technology, the functions of universities and the nature of jobs, change is taking place very quickly. Therefore, there is a need not only for the excellent disciplinary expertise you will gain at university, but also for **transferrable skills**. These skills can help you become problem-solvers, apply your knowledge and influence your approach to new situations.

In order to prepare and succeed in these ever-changing situations, you need to be confident not only in developing and using transferable skills, but in being able to reflect on the skills you have. You can understand transferable skills simply as abilities that are applicable in multiple situations.

An academic example of a non-transferable skill or specialist skill would be using a specific piece of equipment such as a microscope or being able to identify a specific linguistic feature.

A transferable skill is one that can be used in different circumstances. For example, a transferable skill would be the ability to write concisely and clearly: you will use this skill throughout university across multiple modules, and, as you developed it at university, you can then *transfer* this skill to your future career, as nearly every job requires you to be able to write concisely and clearly.

ACTIVITY 3.5

Transferable and non-transferable skills

- Use the table below to think of three specialist skills and three transferable skills.

Examples of specialist/non-transferable skills	Examples of transferable skills
1.	1.
2.	2.
3.	3.

One of the most fundamental aspects of transferrable skills is the ability to recognise them and then apply them to changing circumstances. This means you understand that because you can write well in your Introduction to Philosophy module, for example, you can use these writing skills in your Modern History module and when you are writing for the university newspaper. We have seen so many students who participate in a wide range of activities, and have excelled in many areas, but can't articulate the transferable skills they have developed to undertake these activities.

Being able to recognise your skills means you can share these with potential employers, but it also means that you are able to further develop your skills, as you will be able to identify your strengths and limitations. This is vital in navigating our changing world, as when you are aware of your transferable skills and how to apply them, you will be able to adapt to new technologies or environments more quickly. This will also help you to develop your resilience and adaptability. As we have highlighted throughout this chapter, your university experience will be ever-changing, sometimes even surprising. Understanding where you thrive and where you need further support is essential in navigating these changes. This means knowing when you are happy to jump straight into a task or when you may wish to think about what is ahead of you. Beyond this sense of achievement, developing and reflecting on your transferable skills is imperative when entering into an ever-changing workforce. It's unlikely that 'pure' knowledge or an understanding of a subject is enough to have a successful career. It is likely that you will have many different career roles throughout your life. If you remain in one role for a long time, that role will evolve as new challenges emerge, both within the company or organisation where you work and in the wider world. The beauty of transferable skills is that they are not linked to a single situation, job role or career. Many companies are now even hiring 'generalists' who don't have specialist knowledge of the company's area but have a breadth of skills they can use to undertake challenging roles (Epstein, 2020).

Whether you would prefer to be a specialist or generalist, adapting to new roles through your transferable skills is important.

We will return to transferable skills throughout this book, especially in the next chapter where you will have the opportunity to reflect on these using a skills wheel.

STUDENT INSIGHT

Gitika Sanjay, modern history, first year

University is a massive change in many ways. It can mean new friends, new subjects, new schedules – and for some, like me, even a new country. In the face of rapid, sudden change, it's easy to slip into coping mechanisms, even if they aren't healthy. For instance, when I started university, I started to work obsessively; I was convinced that the more hours I spent reading articles or studying graphs, the more settled I would be. It became clear over time, though, that my incessant work was a way to distract myself from the changes around me. My challenge over my first semester was learning to combat this, largely through finding ways to ground myself. I spent more time with friends, but I also made a conscious effort to make time for myself – self-care is incredibly important! Find what anchors you and use it to create a space for yourself.

CHAPTER SUMMARY

We started this chapter by looking at how the world is changing. Of course, the world has constantly been changing, and there have been huge shifts throughout the course of history. What we are noticing now is how quickly change is taking place, from society to the environment and the impact this will have on you as a student. This brief overview of our changing world provided us with a lens to look at how to navigate these external changes using the FAR framework.

F – Flexibility

A – Accepting the challenge

R – Resilience

We looked at each factor in the framework, starting with flexibility and the need to be adaptable to change. Here we thought about moving with change, rather than trying to resist it. The second factor was accepting the challenge we are presented with. Here we considered reframing challenges to think about them more positively, understanding what we are dealing with in order to make a plan to move forward. This led to our final factor: resilience. We explored how to come back from adversity and how to use the ABC model to try and gain a positive outcome from difficult change.

Before concluding, we explored the need for transferable skills in our changing world, and how these are not only important in a changing workplace but also for our own sense of achievement!

TOP TIPS AND NEXT STEPS

- Reflect on changes that are taking place in the world (both locally and globally).
- Use the FAR framework to help you navigate changes.
- Focus not only on developing your specialist skills but your transferable skills too.
- What would you say to a friend to encourage them to be resilient?
- Use the questions in section 3.3: Accepting the challenge to reframe a recent challenge.
- List five of your transferable skills. Which do you think is/are most important?

PART 2

Where are you going and how will you get there?

CHAPTER 4
YOU AS A STUDENT: HOW TO BUILD A LEARNER

CHALLENGES WE EXPLORE IN THIS CHAPTER

In this chapter we consider what it is to be a student. The transition to university is a significant change, regardless of your previous educational experience. Often the biggest shift is the move to become an effective independent learner. We explore this shift throughout the chapter and outline some strategies for you to navigate the transition. This builds on what we explored in Part 1 of this book, where we looked at where you are right now. This chapter signifies the start of Part 2, where we will ask, '*Where are you going and how will you get there?*'

To begin to answer this question, in this chapter, you need to reflect on how you have previously learnt, what worked well and what you would like to change. If you have not yet started university, then you will need to reflect on your different practices to find a way to learn that suits you and your degree. This chapter will give you the tools to reflect as well as strategies to be more effective at studying, but as everyone is different you will need to find the strategies and techniques that work best for you.

We begin by looking at how we learn. We are continually learning and taking in new information and have been doing so since we were infants. Now that you are learning at such an advanced level, you need to be aware of how you learn. In order to think of strategies to cope with the vast amount of information you are expected not only to know, but to critically analyse. This chapter then reflects on the importance of feedback, how to understand this feedback and how to use it to build on your success.

INTENDED LEARNING OUTCOMES

By the end of this chapter, you should be able to:

- identify your preferred approach to learning based on the science behind it;
- employ time management techniques to become a more confident autonomous learner;
- develop your confidence in studying and ascertain which study skills techniques would be most useful to you.
- understand the importance of feedback and how to use it effectively.

4.1 WHAT IS A STUDENT?

ACTIVITY 4.1

What is a student?

- To begin with, please fill in a copy of the mind map below with seven different words or phrases that you think describe a student.

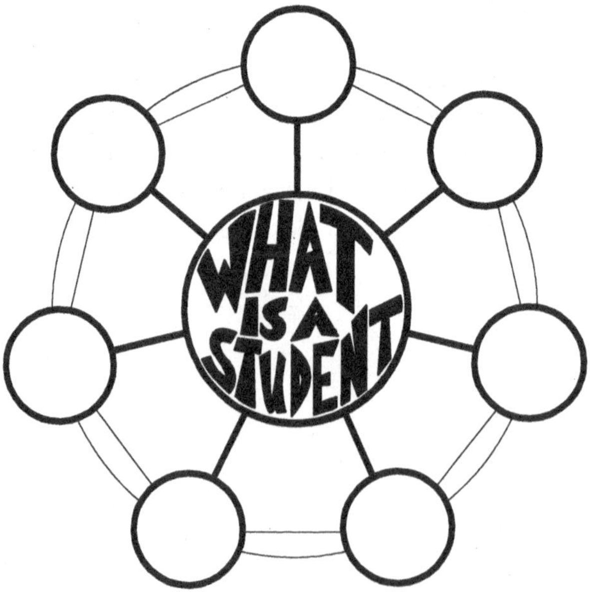

You could have included a whole range of different words to describe what a student is; you may have chosen words relating to learning or education, possibly including school or university. You could have included certain behaviours, such as attending classes, or skills students may acquire, or you may have included discipline-specific ideas about the subject that you will be studying.

Throughout this chapter we explore 'what a student is', with a specific focus on learning. You can use your seven words or phrases to reflect upon this and guide your thoughts.

4.2 LEARNING AUTONOMOUSLY AND THE SCIENCE OF LEARNING

Many students hope that simply reading a textbook or listening to a lecture will allow them to absorb all the information they need (when Cat and Rebecca first started studying at university, we were these students). In fact, in our day-to-day lives, this is how we receive most of our information. We don't create mind maps on videos we watch or practise recall on shopping lists.

Yet, at university there is a need to not only remember the vast amount of information you will encounter, but to engage with it as well by **analysing**, evaluating and interpreting it so that you can create new knowledge. Although for many this may be a daunting task, becoming a 'scholar' is one of the exciting parts of higher education. The term 'scholar' is more than an old-fashioned term for university student; it can be understood as a learned individual who undertakes academic activities. In order to engage with the information you receive at university, you need to be confident and comfortable with the material, and the best way to do this is to reflect on how you learn.

Imagine we asked you to paint the room you're currently sitting in. Even if you have never decorated before, you could think about the separate steps involved. Firstly, you would need to prepare the room: cleaning any surfaces, taping around windows and doors, and protecting any flooring or carpets. Then you would select your tools, most likely using a roller for large sections and a small paintbrush for intricate details and corners. The idea of breaking this task down into different components and reflecting on the best tool (or paintbrush) for the job would not seem strange. We would encourage you to take this same approach to your learning: think about how you will engage with materials and the different steps or tools required to get there. The next section of this chapter looks not only at the science behind why this is important, but some of the activities you can undertake to facilitate this learning.

SCIENCE OF LEARNING

In order to understand how we learn, we must look at **cognitive science**, which focuses on the mind. Here, we can take a very brief exploration of the science of learning in order to understand how to become effective learners. We can consider how information is received, processed, stored and, subsequently, how we retrieve it again, such that it is considered 'learned'.

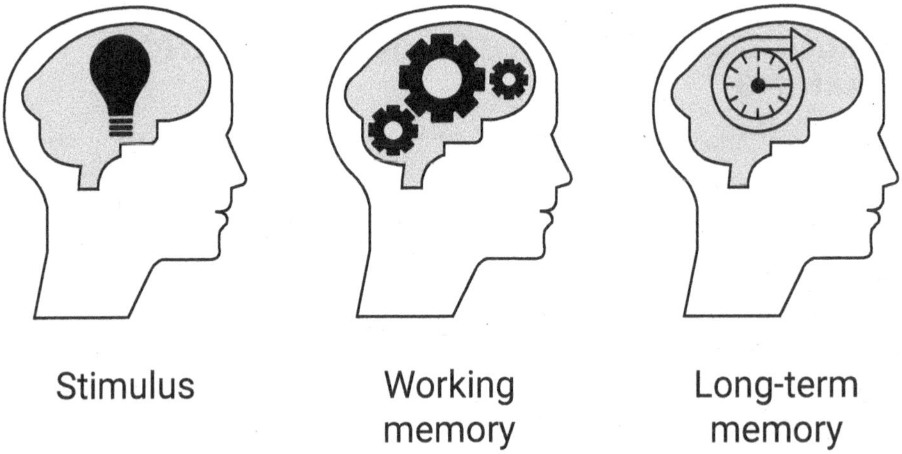

FIGURE 4.1: Stages of memory

We constantly receive information from our environment, which stimulates our sensory registers, yet only if we pay attention to a **stimulus** will it move to our working memory. We are constantly receiving information that we unconsciously decide not to process (Roediger et al, 2014). For example, if you walk upstairs regularly you will receive information about the next step, but it is highly unlikely you will know the total number of steps despite the fact you have walked them so regularly.

Your brain consciously or subconsciously chooses whether to pay attention to information and, if you do pay attention, it will move the information into your working memory, the next stage in the cognitive process. Our working memory has limited capacity and duration: on average it can only hold around seven chunks of information which need to be kept fresh or we will quickly forget them (Weinstein et al, 2018); however, this will differ in each person, especially if you are neurodiverse.

In order for the information we receive to pass into our long-term memory, it must be encoded, which can only happen if we are continuously and consciously engaging with it. When new information enters into our long-term memory, it is connected to existing knowledge and the more connections there are to a piece of information, the easier it is to recall (Roediger et al, 2014).

Therefore, when learning we need to effectively encode information so that we commit it to our long-term memory and can easily retrieve it when required. This means that we want to focus on how our learning is connected to our existing knowledge, with lots of detail and, if possible, have dual sensory stimuli such as an image and words to help us retain the information (Roediger et al, 2014). In order to implement these methods to learn effectively, you need to consider how you are studying (and not simply how long you are studying for) and engage in active learning.

COGNITIVE EFFORT AND ACTIVE LEARNING

In a culture that, unfortunately, often sees stress and working long hours as a badge of honour, it's unsurprising that students proclaim that they have '*spent ten hours solid in the library*'. We will often hear from students that they are spending many hours working but are not achieving their desired outcomes. They share that they aren't getting through the readings, or they are struggling to meet deadlines. Effective learning means working smart, not necessarily working longer. It is far more important to engage in active learning and use significant cognitive effort for a shorter period of time, rather than passively working over the course of a full day and not engaging with the information. This is especially important if you are neurodiverse.

Imagine you could run 5 kilometres in 30 minutes; this doesn't mean that you could run 20k in two hours, or 40k in four hours, or even 80k in eight hours straight. We often apply this same logic to studying. If you can read this one chapter in an hour, you should be able to read eight chapters in eight hours. However, we get tired and our attention span drops, meaning that we cannot concentrate for this amount of time.

Studies have shown that most university students are predominantly practising 'passive studying'; 'active learning' is a far more effective way to study and retain information (Weinstein et al, 2018).

ACTIVITY 4.2

Passive and active learning

- Decide if the common study methods below are active or passive.

Method	Answer
1. Re-reading textbooks and lecture slides	
2. Highlighting texts	
3. Creating and practising flashcards	
4. Rewriting notes	
5. Practising past papers	
6. Creating mind maps	
7. Creating summaries	

The correct answers are 1. passive; 2. passive; 3. active; 4. passive;
5. active; 6. active; 7. active

If you have ever been sat reading a textbook or listening to a lecturer or teacher speak and can't remember what was just said, then the likelihood is that you were undertaking **passive learning**, and not engaging with the information. Instead, you should aim to undertake **active learning**, where you actively question and process the

STUDENT INSIGHT

Carla De Oliveira Santos, psychology, foundation year

I returned to education as a (very) mature student, despite my SpLDs (specific learning differences). If you find yourself in the same position, embrace active learning. With a life full of experiences behind you and having optimised your mental resources to cope with your SpLDs, these become tools that active learning enables you to use to your advantage. Because active learning uses a greater diversity of educational tools, you can learn in the way that suits you best. The creative freedom it provides, guided by your teachers, allows you to use your background and your best skills without being bound by rigid models that cater to the majority. Moreover, the opportunity for constructive feedback enables you to develop your work in the right direction. Active learning puts you in the driver's seat, allowing you to immerse yourself in your exploration and even change an assignment you had to do into something you loved to do.

information given. Here, the aim is to understand it, review how (and if) it is correct, why it is correct and how it links to other information you know.

UNDERSTANDING YOUR UNDERSTANDING

When engaging in active learning, it is important to reflect on whether you understand the information you are receiving. Here, you can ask: do I understand this information or is it just familiar? Our brains can sometimes trick us into thinking we have a grasp of a complicated topic when actually it's just familiar because we have read it before or it might be similar to something we already know.

At university level, you need to not only be familiar with the vast amount of information you will learn but be able to recall it later! You will need to be able to remember this information for your exams and assignments, and understand it enough to critically engage with it (we look at critical thinking in detail in Chapter 7). To unpack this further, look at the statements/questions about capital cities below.

- *The capital of Poland is Warsaw* – it would be easy to think you know this, but there is a difference between reading something and understanding it and recalling it later.
- *True or false: The capital of Columbia is Bogotá (true!)* – here, there is already an element of testing, meaning you need to reflect on the information rather than simply reading it.
- *Is the capital city of New Zealand Wellington, Auckland or Christchurch? (Wellington)* – this is more difficult than a simple true or false answer, especially as all three options are cities in New Zealand.
- *What is the capital of Malaysia? (Kuala Lumpur)* – this is even trickier; you could possibly guess if you knew some Southeast Asian cities, but you would need to know Malaysia is in this region. You have a small clue in that you have the country, but nothing else. For example, if you struggled with this, would knowing the city started with K help?
- *Name three capital cities of East African countries. (Kampala, Uganda; Kigali, Rwanda; Nairobi, Kenya)* – firstly, you need to know at least three countries in East Africa, and then you have to recall the capital cities of these countries. Here, there are minimal cues to recall this information, as you don't even have access to the country names.

You can apply this to your own subject, reflecting on whether what you are learning in class is familiar and if you could recall it at a later date. For example, returning to our capital cities, it's useful to not only have surface knowledge of the names of these cities but to understand the concept of a capital city (ie a capital city is not necessarily the biggest city in a country, but is where the government sits). This is useful when thinking about our New Zealand question as Wellington is not the biggest city in the country.

There are different levels of understanding when we receive information, and identifying what is essential to understand deeply is a skill in itself, which, throughout the course of your degree, you will gain confidence in. It is likely that your lecturers will help you too. Think about the objectives or intended learning outcomes for the class. Are there concepts or theories that appear in many classes or that are fundamental to completing your assignment? Textbook chapters will highlight key ideas too. Once you have identified these objectives or learning outcomes, you can use the following section to engage in active learning to help you understand these further.

ACTIVE LEARNING IN PRACTICE

You can use active learning principles to focus on practices that will encourage encoding and easy recall of information from your long-term memory. You need strategies to remember this information, be able to recall it, and ultimately understand it enough to use it to analyse and evaluate. This book will focus on three strategies.

1. Retrieval practice (testing yourself).
2. Distributed practice (reviewing material over an extended time period).
3. Interleaved practice (mixing the type of problems you are focusing on and the topics you are studying).

We will look at these three strategies before exploring some activities you can undertake to practise them.

RETRIEVAL PRACTICE

Retrieval practice is one of the most effective ways of studying. This method helps us to move information from the working memory into the long-term memory; it is therefore an excellent tool for learning subject matter, and for retaining the information you need to understand that subject. Studies (eg Koriat and Bjork, 2005) have shown that even if we don't remember the material correctly when practising, using recall techniques can significantly improve performance in exams. Retrieval practice will also provide you with an overview of your current learning. Generally, we are not good at predicting our performance when learning a topic and overestimate our future memory; this is called an illusion of competence (Koriat and

Bjork, 2005). When we are passively re-reading a text it can be very easy to think we have memorised the information as it's familiar to us. However, there is a big difference between something being familiar and being able to recall it at a later date.

Retrieval practice can be very easy to implement into your study sessions. Some easy methods are the following.

TABLE 4.1: Recall practice

Flashcards	Digital or paper cards which enable testing.
Creating a one-page summary	Summarising key information, such as a lecture, into a single page.
Answering past exam papers	This could be answering the paper fully or, if it's an essay question, planning an answer. A good way to practise this is to draw a mind map and time yourself (perhaps for ten minutes), and then write everything you can remember on this topic. Subsequently, you can spend time afterwards going through your notes, adding any missed information, or correcting anything you may have remembered wrongly and thinking about how you would use this to formulate an answer.
Cover and test	A simple technique is to cover the summary page of a textbook or the learning outcomes of a lecture and then try to write down as much as you can remember or tell it to a friend. Then check to see what you got right.

Top tip: When practising recall, it's more useful to speak out loud or write down what you are testing yourself on, as it's easy to cheat when you simply say it in your head.

DISTRIBUTED PRACTICE

Distributed practice is the opposite of cramming: it's the idea that you spread out your learning of a topic over a given time period. The likelihood is that when learning at school you would have had distributed practice built into your lessons and would review topics over weeks and months. In comparison, when you become responsible for your own learning at higher education level it becomes more difficult to implement distributed practice. Typically, you will be taught a topic once and it becomes your responsibility as a student to ensure that you retain this information.

INTERLEAVED PRACTICE

Interleaved practice is similar to distributed practice, but you need to consider the types of studying and mixing up the problems you are considering. In practice, this means rather than simply studying for a single module all day, you would switch between different modules. For example, studying ecology for two hours, having a break, then studying zoology for two hours rather than simply studying ecology for an entire day.

It also means mixing the type of problems you are looking at. So rather than simply re-reading a textbook for two hours (as we have already highlighted, this would be passive learning), you could spend time reviewing the material, creating and using flashcards, and then creating a flowchart before summarising the lecture.

The third level of interleaved practice is ensuring you are changing how you are engaging with and learning new information. A simple understanding of interleaved practice would be: 2 × 2 =? Once you know the answer is 4, you can start rearranging the problem to ask 2 ×? = 4, not only memorising the information but asking why this is the answer.

When implementing distributed and interleaved practice, you will need to be organised and create a schedule of what you need to learn. This could be based on the lectures/topics you are studying that week. Having a weekly and monthly review will help greatly.

LECTURE REVIEWS

One way that active learning can be implemented is through a day, week, month and semester review. The overarching idea is that you review your core information (whether this be a pivotal textbook chapter or, more likely, a lecture) the day after you first hear or receive this information. We would encourage you to try and condense this information into a single page of A4 (the split-page method outlined in Chapter 7 is a great way of completing this).

After each lecture:

- create a one-page review;
- outline key concepts.

Weekly (if you have more than one lecture per week for a module):

- review one-page lecture reviews;
- condense all one-page reviews into a one-page summary.

Monthly:

- review the weekly summaries for the month;
- look at connections;
- test yourself on key concepts;
- create a condensed monthly summary;
- review previous monthly summaries.

End of semester:

- review condensed monthly summaries;
- test yourself on key concepts.

Within each review we would strongly encourage you to undertake a retrieval practice so you are engaging in active learning. The simplest way to undertake this would be to read through the summary sheet, and then cover it and try to write down as much of the information as possible from memory. Then check what information you missed or any areas you got wrong.

This will not cover all content of the module; however, when you create the summaries you will be actively engaging with the topic. The repetition of the content will help facilitate moving the information from your working memory to long-term memory. While this may seem daunting when you already have a large workload, here you can set yourself up for success by having organised summaries. This means that at the end of the semester or year, you should still remember all the content (and be able to actively engage with it), compared to having to teach yourself something you don't remember from six months ago.

FLASHCARDS

Another method that can be used is to practise spaced repetition by creating and regularly using flashcards. For flashcards to be effective, make sure you are testing yourself and not simply reading the information, as we want to engage in active, rather than passive, learning. When designing the cards, ensure that there is a question or cue on one side of the card and recallable information on the other. When you see the cue, try to remember as much of the information on the other side of the card as possible, ideally either writing this down or speaking it aloud. We would encourage you to create flashcards throughout the semester, which could be incorporated into your weekly review.

An effective method to ensure that you are engaging with all your flashcards is the Leitner system (shown in Figure 4.2), created by Sebastian Leitner in the early 1970s. The system works by categorising your flashcards into a series of boxes (physical or digital). All cards start in Box 1; when they are answered correctly, they progress into Box 2 and continue to progress into a higher box with each correct recall of information. If a card is incorrectly answered, it returns back to Box 1. The higher the box, the less frequently the flashcard is practised. For example, Box 1 may be practised every day, while Box 2 is every other day, Box 3 every three or four days, and so on.

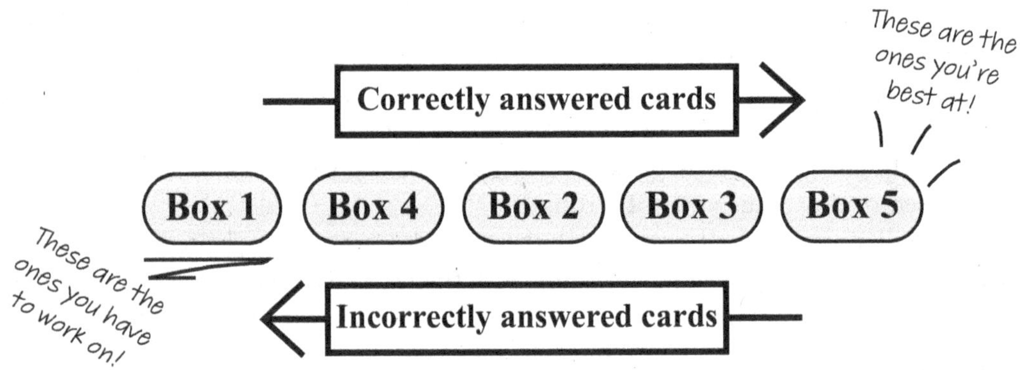

FIGURE 4.2: Leitner system

What is surprising is that these active learning practices are not commonly used by university students. Multiple researchers (eg Weinstein et al, 2018), in addition to our own anecdotal experiences, have shown that students tend to primarily focus on re-reading notes/textbooks and, to a lesser extent, rewriting notes. While this may seem odd when there is an extensive amount of research proving these are not the most effective ways to study, we can speculate a number of reasons why they are so popular. Firstly, as you will see throughout this chapter (and this book), applying effective learning strategies takes time and organisation. While long term they should save you time and even make learning more manageable, if they are not implemented early on it is easy to need to quickly retain information in order to pass the next assessment. Secondly, old habits die hard; if students have found previous success in simply trying to remember information, then they may wish to continue this rather than try new practices. Thirdly, students may not even be aware of more effective practices, especially if they have not had the opportunity to learn them at other education institutes.

4.3 LEARNING AUTONOMOUSLY: MANAGING YOUR TIME

In the workplace it is most likely that your boss (or colleagues) would hold you accountable if you did not meet deadlines. Similarly, at school your teachers would have supported you in meeting regular deadlines and often there would be immediate consequences if you handed in your homework late.

Yet at university you have to become accountable to yourself. Assessments usually take the form of large tasks such as writing a report or essay. There are, however, several steps that need to be undertaken before an essay or report can be submitted. You may have the opportunity to practise your accountability if your module is designed with smaller tasks built into the assessments. For example, you may have a weekly problem in maths or computer science you have to complete and bring to your lab before each session, or you may have to create an annotated bibliography for a classics tutorial. You will also have to take accountability for your learning in other ways; it is most likely that you will be responsible for accessing your own learning materials, whether that is borrowing or buying specific books or ensuring that you have the correct safety equipment for the lab. Similar to holding yourself accountable, another big shift when you start university (and often the most difficult) will be managing your time. Your weekly contact hours will be hours that you must be present at the university for and typically take place in the form of lectures, tutorials/seminars or labs. In addition to these slots, you will have other activities you have to or choose to undertake, for example part-time work, family or care responsibilities, co-curricular activities, sports clubs and society events. On top of these commitments, you will have 'life admin' such as arranging accommodation, buying food and looking after yourself (cooking, washing clothes etc), all in addition to spending time socialising and enjoying your time at university. There will always be many commitments to manage and some of these will clash; unfortunately, you will have to make

compromises. This transition is particularly difficult if you previously had a very busy, structured life, whether that be in a school or workplace with a rigid routine, and have then moved to a very flexible schedule with few fixed times. For example, if you are studying an arts degree you may have less than ten contact hours a week and a significant amount of independent learning, which may take some time to get used to.

There are some steps you can take to mitigate the difficulties of having a large amount of accountability in order to study effectively and enjoy your time at university. A lot of these will vary from person to person and you will need to adapt them to your own habits. As we outlined earlier in Chapters 1 and 2, there is a certain amount of trial and error while adapting to university study and often something will not stick until you have failed; someone can tell you the plate is hot, but often we still want to touch it!

This chapter looks at larger organisational tools for managing learning. You may also wish to reflect on the day-to-day time management techniques outlined in Chapter 6.

KNOW WHAT YOU NEED TO DO

At the start of each semester, create a detailed list of all your commitments and deadlines for that period. This could be in a Word document, Notion page, or on a wall planner or a sheet of paper you hang next to your desk. This list should include:

- all assessment deadlines;
- exam periods;
- other non-moveable commitments (such as sport tournaments);
- holidays or time away from study (such as visits to family or friends).

We would encourage you to put the list somewhere you will see it regularly, so deadlines do not surprise you.

RHYTHM AND ROUTINE

It can become easier to study if you create a routine for yourself where you complete the same tasks on working days. For example, if you can complete 30 minutes of reading at the start of every day, although this may seem like a chore at first, it will soon become a habit. By focusing on change principles (as outlined in Chapter 2), you can incorporate small activities into your daily routine that will help you to study.

Traditionally, study skills literature advises that you should approach studying like a 9–5 job, working these times Monday to Friday. Now, as many companies are moving to a more flexible working week, we think this advice should also reflect how to manage your time. Equally, we know very few students who work 9–5, and those who do are normally the ones who live with a person working these hours and thus they mirror them. We would highly advocate that during the semester you take at least one day per week away from study, and two days if possible (for example, the weekend). Instead of working 9–5, we have heard of students approaching their working days in three blocks: morning, afternoon and evening. On working days, they would dedicate two of these blocks to work and the other would be social and activities time.

It is important to be aware that there will be negative implications of studying at night. Most notably, that it is likely that your classes will take place during the day and you will need to be well rested to attend them. However, our bodies have preferences of when we work best, so be aware of these times and complete the most challenging tasks during these times while being aware of the larger impact this has on your week and day.

BEING PREPARED

Although 'being prepared' sounds like the simplest action point for time management, it's often the most difficult to complete. This will take into account planned actions such as ensuring you know which reading materials you will need for each week. At this stage, things can get complicated; for example, if there is a useful text required to complete an assignment but there are limited copies available in the library, you need to be organised enough to allow time to find a copy and use it. Being prepared also includes allowing time in weekly and semesterly schedules for things to go wrong, such as when computers break down or when you catch a sickness bug. By allowing this extra time, you can help mitigate often highly stressful situations.

PRACTITIONER INSIGHT

Professor Wendy A Garnham, professor in psychology, University of Sussex

Engaging with your subject by investigating, creating and doing has been shown to promote understanding, increase grades and boost motivation. This type of learning is fuelled by curiosity and enables you to move beyond mere rote learning to develop a stronger understanding of concepts and theories.

Students often mistake the increased effort associated with this type of learning to mean they have not learnt effectively. It can seem 'easier' to sit and listen instead. However, it is exactly the increased effort required in active learning that leads to the positive effects.

It isn't just academic benefits that have been associated with active learning. As you are working in collaboration with peers, it can also help to foster a sense of belonging. It has been associated with reductions in anxiety and reduced stress around assessments, and it can empower you to excel in the workplace by building your confidence and equipping you with valuable skills.

4.4 DEVELOPING YOUR CONFIDENCE IN EXAMS

Developing your confidence in your academic work can be very daunting but is essential for becoming an effective learner.

When marking exam papers and speaking to colleagues, we have found there is a common mistake students make when answering exam questions: they don't answer the question! This mistake often comes from students who have actually done a lot of great research around the topic and are so excited that they know the topic that they overload the answer with any bits of information they can recall that are even slightly related to the question. While this technique is better than not answering the question, it will always have limited success as your examiner wants you not only to remember this information, but to use it. They want you to critically engage with the great research that you have performed to analyse the prompt given and produce a thoughtful answer. We explore this further in Chapter 7.

When receiving an exam question (or any assessed coursework), there are some important first questions to ask.

1. What is the verb in this question? Typically, these are *examine*, *describe* or *compare*. Additionally, there may often be adverbs such as *what*, *why*, or *how*. By

firstly looking at this instruction, you can focus your attention on how you will use the information and not simply what information you need to recall.
2. Next, look at the topic of the question, such as 'nationalism' or 'animal adaptation'.
3. Finally, identify the limitations of the question. Is it asking you to focus on a specific time period, location or case study?

By taking a moment to answer these questions and then create a plan, you reduce the risk of informational overload in your answer.

It's important to note that exams have changed considerably in recent years. Open-book exams are far more common; although open-book exams come in different formats, the uniting feature of these is that you will have access to notes or possibly a host of resources (such as the internet). On the surface this may seem like the exam will be considerably easier; however, this is not the case and the format can be very different and challenging. It is unlikely that you will be asked simple recall questions (anything you can 'google'). Instead, exams will focus even more on analysis and evaluation of information. Here you will be asked not to simply recall information, but to interpret it and ask why or how it has happened.

To prepare for these exams, you will still need to understand and process the information in the same way you would prepare for a traditional closed-book exam. Even if you have a couple of days to answer the question (which is common for essay-based subjects), you will not have time to teach yourself the topic and write an essay. Instead, you will be using this time to construct your answer based on work that you have been completing throughout the semester. It will be important to have detailed notes (which we look at in Chapter 7), which are organised in a way that you can quickly access them.

When preparing for open-book exams, we advise students to practise finding the resource they need in a timed situation. A good way to do this is to find a past paper for your module, use a question you have discussed in class or create your own question based on your subject material (a great way to practise active learning), and then give yourself a set amount of time to answer it using notes that you will have access to during the exam. This will give you the opportunity to see, in a simulated environment, how easy your notes are to find as well as how confident you are with the topic and creating an answer. If it's a long question or an essay, you could also practise this by simply planning the answer.

With open-book exams, it's important to retain a balance between research and your own knowledge. After recently completing a short two-hour open-book exam for medicine, a student shared that they were looking up the equivalent of $2 \times 2 = 4$, purely because they had the option to. However, due to the extra time spent on looking up basic information, the student's timings were off and they struggled to answer all the questions. This shows the importance of knowing the subject material in detail even if you will have access to notes.

How you approach studying is just as important as the techniques you actually use to learn. Here you can boost your confidence and have an open mind to overcoming challenges, or you can have limiting beliefs which can hinder your ability to be successful at university. It's important when you learn that you engage a growth mindset (as we explored in Chapter 2). This means that if you are struggling with a topic, you understand that with time and effort you can gain a greater understanding of it. It also means that you should question your limiting beliefs; for example, it's easy to decide that you are going to fail an exam before you even sit it. This can become a self-fulling prophecy: you think you are going to fail so don't see the point of revising and thus don't do as well as you could have on the exam. Instead, you need to see challenges as an unavoidable part of your degree. A big part of applying this growth mindset is how you engage with feedback, which we will explore now.

4.5 UNDERSTANDING AND USING FEEDBACK

One of the biggest frustrations felt at university is that of feedback. It's interesting that feedback on learning is consistently one of the lowest-scoring areas in the National Student Survey (Office for Students, 2024) across UK universities. When we speak to new students, they feel that they have less feedback than they are used to receiving in school, college or the workplace. However, many of the lecturers we speak to are also frustrated and they feel they spend time giving feedback to students who then don't implement these actions.

Anecdotally, we think this frustration on both sides of the feedback relationship comes from a translation problem. Students haven't learnt the language of their discipline or the rules of university assessments, while academics are such experts in this area that their comments can seem alien to a new student. While this may not be true for all students and lecturers, it's a student's responsibility as an autonomous learner to engage with their feedback and build on it in the future. But this doesn't mean that you can't get help to do this!

In order for you to get the most out of feedback, we need to take a step back and think about what feedback actually is. The notion that you are receiving thoughts on your performance can be anxiety inducing. But you actually get and give feedback every day, just in a less formal setting. Your friend telling you they like your scarf is feedback and asking for more sauce on your chips is feedback. If you can simply think of feedback as information to change a situation (such as wearing an item of clothing again or the need for more mayonnaise), then hopefully the idea of receiving it can be less daunting.

In an academic setting you will also receive informal feedback about your learning; this will mainly be in the form of verbal feedback in seminars, tutorials and labs. You will of course receive formal feedback on assessments. It is likely that most of your feedback will be on a final unseen assignment (such as a lab report or essay). Although you may get the chance to receive formative feedback on an assignment before you submit it, this is quite rare and normally your marker will be seeing this piece of work or exam script for the first time. **Formative feedback** is often informal and takes place throughout the course to help you understand your process, compared to **summative feedback** which examines your knowledge at the end of a course, such as a final exam.

Therefore, when you get formal feedback, you need to think of it not just as a comment on the work you have done but, most importantly, how it will help you to improve your future work. This approach to feedback is essential for developing a growth mindset, which we discussed in Chapter 2. When looking at your feedback, you need to think about how you can build on this success, considering both how you can continue to do the things you did well (this is an important step we often forget), as well as anything you can do differently next time.

It's important to reflect on your expectations; it would be strange if you got something perfect the first time. Where would you go from there? This is especially true at the start of your degree when you are learning new content and navigating a new system of assessment.

It's very frustrating for both students and markers when students continue to make the same mistakes. What's even more frustrating is when you do something great in one assignment, and then you don't do it next time. In order to help mitigate this and use your feedback effectively, it's useful to read it carefully before creating an action plan.

ACTIVITY 4.3

Feedback action plan

- Based on a model created at the University of St Andrews, we suggest you create two tables: one that looks at your success and how you can continue to do this, and a second looking at improvements and listing practical actions you can undertake. Our feedback action plan has three steps.

1. Select a piece of feedback (it's likely that you will receive multiple comments/actions for each piece of work, so you'll have lots of rows on your tables for each piece of work).

2. Translate this into your own words, meaning that you fully understand what it means (if you struggle with this, it may be worth speaking to the marker).
3. Think about the practical steps you need to take to make sure you do that again in the future (for successful aspects) or do something differently (for aspects that could be improved).

Here is an example of a filled-in feedback action plan.

Feedback	**What does this mean?**	**How I can do this again in the future**
You have engaged well with the text and have a clear understanding of the subject matter. This expertise is evidenced in your choice of quotations and your analysis of them.	I understood the materials that I read and used them in my report. I chose appropriate quotes in my report and commented on them using my wider reading and own thoughts.	I will make sure to keep taking detailed notes when reading, which help me understand the text.

Feedback	**What does this mean?**	**How I can improve this in the future**
Your structure in this essay is a little confused. Sections 2 and 3 link together well, but Sections 1 and 4 seem out of place. It does not follow a logical order, nor one that supports your argument. I would encourage you, in the future, to aim for a more coherent piece of work.	My essay did not flow from one section to another. The order of the essay did not help the reader understand my point. I need to think about the best way to structure my essay in the future and allow time to do so.	I need to allow more time to work on my essay, to make sure that I am not rushing the editing process. I also need to ensure that I produce a plan before I begin writing, to get my ideas in order. I will book an appointment with the university writing coach to learn more about structuring my work.

Here's a blank copy for you to use.
Things to continue doing:

Feedback	What does this mean?	How I can do this again in the future

Things to do differently:

Feedback	What does this mean?	How I can improve this in the future

CHAPTER SUMMARY

We began this chapter by thinking about what a student is, and how you would engage with this identity. The first part of the chapter looked at learning autonomously and the science of learning. Here we briefly looked at cognitive science in order to understand how our brains process information, employing this to ensure that you engage with active learning and summarised some principles about how to do this in practice. Building upon this, we examined how to learn autonomously and the shift that you will face when attending university. The chapter concluded by looking at developing your confidence in undertaking exams and assignments and exploring feedback at university.

TOP TIPS AND NEXT STEPS

- Reflect on how you approach study; think quality not quantity.
- Use the feedback action plan to reflect on past assignments and build on this success in the future.
- What current methods do you use to study? Are these active or passive techniques?
- Reflect on whether you are an autonomous learner. What obstacles do you suspect will hinder you from being an autonomous learner?

CHAPTER 5
YOUR SKILLS AND ATTRIBUTES

CHALLENGES WE EXPLORE IN THIS CHAPTER

This chapter gives you the opportunity to answer two big questions: where are you going, and how will you get there? You will then have the opportunity to reflect on these questions to think about your skills development, goals and plans.

If you're reading this book in the order it's presented, you will have just learnt about the best ways to build a learner and will have reflected on the importance of becoming a confident and autonomous learner yourself. One of the key challenges university students face is how to know what to spend their time on and where to focus their learning. This chapter helps you with this by focusing on the importance of planning and setting goals. You will learn some goal-setting strategies and how to plan using a **Gantt chart**. This chapter also helps you to think about all the different skills you could develop while at university and where you might want to put your focus. To do this we introduce you to a **skills framework** and invite you to think about where you currently are with regard to developing each of these skills. You should finish the chapter feeling clearer about the importance of developing skills and with a plan for where you want to develop your skills in the coming year.

INTENDED LEARNING OUTCOMES

By the end of this chapter, you should be able to:

- reflect on the importance of purposely developing a set of transferable skills;
- value the breadth of ways you can develop skills while at university and the range of skills you can develop;
- set some goals for the year ahead using the goal-setting strategies discussed in this chapter;

→

- plan your assignments using a Gantt chart;
- identify ways in which you are developing both a breadth and depth of skills;
- understand and relate to the five categories which form our skills wheel;
- complete a reflective skills analysis against the skills framework and highlight skills to develop in the coming year.

5.1 ANSWERING THE TWO BIG QUESTIONS: WHERE ARE YOU GOING, AND HOW WILL YOU GET THERE?

The two questions '*where are you going, and how will you get there?*' seem like fairly big questions, don't they? If you stopped someone in the street and asked them that, they might look at you a bit strangely and say '*I'm going to the shops and I'm going to take the number 38 bus*', in which case the questions aren't all that big, but if you pressed them to answer in terms of their *life* or their *career* or their *aspirations* and *goals*, it's likely they might not have the answer at their fingertips.

The truth is most people don't have everything figured out with regard to where they are going and how they will get there. In your university class there might be a minority of people who have a very clear idea of where they are going and how they plan to get there. Perhaps they've had their heart set on a particular career path for a very long time or have returned as mature learners to further an already established career. If so, they might have worked with a singular focus to get the grades or experience needed to get onto this particular course and have the next several years of their lives mapped out. Perhaps this is you! If it is, that's great. You have a clear plan and motivation to achieve it.

However, in your university class, you might also find that the majority of students have no idea at all about where they are going and how they are going to get there. Is this you? That's also great! You have time on your side and so many opportunities to try things out and see which direction you might want to head in.

Finally, in your university class, there will likely be a third group of students who have a rough idea about where they might like to go and a few thoughts about *maybe* what they could do to head in that vague direction. Is this you? We have good news: that's also great! You are starting from a position where you have curiosity and there is plenty you can do to investigate further.

Here's the thing: you don't need to know which career area you want to go into on day one of university, but what you *can* start doing is thinking about your skills.

You can think about the skills that have brought you here – to become a university student. The skills that you enjoy building, and which come easily to you; the skills that you enjoy building, but which *don't* come easily to you; and the skills that you have little interest in developing. These will help you to work out where you are going and how will you get there.

5.2 VALUING THE BREADTH OF SKILLS DEVELOPMENT

Being at university presents many opportunities to develop skills, and you will find that developing a particular skill allows you to improve across multiple domains. Many students find it difficult to make connections between what they are doing as a regular part of student life and how it is helping them develop a skillset that is going to benefit them in the future. For example, completing an assignment for a class will help to develop a whole range of skills such as organisation, time management, research, creativity, team working and resilience. If you don't *know* that something is happening, then it's really hard to describe it to someone else, like an employer in a job interview, for example. Chapter 6 focuses on how reflection allows you to become more self-aware about your skills and make these connections, and Chapter 11 covers how to articulate your skills, but for now let's focus on thinking about what you might be doing as a student, and if these activities could be helping you develop useful skills.

The first thing to do is to set a wide scope when thinking about what kinds of skills you might develop and where you might be developing them. If you say the word 'university' the first place your mind might go is to a large group of students in a lecture hall and, yes, here is exactly where you might be developing a range of **academic skills** to help you become a better student, but you will also develop a range of academic skills outside of the lecture theatre (for example, through lab classes or field trips). You might also develop a range of academic skills far from the traditional 'classroom' environment. For example, developing your research skills through your hobby of tracking down rare vinyl records, or developing your academic resilience because you failed your driving theory test and are now focusing on the areas in which you need to improve in order to pass. The point is that academic skills such as data analysis, critical thinking and synthesising information can be developed in lots of places and by undertaking activities that might not seem very 'academic' at first glance.

It's a similar story for developing professional skills like managing a project, team working, leadership, or IT and digital skills. A skillset that's becoming increasingly in demand due to how quickly the world is changing is entrepreneurial skills such as creativity, problem-solving and being able to recognise opportunities. These too can be developed in a great range of places.

So, the good news is that almost everything you do during your time as a student will generate skills development in you – studying, joining university clubs and societies, volunteering, part-time working, socialising, living with others, caring for others, commuting, hobbies, taking part in optional workshops and courses outside of your own degree course: it all counts! Your job is to become skilled at making the connections and spotting which skills these activities are giving you.

All of these skills development methods can be effective, and it's valuable to use and appreciate a range of ways to develop your skills. Being mindful of how you might develop through a blend of curricular, co-curricular and extra-curricular activities helps you appreciate the holistic nature of skills development and recognise the fact that opportunities to develop are everywhere.

5.3 SETTING GOALS

In order to give the process of working out where you are going and how you will get there a little bit more focus, this section explores how setting goals might help you build your skills and get the most from your university experience. You're probably also aware, however, that people often struggle to achieve goals (DiSalvo, 2020), so let's first look at some of the reasons why this may be.

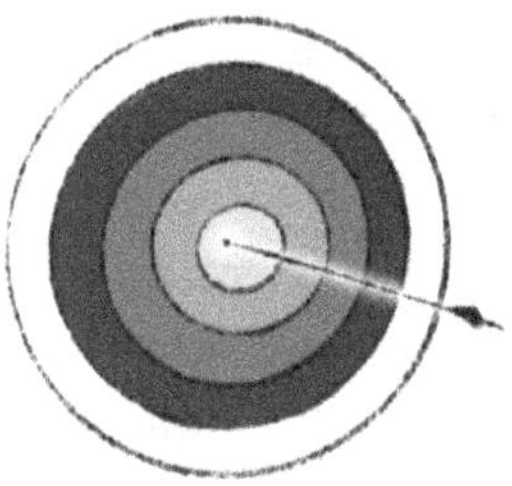

Think about goals you might have set yourself in the past that you didn't achieve. Most people have quite a long list of these. Do you know why you didn't achieve them? Perhaps you simply lost interest because your goal wasn't motivating enough, or maybe your goal was too ambitious, or so vague you weren't sure what success looked like in the context of that goal.

So, what might be happening in those cases where people *do* hit their goals? Last year for Cat's birthday she received two presents, both of which gave her opportunity to develop her skills. Her friends gifted her a ukulele because she always wanted to be able to play a musical instrument, and a ukulele seemed like an easy choice. The second was that she gifted herself a mindfulness app, which she'd heard a few people talking about. Fast forward a year, and one of these gifts is now a part of her routine and forms a skill she practises daily, whereas the other didn't last a month. Two gifts, two goals, related to developing two skills (playing an instrument and being mindful), yet only one was successful.

Reveal: she is not a proficient ukulele player; this was the goal that failed. When she reflects on why, it was because it required quite significant effort (daily tuning and practising); nothing bad happened if she didn't meet her goal (there was no one there to hold her to account); it was a solo goal (there was no one else there to make it fun); and there wasn't much positive feedback (the noises she was producing were not good).

But she is getting better at the skill of being mindful. This goal was met. She thinks the factors which helped her achieve this goal included:

- that she was invested in it (she bought the app for herself);
- others were practising the skill with her (some of her friends practise mindfulness so she had social support);
- the goal was visible (every time she looked at her phone, the app was there and reminded her of her goal);
- it didn't require much effort (she only needed to complete one ten-minute lesson per day);
- the goal was incentivised (once she finished a lesson, the app would give her a reward in the form of a big green tick and tell her how many days in a row she had practised for);
- she was clear about the benefits (she had read and heard how being mindful can be helpful with focusing attention and decreasing stress).

These factors of investment, social support, visibility, low effort, incentivisation and clear benefits can be important in helping us to set and achieve goals.

We tend to set goals because we want to elicit a change or improve something in some way. One way to conceptualise how we can change is to look at something called the Beckhard–Harris change equation (Beckhard and Harris, 1977), shown in Figure 5.1.

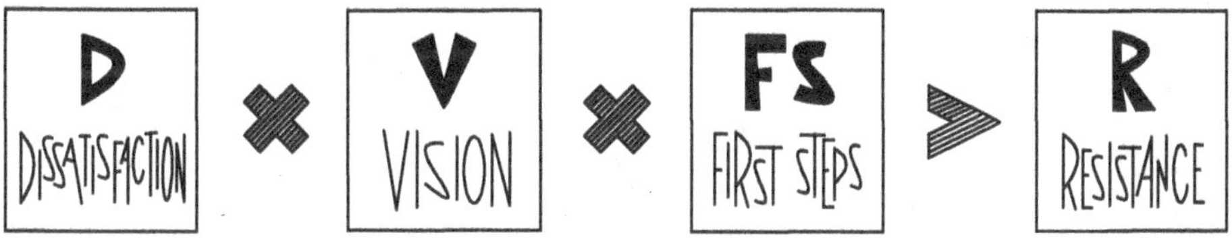

FIGURE 5.1: The Beckhard–Harris change equation

On the right-hand side of our 'equation' is R, which represents resistance to change. This is the notion that most of us quite like things as they are and don't want to expend effort to change. To overcome this built-in inertia, we have to ensure that the three things on the left-hand side of the equation are big enough to overcome our resistance. The first of these is 'D', which refers to dissatisfaction with the current situation. We have to be really honest with ourselves about why we're not totally happy with things as they are and why we shouldn't wait to take action. Then we have to imagine a clear vision, the 'V', about what the future could look like: what would be the benefits of reaching our goal or developing our skill? The clearer and more specific we can be about this, the better. And then we must have some simple and easy first steps, the 'FS', practical and small things we can do to move us a little bit closer to our imagined vision.

This could be a good starting point for thinking about some of the goals you might have right now as you begin or continue your university studies. Start with 'D' – which areas aren't as good as they could be and you would like to make improvements in? It might help if you think about various categories that could be relevant to your life; for example, it could be study skills, managing money, physical or mental health, friends, becoming part of new communities, finding new interests, moving towards a potential career area, helping the environment, or more besides.

If you have some categories that you'd like to develop in, you can then start to formulate some goals that sit within these categories. For example, if your category is 'study skills', your goal might be to improve your note-taking technique in lectures or to learn how to structure an essay. If your category is 'friends', your goal might be to make some new friends on your course but also to not lose touch with your existing friends, and perhaps even to make friends who aren't on your course but who share an interest with you.

ACTIVITY 5.1

Getting ready for change

- Think about a goal you have, or a goal you would like to work towards, and use the table below to identify the 'D', the 'V' and 'FS' related to that goal.

My goal is ...	
I am dissatisfied with ...	
My vision is ...	
The first steps I could take are ...	

USING THE SMART ACRONYM AND PRIORITISING GOALS

Once you have some ideas for goals, your work is not done! To really increase the chances of you reaching these goals, we're going to use the **SMART acronym** (Doran, 1981) to make it easier for you to be successful.

Ask yourself. Is this goal ...

- **S**pecific – be really clear about what it is you want to do; we don't want any vagueness here!
- **M**easurable – how will you know if you have reached the goal?
- **A**chievable – is it possible to meet this goal?
- **R**ealistic – is it likely that you will meet this goal?
- **T**ime-bound – when will working on this goal begin and end?

So, in our example our goal might change from '*I want to improve my note-taking technique in lectures*' to become '*I want to research different note-taking techniques and try a new technique in a lecture by the end of the month*'. Suddenly we have a clear task and timeframe, and we have checked that it feels both achievable and realistic.

Another thing to think about at this stage of finessing our goals is whether our goals are related to outcome, performance or process.

Outcome goals are based on wanting a successful outcome, such as landing a part-time job or winning a competition. **Performance goals** are based on you performing to a high(er) personal standard, such as gaining a first-class grade in your module. Outcome and performance goals can be hard to have control over – there are often other factors at play. Instead, try to focus on *process* goals. **Process goals** are the specific actions or processes that can help you to perform, and lead to successful outcomes, but that you have more control over. So, if your goal is to achieve a high grade in your module, this could change to '*I want to set aside one hour every weekday to read an optional source from the reading list*'. This will help you towards your performance goal, but you are focusing on a process you have autonomy over.

ACTIVITY 5.2

Generating SMART goals

It's your turn now to practise writing some SMART, process-focused goals for the coming year. You could use the goal you identified in Activity 5.1 as one, if you like.

- Take two or three blank pages and divide them into two headings: one heading stating 'Categories' and another 'Goals'.
- Start by identifying some categories that you'd like to improve in, and then generate some goals using the guidance in this section.
- Your goals should be written using the SMART acronym.

If Activity 5.1 is leading you to think of lots and lots of goals you might want to set yourself at university, that's excellent! However, be careful not to overwhelm yourself. When Cat has a list of goals, she applies a **prioritisation** process to help her slim down to those goals that she's most invested in.

1. Step 1: Give your goals a ranking of 1–10 (1 is not very important and 10 is incredibly important).
2. Step 2: Write down what cost you're willing to pay to achieve the goal. If you feel the costs of achieving the goal are too high, the chances are you won't be successful. You may have to revise or break up your goal into smaller chunks and go back to the drawing board on it.
3. Step 3: Write down the first steps required to get moving – the easier and smaller the better.

Here's an example.

TABLE 5.2: Example of a table to help prioritise goals

Goal	Importance ranking	Costs	First steps
Research different note-taking techniques and try a new technique in a lecture by the end of the month.	8	Set aside an afternoon for research, and have a few failed experiments in lectures if a new technique I try doesn't work.	Do an online library search for a book on note-taking techniques.

The prioritisation process helps Cat whittle down her goal list to those that she is very invested in and willing to meet the costs of. Oh, and you're much more likely to achieve your goal if you tell someone else about it, so make sure you let a friend know what you're hoping to do.

ACTIVITY 5.3

Prioritising goals

- Revisit your goal list and for each goal think about giving it a priority ranking (on a scale of 1–10), consider the costs you're willing to invest to achieve it and what first steps you need to take to get things moving.

So far, we've created a vision for where we want to improve, we've identified categories and goals within those categories, and then we've made them SMART and process focused. We've also prioritised our goals and thought about costs, and we've even made it easy for ourselves to begin because we have simple first steps. That has to be it, right?

Not quite! There's still a good chance you won't meet your goal. We need to be prepared to deal with failure if things don't quite go as we hope. Failing is perfectly normal. When it happens, it's a good chance to go back to the '*why is this goal important to me*' question. If the goal is no longer important to you, it can be deleted from your goal list. If it is still important, then the failure has been an important piece of feedback to you about what *doesn't* work. It's an indicator that you need to change your approach in some way.

We all fail with goals, but we're not always kind to ourselves when we do. It can help to think about what you'd say to a good friend if they came to you and told you that they'd failed in a goal. You would likely be kind to them and tell them it's okay and not to worry, and that they can dust themselves off and have another go. This is also what you should be telling yourself.

If you have failed in a goal and want to have another go, there's some science that can help us with making our intended changes stick. Author and researcher BJ Fogg found that you will have more likelihood of success if you pick a small action and in some way connect it to an existing habit (Fogg, 2019). So, in the example of our goal to do an hour of optional reading every day, is there something else you do every day as a habit that you can link this goal to? Most people eat lunch every day, so perhaps you can link your goal action to this. As soon as you finish lunch you start doing your reading.

It can be helpful to make the new action easy by setting it up in advance. So, if you want to do your optional reading straight after lunch, you set it up right before lunch by pulling up the reading list on your computer and loading the first article so it's all ready to go. Just a little nudge to make it easier can make a big difference to the likelihood of you doing it.

At this stage you have a set of goals that you want to achieve as part of your university experience, so the next thing to think about is how these goals form part of your short-, medium- or long-term plans.

5.4 HAVING A PLAN

Now you're armed with some realistic goals to help you focus your energy at university, we can think about the value of making plans. While your goals help you be clear about where you want to get to, a plan helps you work out exactly *how* you're going to get there.

Just as some people in your lecture or tutorial will be certain about where they want to get to, and others might have no idea, there will also be a mixture of how much people use planning to help them work towards goals. Having no plan at all is a risky strategy, but so too is having a plan so rigid that you panic when it gets knocked off course. Because this is the thing about plans; they rarely execute themselves exactly as you hope they will. Plans in real life involve lots of variables which you don't have control over. Therefore, ideally you need a plan that's clear enough for you to follow, but also roomy and flexible enough to bend a little bit in unexpected circumstances.

You can think about having plans that have short-, medium- and long-term horizons. This will likely match some of your goals. For example, making some new friends might be a short-term goal for you in your first few weeks of university; taking more effective notes in lectures might be medium term – perhaps it will take a whole term or semester; setting aside an hour every day for optional reading might be a long-term goal that you want to embed across your whole degree. In order to keep track of everything, you might want to think about how you break goals down into specific tasks and plan for them to happen. We will consider how to keep track of these goals and tasks by looking at **sequencing, scheduling** and **contingency time.**

SEQUENCING, SCHEDULING AND CONTINGENCY

Sequencing is where you think about all the steps or tasks that are involved in working towards a goal or completing a project, and then figuring out which order they have to go in. This stops you doing a task too early or too late. Let's use our example of wanting to take more effective notes in lectures. First of all, we need to break the goal down into the constituent tasks. In this case the tasks might be:

- trying out a new note-taking technique in a lecture;
- learning about different ways to take notes;
- knowing where to find out about note-taking techniques;
- reflecting on how effective the new techniques were and choosing which to adopt.

Next, we need to sequence these tasks into an order that makes sense. This example is very simple, but you can imagine things might get much more complex if you had a substantial project which you needed to break down into its individual component tasks. Clearly, we can't try out new techniques if we don't know what they might be, nor can we learn about different techniques if we don't know where to look. So, the sequence of these tasks that makes sense to reach the goal is:

- finding sources for learning about note-taking;
- reading and researching these to learn about different techniques;
- practically experimenting with the new techniques in a lecture environment and reflecting on their effectiveness.

A tip for working out what your tasks might be and how best to sequence them is to start not at the beginning but at the end. Imagine you've just finished your project or completed your goal. What was the very last thing you would have needed to do? And the step immediately before that? And so on.

When you sequence tasks, you might notice that some are contingent on others – that is, you can't do one task without having done a preceding one. But you will also find that there are tasks that can be done concurrently, and your sequencing might reflect that.

This leads us on to the notion of scheduling: putting a timeline to your sequence. You're getting into the nitty gritty of planning here, figuring out what time you need to allocate to each of the tasks or steps you've identified and when this is going to happen. Again, you can do some scheduling at a zoomed-out level or a zoomed-in one. You could theoretically schedule your entire semester with some key milestones that you've identified as part of the sequence towards your project or goal. Perhaps more manageably, you could schedule out a month or a week. And at a micro level, you can have a plan for a single day.

At university you might find that you have a glut of deadlines for assignments and exams all lined up for around the same time. Time management is one of the aspects of university that, in our experience, students find the most difficult. We work with a lot of students who are very able and committed to their studies but who find it difficult to manage their time, and their performance suffers as a result. A key part of this is poor planning.

GANTT CHARTS

When you're working on multiple goals and projects simultaneously, which have similar deadlines, you might want to employ some tools which help you keep track of the planning. These tools don't have to be fancy. Project planners, who have to stay on top of lots of moving parts, often use something called a Gantt chart. This is a way of laying out all the tasks you've got going on against time, and seeing at a glance which tasks can happen simultaneously.

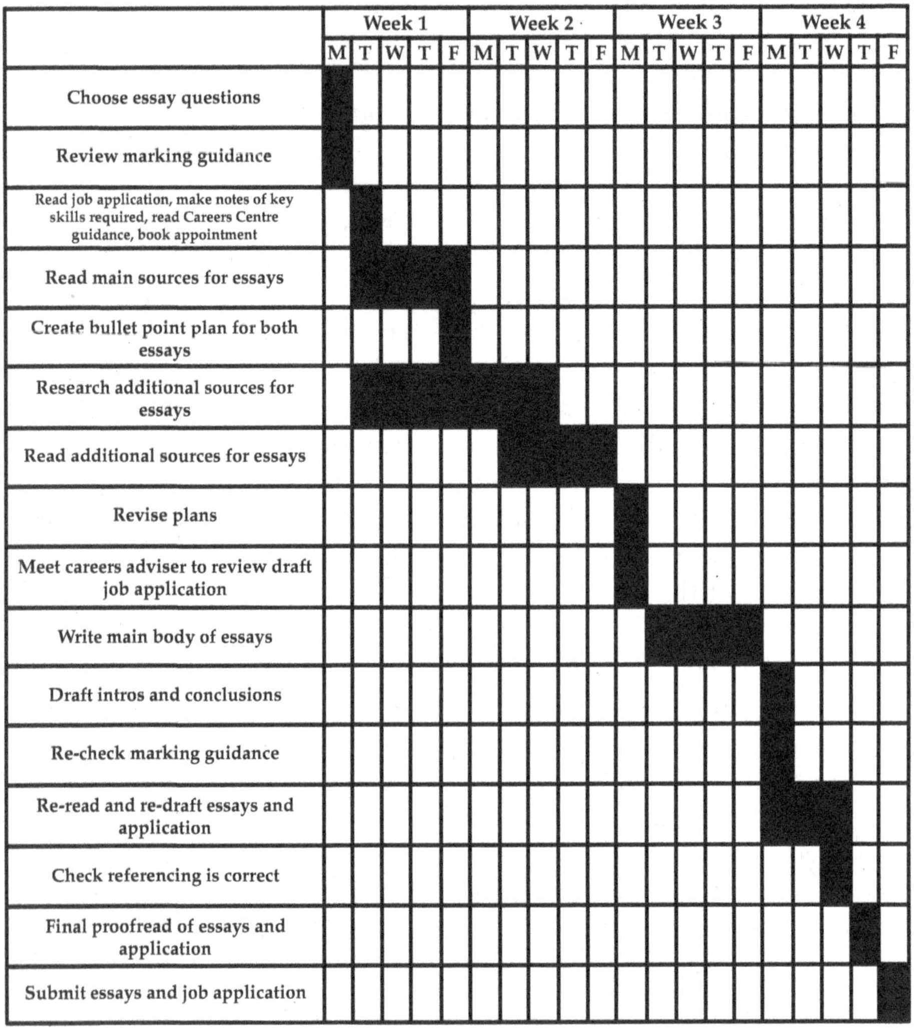

FIGURE 5.2: An example Gantt chart showing one month of a student's assignment planning happening alongside a job application

A Gantt chart has some form of timeline along the top: it could be days, weeks or months. Down the side it has the component tasks that make up the project or goal. In the centre it shows blocks of time set against each of these tasks. Have a look at the example in Figure 5.2. It shows the month in the run-up to a student having the same deadline for two different modules they are studying and an application for a part-time job that they want to submit.

Gantt charting can help you work out what is a realistic amount of time you need to complete your project or goal (also helped by our top tip of starting at the end when sequencing). You can read more in Chapter 6 about managing time and energy, but one of the most common mistakes students make is not starting their projects with enough time and either not having solid plans or not following them!

There are apps you can download to help you create a Gantt chart (such as Asana, Wrike or GanttPro, among others), or of course you can do it on an Excel spreadsheet or even with a piece of paper and pen.

STUDENT INSIGHT

Martin Ladekarl, social anthropology, second year

The benefits of having a plan and being organised are fourfold. Not only does planning lead to more holistic approaches towards work, but it also allows for revision and adaptation as you work. On a simpler level, planning adds a layer of security knowing that you are on top of your objectives.

I tend to get sidetracked when I do research by potentially unimportant details. Knowing this, I include references back to my research question throughout my plan.

I plan in advance based on the size of the project. For smaller projects I like to give myself five days and for medium and large projects I like to give myself a week or ten days, respectively.

Planning ahead as a student is important for both your academic achievements and your ability to actually learn the course material rather than loosely retaining it.

WEEKLY PLANNER

A common companion to a Gantt chart would be a good old weekly planner. This can be such a powerful tool to keep you organised and heading in the right direction. All the thought you've already put into breaking down your goals and projects into work tasks, placing them in a logical sequence and thinking about how long each task takes means that by the time you come to fill in your weekly planner, all the hard work is done.

Here are some key tips.

1. There is only one you, so only have one system of planning, whether that is a paper diary or an app on your phone.
2. Build in contingency time – things become stressful when you can never keep up with your plan.

3. Remember to allow time outside of your academics for life admin, commuting, socialising, exercise, and of course some downtime for yourself.
4. Protect time for the activities which are important to you – this should include learning but will also be your hobbies and interests.
5. Find a routine that works well for you, and this can make life easier.
6. Neurodiversity can make planning and sticking to a plan much harder – it's important to be kind to yourself and try different systems until you find a good fit.

Figure 5.3 shows an example of a student's weekly planner.

	Monday	Tuesday	Wednesday	Thursday	Friday	Saturday	Sunday
7:00		Wake up		Wake up			
8:00	Wake up	Morning Run	Wake up	Go to the Gym	Wake up	Wake up	
9:00	Maths Lecture		Maths Lecture		Maths Lecture		
10:00				Reading List			Wake up
11:00	Library	Biology Lecture	Library	Biology Lecture	Biology Tutorial	Cycle Ride with Team	
12:00							Brunch with friends
13:00	Lunch	Lunch	Lunch	Lunch	Lunch	Lunch	
14:00	Lecture Review	Library	Reading List	Lecture Review	Lecture Review		Library
15:00		Biology Labs		Biology Labs			Call friends
16:00	Reading List		Lecture Review		Reading List	Catch up time for Lectures & Notes	
17:00			Maths Tutorial		Dinner		Summarise Lectures
18:00	Dinner	Washing		Grocery Shop	Club Run		
19:00		Dinner	Dinner			Dinner	Dinner
20:00	Movie Night	Lecture Review		Dinner	Pub with Team	Reading List	Movie Night
21:00		Sleep		Sleep			
22:00	Sleep		Sleep		Sleep		
23:00						Sleep	Sleep

FIGURE 5.3: Example of a student's weekly planner

ACTIVITY 5.4

Plan your week

Have a go at scheduling your coming week. Put in everything that's relevant for you: work, studying, sleeping, eating, exercise, socialising, reading, planning and anything else you can think of.

- See if you find it easy or difficult to make room for everything.
- How easy is it to know what's happening day to day?
- Do you need to build in contingency time for the unknown? How would you incorporate this?

In a week's time you can revisit your plan and see how well you were able to stick to it.

	Monday	Tuesday	Wednesday	Thursday	Friday	Saturday	Sunday
7:00							
8:00							
9:00							
10:00							
11:00							
12:00							
13:00							
14:00							
15:00							
16:00							
17:00							
18:00							
19:00							
20:00							
21:00							
22:00							
23:00							

If you find that planning can be especially challenging, you might find value in trying different versions of planning tools and using the ones that work best for you. While you might not find a system that 100 per cent works for you, any planning system, even an imperfect one, is better than none at all. There may be a learning support team at your university that can offer you further help and support with planning.

5.5 BUILDING A BREADTH AND DEPTH OF SKILLS – BECOMING A T-SHAPED STUDENT

In the previous section, we talked about valuing the breadth of skills development and some of the many ways that you will develop skills. In this section, we will now think about the importance of developing both a breadth and depth of skills, and how you can conceptualise this as becoming a 'T-shaped' student (Guest, 1991).

The new subjects and topics you are learning will be expanding your overall *breadth* of knowledge, whereas the continued studies in areas you already have a grounding in are expanding your *depth* of knowledge. When you put this 'horizontal' learning and 'vertical' learning together, you can imagine the shape of the letter T, as shown in Figure 5.4.

FIGURE 5.4: A 'T'-shaped concept for student development: a combination of generalist skills and wide learning (breadth) with specialist skills and deep learning (depth)

Having a good *breadth* of skills and knowledge allows you to make connections between different areas and tie different elements of learning together. This ability to connect different areas of learning often breeds creative thinking and can help you conceptualise new ideas or envision solutions to problems. It's a great asset to have. Having a good *depth* of skills means that you are becoming an expert in your field and building specialist knowledge that not everyone has. The more you study a specific subject or work to develop a specific skill, the more you learn and the deeper your pool of knowledge is to draw on.

Thinking ahead to after your studies when you embark on a career, or in some cases return to one, there will be value in being aware of being 'T-shaped'. Some careers lend themselves to employees having a deep specialism, for example IT developers who become specialists in a particular coding language, or human resources professionals who specialise in employment law, or medics who train to become cardiologists. Other careers benefit from practitioners having more of a generalist approach, for example primary teachers who deliver a wide curriculum, or organisational consultants who work across a number of diverse organisations.

However, even in these examples it helps if people can draw on both the 'vertical' and the 'horizontal'. For example, specialist IT developers might have to work in a team with others who don't share their specialism and need to know how their work links to that of others. A cardiac specialist in the hospital needs to know how the rest of the body works too. Similarly, generalists who have a great breadth of skills might need to know how to drill down and apply learning in a narrower, more expert setting.

Employers are keen to recruit 'T-shaped' students for graduate roles. Being conscious of this as you develop your skills and learning at university, and thinking about how you're expanding your skillset both horizontally and vertically, will put you at an advantage for whatever comes next.

PRACTITIONER INSIGHT

Dr Ben Carter, careers consultant, University of Manchester

What does every graduate have in common? A degree! The disciplines may vary, but from an employer's perspective, it can be hard to tell university leavers apart based purely on their subject. So how do you stand out? By considering your experiences and the different ways they can be viewed.

→

On the one hand, if you want to turn your degree subject matter into your career, depth of experience counts. Seeking relevant internships, insight events and networking opportunities allows you to dive deeper than your degree may allow. It will also demonstrate your commitment to the field and desire to grow.

On the other hand, broadening your horizons is an important part of career development. How will you know what's for you if you don't search around? The extracurriculars and volunteering; the student advocacy and fascinating-but-irrelevant part-time work – these all serve to enrich your lived experiences and your job applications.

Balance is key here – take either of these options too far, and it can throw your CV out of shape. Start to consider this balance early though, and it can give you the confidence and stability to continue.

5.6 INTRODUCING OUR SKILLS WHEEL: FIVE CATEGORIES, 20 ATTRIBUTES

By now, you should hopefully be aware of the fact that your university experience is going to develop a range of skills in you, that these skills are valuable, and that they will help you move forward in a particular direction – to get to where you're going. You might have ideas about some specific goals you want to achieve and ideas about how you can plan well to make them happen. However, you might also be a little vague about exactly what sorts of skills you might develop during the course of reaching your goals or being part of a university community.

To help give you some clarity, meet our skills wheel. It's a framework to help you think about your skills and how they might relate to one another. Our skills wheel, set out in Figure 5.5, has five important categories that students will need in order to succeed in a changing world. Within each of these categories there are a number of separate yet related attributes: component skills that you should be able to develop during your time as a student.

FIGURE 5.5: Our *University and You* skills wheel

Thinking about skills development within some kind of framework can be helpful for a few reasons.

- It can give you a focus, so you're not overwhelmed by a never-ending list of skills.
- It can give you a structure to benchmark against. You can think about each skill and reflect on your current ability level.
- The framework can help you decide where you want to go.
- Seeing the skills laid out next to one another can help you think about the connections between them and how they might interact with one another.

We present the five categories: **self-leadership**, **research**, **diversity**, **connectivity**, and **agency** and **community**.

SELF-LEADERSHIP

Developing leadership can be a life-long activity and comprises not just leading others, but also the ability to lead yourself. Leaders are responsible for helping to identify change they want to see in the world, setting a vision that others can buy in to, galvanising others to engage, and steering and shaping the resultant change. But leadership has to start from within, and your ability to lead yourself, in terms of being aware of your values, understanding what motivates and drives you, managing your time and energy, and knowing how to use your preferred leadership styles, is a foundation which needs to be in place before you can effectively manage others. The problems that the world faces are complicated, and the students who are going to play a part in solving them are going to need to display leadership – be that in their academic discipline, professional work, social circles or within themselves.

RESEARCH

Universities exist to provide benefits to the economy and society and to generate new knowledge and learning. A combination of teaching and research helps to drive universities forward – the teaching informs and advances the research, and the research informs and advances the teaching. Developing the ability to research well is a critical skill, and the ability to know how to research is a transferrable skill that applies to all areas of life, not just academia.

Students at university tend to have the opportunity to develop their research skills throughout their degree, and the majority of programmes will have a significant portion which involves students devising and carrying out research projects.

Being able to engage with information critically and assign credibility to sources can make a huge difference to our lives and decision making in an interconnected world of ever-increasing disinformation. Additionally, being a good researcher involves being able to spot opportunities and pursue them, and to think in creative ways. This creative spark, combined with critical thinking, allows researchers to find new ways to approach and solve problems.

DIVERSITY

You might think of **diversity** as being everything that makes us different from one another – our nationality, age, gender, sexual orientation, political views, educational background, privilege, previous work experience, religion and beliefs, neurodiversity, abilities and disabilities, etc – but this can have the result of dividing us. Part of having a **global mindset** can involve being conscious of just how much people have in common. Did you know that the moral values people hold, such as group loyalty, reciprocity and fairness, are the same across the world? (Curry et al, 2019).

Instead, let's think of diversity as the things that can give us strength in a particular situation: our different lived experiences and ways of seeing the world can be especially valuable in terms of helping us to be creative, solve problems and understand situations more fully. Being aware of what helps you contribute to the diverse make-up of your class or work team is important. So is appreciating the diversity of others and seeking it out where you can.

CONNECTIVITY

Our world seems smaller now than it has ever been. There are more transport hubs and ever-faster journey times to move between cities, countries and continents. There are more efficient and creative technologies that connect us. It's entirely possible to be in a student or work team with colleagues you might never meet in person because you are spread across the globe, yet you can work together in real time on the same document or presentation or talk in the same meeting or tutorial.

Manufacturing supply chains can be truly international. If you are fortunate enough to have a smartphone in your pocket, it might well represent the interconnectedness of the world around us. An iPhone is made from components purchased from suppliers in 43 countries across six continents (Petrova, 2018). This global interconnectedness is highlighted when it comes to the fact that tackling our most pressing challenges, such as the climate emergency, can only really truly work when there is a joined-up global approach.

To be the most effective student today you will need to be a citizen not just of your university town, but of the world. If you can cultivate a mindset that thinks on a global scale as well as a local one, you will be part of the next generation of students who can make a difference. A global mindset, being aware of global issues, being able to be part of global teams and being able to build a **global network** will be necessary skills for the future as you make connections with others.

AGENCY AND COMMUNITY

Being at university will hopefully provide you with a sense of community – you belong to a group of staff and students who share the same goals – and the agency to empower you to make changes within your communities. The likelihood is that you will belong to several communities at once. If you've moved away to university you might be part of a community back at home, or still part of the community of your old school, college or workplace. You might be part of niche communities like a small student society, or part of giant worldwide communities, for example through being an online gamer or supporting a particular sports team.

Communities form because people that like or do the same things exist in the same geographical space, want to take action and change the same things, or because external events have brought them together (Feverbee, 2022). They give us a sense of belonging, and belonging can be hugely important in helping people feel safe and free to contribute. They can also inspire a sense of ownership to make improvements and changes. As a student today, existing in our interconnected, inter-dependent world you also belong to a global community.

THE 20 ATTRIBUTES: THE BUILDING BLOCKS UNDERNEATH THE CATEGORIES

Contained within our five categories are a range of specific skills – we will call them **graduate attributes**. These graduate attributes, 20 in total, will give you a set of skills that employers across all kinds of professions will value. In combination, they will help you become the best possible version of you.

In Chapters 6 to 10 you will learn much more about these attributes and how you can build them. You will find the building materials in all sorts of places and situations – your lecture halls and study groups; your work experience and volunteering; your communities, clubs and societies; your friends and hobbies; your travels and adventures, and others that you haven't even thought of yet.

Not everyone will develop all 20 of the graduate attributes by the time they leave university. In fact, it would be really unusual to do so. What's much more likely is that you will develop a range of attributes dependent on what you're studying, what you do outside of university, where your journey has taken you to get to this point, and the sorts of goals you have set for yourself. Your own combination of attributes belongs to you. It is what makes you unique and therefore gives you strength and helps you to stand out. Knowing your own attribute combination is can be important; if you don't know it, how can you explain it to anyone else? The end of this chapter helps you think about what your attribute profile looks like at the moment, but first let's take a look at our attributes which we have listed within our five categories.

AGENCY AND COMMUNITY ATTRIBUTES

1. INTEGRITY

The ability to conduction yourself honestly and be guided by moral principles.

2. CHANGE MAKING

The ability to identify things you would like to change, and take ownership for the planning and implementation of actions as a result.

3. ETHICAL AWARENESS

Ensuring you conduct yourself truthfully and do the right thing.

4. DISCIPLINE-SPECIFIC IDENTITY

Holding yourself to the highest academic standards and contributing positively to your discipline.

SELF-LEADERSHIP ATTRIBUTES

5. TIME AND ENERGY MANAGEMENT

Planning and prioritising in order to meet deadlines and deliver under pressure – including being able to work on multiple projects simultaneously, anticipate periods of peak demands, and organise appropriately whilst minimising procrastination.

6. EFFECTIVE FOLLOWERSHIP

Being active and engaged when in a follower role, and able to think critically while also demonstrating commitment to the team's goals and vision.

7. LEADING OTHERS

Articulating a vision to others, and coaching and motivating team members towards achieving goals. Co-ordinating team effort through understanding the skills and talents of team members, and being able to do this in challenging environments.

8. SELF-MOTIVATION

Being aware of the values that drive you, the goals you are striving for, and having the ability to persevere in tough times.

9. REFLECTION

Using your experiences as an opportunity for feedback and learning, and being able to increase your self-awareness through the habitual act of reviewing, extracting learning and applying that learning to future experiences.

VALUING DIVERSITY ATTRIBUTES

10. CULTURAL APPRECIATION

Having an openness to learn about cultures different from your own, and seeing these differences as valuable.

11. TEAM WORKING

Being able to strengthen a team's performance by contributing a range of positive behaviours such as being inclusive, communicating well, addressing conflict, offering support, and being results-focused. Having awareness of the strengths and weaknesses of the team at any given point, and being able to contribute accordingly.

12. INTERPERSONAL SKILLS

Understanding the emotions of yourself and others, and knowing how best to regulate your own emotional responses. Feeling empowered to share feedback with others whilst also being sensitive to approaches different from your own. Having a well-developed sense of empathy and self-awareness, and actively thinking about things from other's perspectives.

CONNECTIVITY ATTRIBUTES

13. INFLUENCING AND NEGOTIATION

Employing strong listening skills and respecting the differing opinions of others whilst cogently outlining your preferred course of action.

14. COMMUNICATION

The ability to actively minimise barriers so that information is accurately sent and received. Having an ability to easily be understood in a range of mediums – emails and messaging, written reports, presentations, speech and digital formats.

15. NETWORKING

Seeking and cultivating connections with others, so that you can exchange information, experiences and resources in mutually beneficial ways.

RESEARCH ATTRIBUTES

16. PROBLEM SOLVING

Being able to understand and articulate problems before identifying and evaluating potential solutions, then choosing and implementing an effective course of action.

Having the ability to review the impact of your actions and be flexible and reassess your approach if necessary.

17. ACADEMIC ARGUMENTATION

Understanding how to convey your point in an academic setting, using evidence and incorporating your own analysis of the supporting and contraindicating evidence.

18. CREATIVITY

Practising mental agility by using your imagination to think of new possibilities, and make new connections. Generating ideas, concepts and arguments to help solve novel problems.

19. CRITICAL THINKING

Actively employing clear, relevant and reasonable thinking to judge and evaluate complex information.

20. READING AND NOTE TAKING

The ability to synthesise and capture information accurately, and correctly cite and reference it.

5.7 IDENTIFYING YOUR ATTRIBUTE STRENGTHS AND AREAS FOR DEVELOPMENT: A SKILLS ANALYSIS

The last thing to be done before we move on to the next chapter and start to explore the skills categories in depth is to consider what your own graduate attribute profile looks like currently, thinking about which attributes you might want to develop.

Thinking about your skills profile doesn't have to be complicated. We can use a simple process of looking at each attribute in turn, based on **Bloom's Taxonomy of Learning** (Bloom, 1956), and thinking about how you would rate your familiarity with the attribute. We will use four levels.

1. Awareness – I have heard of this skill.
2. Understanding – I have heard of this skill and know what it means.
3. Application – I have heard of this skill, know what it means and can give examples of when I use it in real-life situations.
4. Expertise – I have heard of this skill, know what it means, use it in real-life situations and can help teach it to others.

This isn't a perfect process. When we self-rate, as opposed to having other people rate us, we can be biased (and are sometimes prone to over or under-rating our true level), so try to be as honest as possible. This exercise aims to help you have an awareness about your current skills and where you want to take them.

ACTIVITY 5.5

Your skills wheel

- For each attribute, make a mark on the diagram to say whether you consider your current level to be awareness, understanding, application or expert. Awareness is the circle nearest to the centre; understanding is next; application is second to the outside; expert is the bold outer circle.

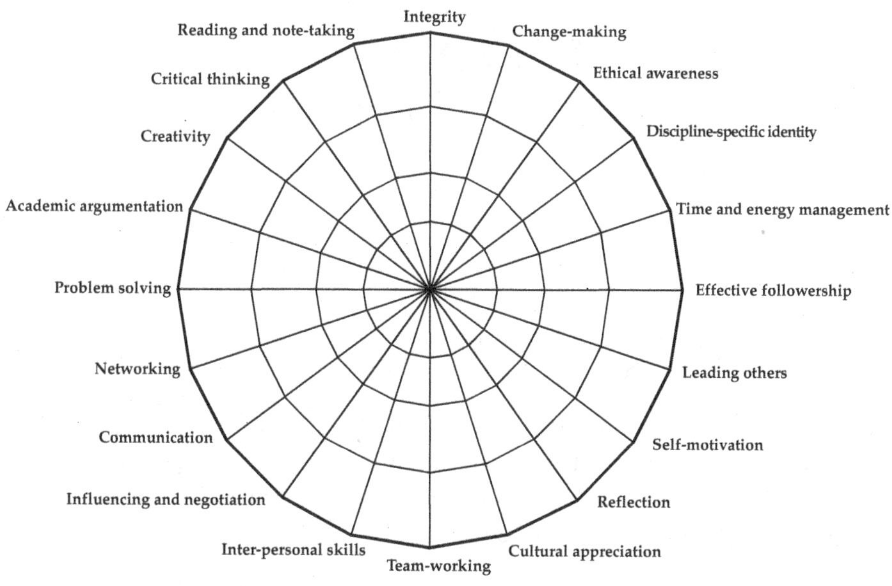

Now join up all of your dots in the diagram to give you a shape. It will look a bit like a splodge. Not just any splodge though. This is your splodge. The next part of the activity is to go back to the diagram and this time for each attribute indicate where you'd like to be by this time next year.

- Are there any you'd like to move up a level, eg from aware to understand, or understand to apply?
- Are there any you'd like to move up two levels, eg from aware to apply, or understand to expert?

It isn't feasible to become an expert in all 20 in a year. This wouldn't be a realistic goal, and we're all good at setting goals now; remember how we want to set SMART goals? This applies to developing your graduate attributes too. By joining up the dots of where you'd like to be, this time with a dotted line, you will create a second splodge, likely taking up more room than the first. Congratulations! This is where you'd like your abilities to be in a year. You have completed an excellent bit of skills development planning. You can see an example of the finished diagram in Figure 5.6.

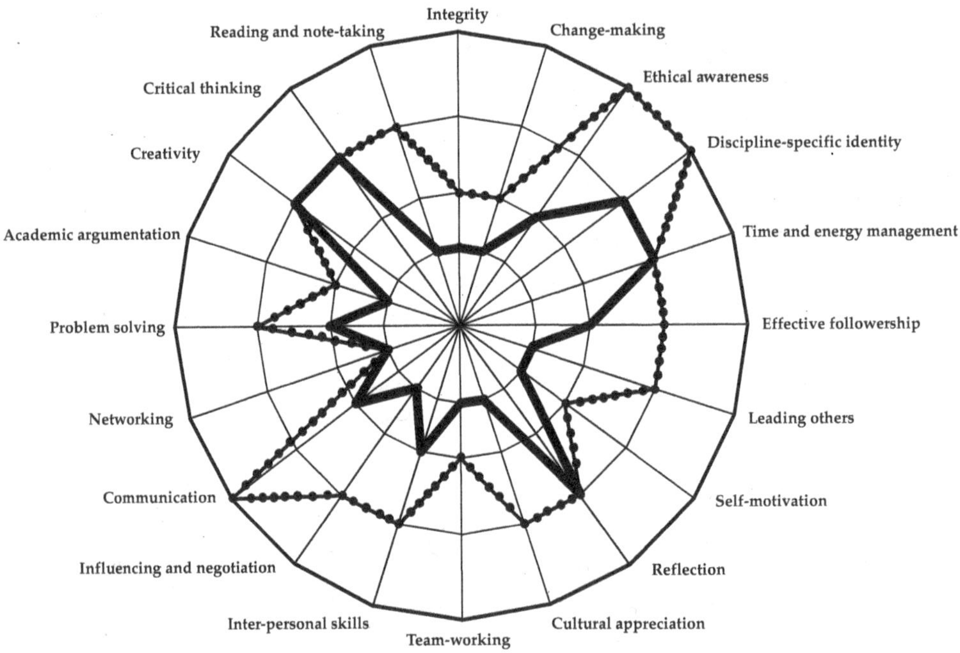

FIGURE 5.6: Example of a completed skills wheel

The solid line is where the student is now, and the dotted line is where they would like to be in a year. You can see that this student would like to improve their skills in change-making, academic argumentation, motivation, followership, team-working and discipline-specific identity the most.

When we started this chapter, we asked two big questions: Where are you going, and how are you going to get there? Part of the answer is right in front of you.

CHAPTER SUMMARY

You will hopefully now have a good appreciation of the importance of developing skills and see that skills can be developed in many different ways, and through many different activities. This chapter has focused on the common challenges of not knowing where you want to invest your time and learning. By completing your skills analysis, you should now have identified a list of skills you want to invest your time in developing and have a list of prioritised goals for the coming year, as well as an understanding of how you can plan and track those goals. We have introduced you to the *University and You* skills framework, which will set the structure for the rest of Part 2.

TOP TIPS AND NEXT STEPS

- See the importance and value in developing a range of skills – academic, professional, research, entrepreneurial, digital, etc.
- Practise setting SMART goals and focus on process goals where you can.
- Use tools to help you plan, such as Gantt charts, a weekly planner or app, and build in contingency time.
- Reflect on your completed skills wheel in Activity 5.4. Think about what you can do to ensure you revisit it regularly.
- Ask yourself what areas of planning and organisation do you feel like you could improve on? How might you do this?
- Think about which of the five categories of the skills framework you feel most drawn to. Which do you feel least drawn to? Why do you think that is?

CHAPTER 6
YOUR SELF-LEADERSHIP

CHALLENGES WE EXPLORE IN THIS CHAPTER

This chapter focuses on our skills category of self-leadership. One of the challenges we see students grappling with the most is being able to organise themselves in terms of staying motivated, responding to setbacks, and managing their time and energy well. In this chapter we explore how these concepts can be thought of as being part of how you lead yourself. You will be able to see the importance of being able to 'self-lead' and how skills like reflection and resilience, and being able to understand your values and motivation, can be incredibly helpful for keeping on top of the demands university will throw at you. The ability to self-lead cuts across everything, and can set you up for success at university and beyond. With this ability to self-lead in place, you are well positioned to become an effective leader of others. We will help you identify your preferred leadership style and identify ways you can become both a valued leader and an effective follower.

INTENDED LEARNING OUTCOMES

By the end of this chapter, you should be able to:

- define the term self-leadership and appreciate its importance for your university journey and beyond;
- understand the importance of reflection in learning and be aware of techniques to help reflect on events;
- identify what motivates you and understand how your values connect to this;
- apply techniques for managing your time and energy;
- identify your preferred leadership style;
- appreciate the value of being an effective follower.

The attributes covered in this chapter are time and energy management, effective followership, leading others, self-motivation and reflection.

6.1 WHAT IS SELF-LEADERSHIP AND WHY DOES IT MATTER?

In Chapter 5, you learnt about how you can approach organisation and planning positively and with a growth mindset. Exactly the same attitude can take you far in your quest to become an excellent leader. If you've got good attention to detail, you may have spotted that this chapter's heading is not about 'leadership' though. It's about *self*-leadership. What's the difference, and why is it important?

In our roles at the university, we help students to develop the skills they need to succeed in their studies and beyond. One of our consistently most popular skills workshops is leadership. It's the skill students seem to want to develop more than any other (or at least think they should develop). But here's the problem: how many opportunities are there for students to take on leadership roles where they are responsible for leading a team of people? Some, but not many. So, we have lots of students who want to learn about leadership, but who will likely lack opportunities to apply their learning in practice.

How about then if, instead of focusing on how best to lead others, we all took a step back and thought about leadership not from a standpoint of leading someone else, but from a standpoint of how you lead yourself.

Self-leadership is about how you present yourself to the world, and how you can be the best version of you. It involves elements of how you think about yourself, how you organise yourself and how well you know yourself. It's a big deal because if you don't have self-leadership figured out, it can be much harder to lead others.

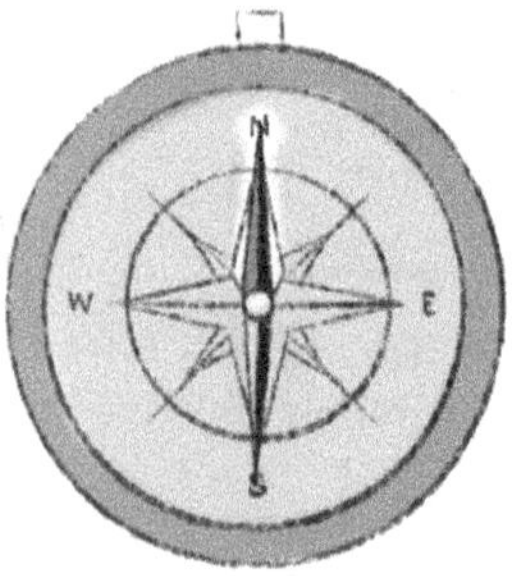

The word 'lead' suggests movement – that there is a place or destination that you are taking yourself or others to. In the case of self-leadership, we can think of this destination as arriving at your goals and being guided by your values along the way. Having clarity of purpose can be very helpful in setting the circumstances for strong self-leadership.

Self-leadership is not about pretending to be someone you're not. It's about being aware of your strengths and accepting your weaknesses. Self-kindness is another important element of being a good self-leader. When we think about inspirational leaders, and list all the traits we think good leaders have, we quickly amass a very long list. It can be demoralising when we see this shopping list of leadership traits and measure ourselves against it – typically we will come up short. Few of us embody *all* the traits. Does this mean we won't be good leaders? No! As long as we are true to ourselves, we will find it easier to build trust with anyone who we might be asked to lead. But to *be* our true self, first we must *know* our true self.

6.2 SELF-REFLECTION

One way to know who you are is to engage in some self-reflection. We can place reflection as part of a larger cycle of planning, doing, making observations and then reflecting on them. Being able to reflect in a way that you find helpful is a skill that will come with practice. You can reflect through thinking about things on your own, writing things down, speaking to others, or through creative outlets such as video creation, poetry, painting or music. You can reflect as soon as you do something, or you can let some time pass first. However you reflect, it's a way to learn more about yourself, your behaviour and how you react. All of this helps you understand who you are and to develop as a self-leader.

Returning to a situation in your mind, examining it and **extracting learning** from it is a useful skill to practise and can set you up with a positive mindset. Extracting learning is a key element of reflection; otherwise it's just you running an event over and over in your head but not properly seeking to understand it and find insights that you can apply in the next situation you encounter. It's quite common for reflection to be part of your university experience – you might be asked to keep reflective logs of projects you're involved in or to complete reflective assessments for your coursework. Reflection doesn't stop at the end of university either – many professions require their members to engage in reflection when they undertake training and development.

One of the classic models about *how* to do reflection is **Gibbs' Reflective Cycle** (Gibbs, 1988). It consists of six stages, and while you could go through them in your head, the deepest reflection might come from writing down your thoughts as you work through the model, shown in Figure 6.1.

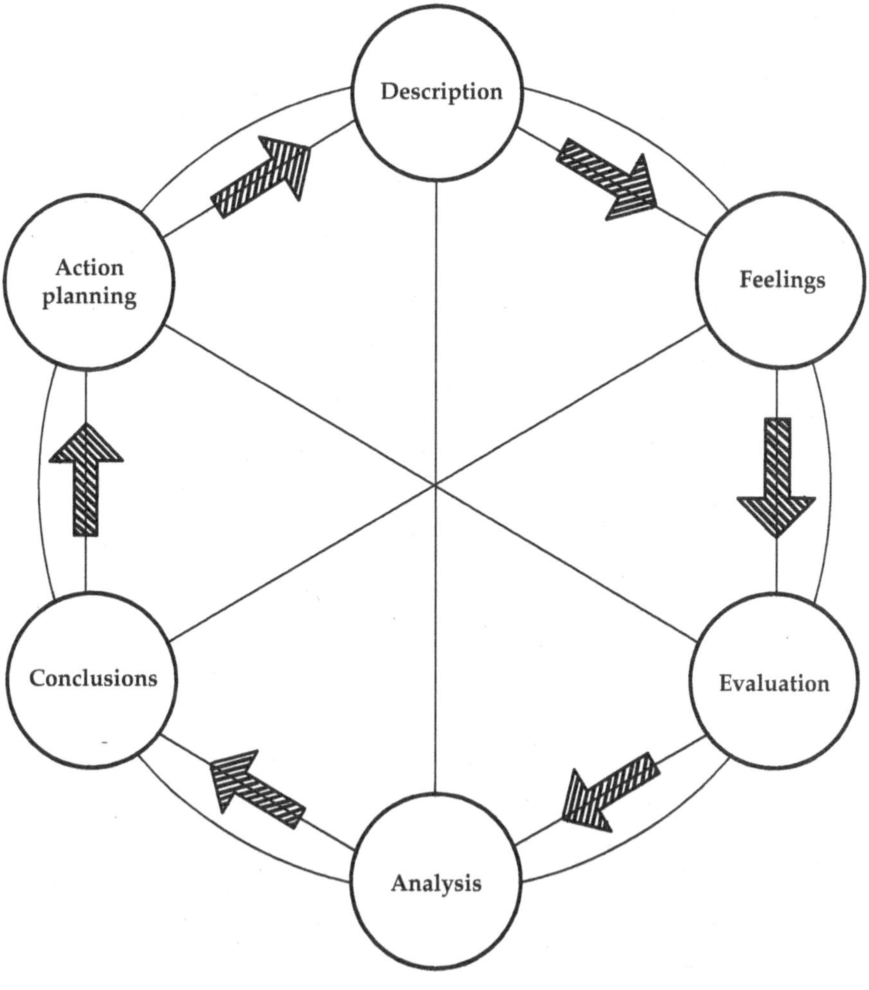

FIGURE 6.1: Gibbs' reflective cycle

1. The first stage is **description**. This is where you write down a factual description of what happened. You don't need to think about any feelings or reactions yet – it's just a case of setting the scene.
2. The next stage is **feelings**. Here is where you focus on how you felt during the event. Again, you don't need to do too much critical thinking at this point, but instead try to be really honest about how you felt at various stages of the experience and how you reacted in the moment. Did you feel positive or negative? Did your feelings change over the duration?
3. The third stage is **evaluation**, and this is where you begin to dig a little deeper and think about how you'd sum up the experience. Was it good or bad overall? What was valuable about it? Did you perform well in the situation?
4. Next, you begin to do some **analysis**, to think about why the situation was good or bad, or why you performed well or not so well. At this point you might begin to recognise patterns in your own behaviour or the behaviour of others. You might be able to use your experience of previous situations to help you make sense of what happened, or to use theories or models from outside the situation to help you interpret it. You are taking a step back from the event, setting aside your feelings and emotions and, like a good detective, trying to objectively understand what made you feel, think and act the way you did and, if applicable, also what made others feel, think and act the way they did.
5. With the situation analysed, you can then move on to making some **conclusions**. This is effectively what you can generalise about the situation and take away for next time. These conclusions can either be general ones or ones very specific to you. For example, perhaps you have realised you tend to behave or think in a certain way in stressful conditions, or you like to dominate conversation when you feel confident about a topic, or that in a group setting there are often some people who don't readily speak up but will if you ask their opinion directly.
6. The final stage is to do some **action planning**, and this is concerned with practical changes you might make to your own behaviour or thoughts the next time you are in a certain situation. You are applying the learning you derived from the conclusion stage.

Becoming accustomed to reflecting on incidents when they happen and, crucially, deriving learning from them is a key element in terms of developing your skills and becoming the best student and self-leader you can be. It's a practice that you can carry with you throughout your studies and career beyond.

ACTIVITY 6.1

Reflection

Think of a situation you were part of recently that you can use as an example for reflection. It could have been a group project, a solo activity you were working on or an interaction you had with someone.

- Take some time to work through the reflective model, ideally writing your reflections down on paper.
- Go through the stages of description, feelings, evaluation, analysis, conclusion and action planning.

6.3 UNDERSTANDING YOUR SELF-MOTIVATION

Becoming an experienced reflector is going to give you real insight into who you are as a person, and it pays to understand what motivates you. Knowing what is important to you, what your values are and what you have passion for can unlock real benefits as you navigate your way through your university experience.

Before we delve into this, first a quick sidenote on passion. It can sometimes feel daunting to identify what we are 'passionate' about. We might feel pressure as we go through life to find our passion, or worry that we are deficient because we don't have something that speaks to us in such an important way. It's really okay! Not everyone needs to have a passion for one particular thing. In fact, perhaps a helpful way to reframe it is to think about not having one giant passion (such as a calling to a particular research area, career, sport or political cause), but to have lots and lots and lots of micro-passions – small things that you really enjoy and are interested in, but which might not be enduring or linked to a big life goal. These can be just as fulfilling and motivating in the moment. Indeed, even if you do identify a passion, it doesn't necessarily link to job satisfaction (Newport, 2018).

Returning to motivation, at the beginning of the book we learnt about intrinsic and extrinsic motivation. There are a number of elements that contribute to becoming and staying motivated. Daniel Goleman researched the concept of **emotional intelligence** (how we perceive, understand and handle our emotions and the emotions of others). Goleman (1995) thought that a key part of being emotionally intelligent was being self-motivated. To be self-motivated you need to be optimistic, committed to your goal, resilient when things don't go to plan and have the initiative to seize opportunities. To be self-motivated you also need to have a sense of meaningfulness about the task or goal you're trying to accomplish. There needs to be some element of it that you can see importance in, even if you don't particularly like it in the moment. To know if something is meaningful, let's take a step back and think about **values**.

VALUES

In order to be a self-motivated self-leader, it helps to know what you stand for – what values you hold. Values influence your beliefs about things; your beliefs influence your feelings; and your feelings influence and drive your behaviour.

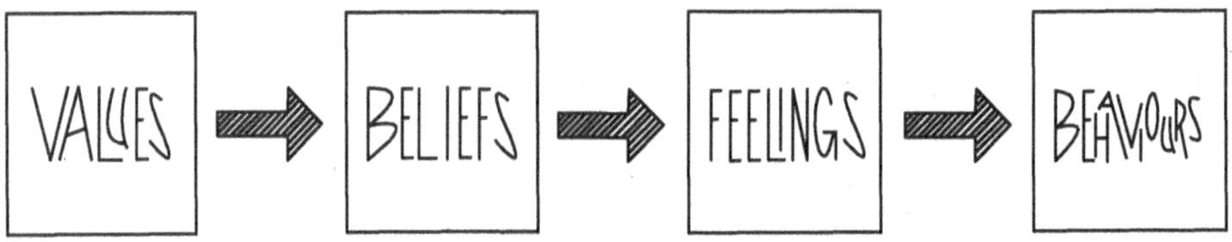

FIGURE 6.2: Values and beliefs underpin feelings and behaviours

When we reflect on our behaviour, often we get stuck at the feelings level. It's easy to see why – feelings can be overwhelming and if we are very upset or sad or excited or happy, that can occupy most of our brain. However, to fully understand why we feel the way we do, we might have to dig a bit deeper into the underlying beliefs and values that we hold. Particularly when we're upset or struggling, it can often be because our values are not being adhered to, or a belief we hold about ourselves or others has been disrupted. When we work with students and ask them to think about their values, they can find it hard to think of them straight away. Sometimes it can be helpful to start with a long list. We can ask them to look at the list and tick all those that are important to them. We then ask them to look at all the values they have selected and narrow the list down to ten. This can really force people to reflect and focus. Then we ask them to look at their top ten list of values, and cut it down to just six. And then, to be really mean, we ask them to rank the six in priority order. You can have a go at this in Activity 6.2.

ACTIVITY 6.2

Values

- Take time to read through this list of 99 values and tick all that are important to you.
- Go through them again and select your top ten.
- Finally, choose a top six from your top ten and rank them in order.

Alongside finding value and meaning in what you're doing, there are other things you can do to become and stay self-motivated, which are all part of being a good self-leader:

- setting challenging but achievable goals for yourself;
- having a growth mindset and being open to feedback;
- looking for opportunities and taking them on when you find them;
- being able to work through setbacks in a resilient way.

accountability	exploration	optimism
achievement	fairness	order
adaptability	faith	passion
adventure	family	patience
affection	forgiveness	perseverance
ambition	freedom	play
authenticity	friendship	power
balance	fun	quality
belonging	generosity	recognition
boldness	giving back	reliability
caring	gratitude	reputation
challenge	growth	resourcefulness
collaboration	happiness	respect
commitment	harmony	responsibility
community	health	risk-taking
competition	honesty	security
connection	honour	self-expression
contentment	humility	service
contribution	humour	simplicity
cooperation	inclusion	spirituality

→

courage	independence	stability
creativity	influence	success
curiosity	integrity	teamwork
decisiveness	involvement	trust
dignity	justice	truth
discipline	kindness	understanding
effectiveness	knowledge	uniqueness
efficiency	learning	vision
empathy	legacy	vulnerability
equality	loyalty	wealth
ethics	moderation	well-being
excellence	nature	wisdom

RESILIENCE AND GRIT

Being resilient and having **grit** is something that won't just help you to be self-motivated; it is something that will help you to be an excellent leader, and a much more successful student and all-round human. As a student, you have a fantastic opportunity to practise resilience and grit regularly and become really good at them.

Resilience is one of those terms that is everywhere but can be tricky to define. When we look at dictionary definitions, they usually include the concepts of 'recovery' and 'toughness' with some referring to the idea of 'buoyancy'. When we think of people we know who we might consider to be resilient, we might picture someone who is able to accept change, find a way through tough situations and who exhibits flexibility. Resilience isn't about avoiding adverse events, but about navigating *through* them. Sometimes resilience is described as an ability to 'bounce back' from something, but at its most powerful resilience can actually be about bouncing forwards – reflecting and taking learning from the experience and using it to grow. Being resilient is also about being able to live, operate and study with uncertainty around you. You can see why it's such an important component of self-leadership.

You can conceptualise having a fixed amount of resilience within you – like a water tank or reservoir, as displayed in Figure 6.3 (Dunn et al, 2008). The water line represents your coping ability, and this can go up or down depending on how much water goes in and how much water goes out. There's a variable flow of water out of the tank, caused by internal and external stressors, but there's also a variable flow of water going into the tank, caused by things like supportive friends and family, having a sense of purpose, a motivating goal or an optimistic outlook. The trick is to try and ensure the flow of water in is greater than the leakage of water out. This metaphor ties in well with our growth mindsets: resilience is something we can cultivate and improve.

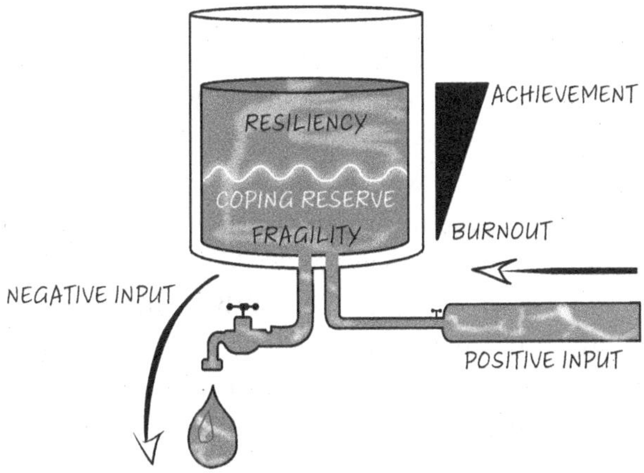

FIGURE 6.3: Resilience as a water tank concept – your water level can be topped up or drained.

Resilience comes not from the events you experience, but from the *attitude* you take to these events. The ABCD model, outlined in Chapter 3, gives a very helpful framework to think about the impact beliefs and attitudes can have on outcomes. So, how can we take a more positive view of the things that happen to us and develop our resilience?

The beliefs we hold can make all the difference to how we react to situations. Often we hold beliefs that don't help us: our thinking is not perfect and it's common for us to engage in some faulty thinking which gives rise to beliefs that hold us back.

STUDENT INSIGHT

Jonathan Tarquinio, management and modern history, second year

Developing effective time management skills is the biggest positive shift in my approach to university life. Managing coursework with extracurriculars, a student job and a social life has required me to step up my efficiency at managing tasks ahead of time. In high school, I was able to procrastinate until final deadlines. In university, I have found it much easier (and less stressful!) to begin working when I am assigned a new piece of coursework and spread the work over a period of weeks. This way, I have enough time and energy to put the same amount of effort into every part of my university life, without suffering periods of burnout after binge work sessions.

Resilience isn't the whole story though: what about a type of resilience that keeps us going for a very long time towards the longer-term goals we set ourselves. Having a passion and perseverance for long-term goals is what researcher Angela Duckworth (2016) calls 'grit'. A small word with huge self-leadership power.

In her TED talk, psychologist Angela Duckworth explained her research behind the concept of grit. As a teacher she noticed that intelligence (measured by IQ) wasn't the best predictor as to which students performed well or badly. She believed that while the topics she was teaching in class were demanding, all students were capable of understanding them if they were willing to put in the effort. Duckworth says that *'grit is living life like it's a marathon, not a sprint'*. While university might feel like it's a sprint, really and truly it's a marathon. If you fall over at any point, there's still time to pick yourself back up and get back in the race. You also don't need to be a particularly skillful runner – Duckworth's research suggested that there wasn't always a positive correlation between grit and talent. If you have talent, it does not mean you also automatically have grit. In fact, it might even mean you have less of it (Duckworth, 2016, p 14).

To develop grit, the best thing you can do is to adopt a growth mindset, as outlined in Chapter 2. That is, as Duckworth says, *'you hold a belief that the ability to learn is not fixed, it can change with your effort'* (Duckworth, 2013). Putting in effort in the pursuit of long-term goals is a great skill to cultivate. We can think of good performance as talent multiplied by practice effort, multiplied by **performance effort**. Effort is there twice: the first effort is *practice* effort – the effort you put in to develop your talent into a skill. The second effort is *performance* effort – the effort you put in to use the skill when it's needed. In trying to predict who's going to become the high-performing students, we don't need to look for who has the talent but who is willing to put in the effort.

6.4 HOW TO MANAGE YOUR TIME AND ENERGY

If you think of university study as running a marathon, you'll quickly realise how important it is to manage your time and energy. You don't want to risk burning out within the first few miles, and you don't want to be so far off the pace that you don't finish. Typically, university does not provide perfectly balanced weeks for students in terms of time demands. There are peaks and troughs. There will be weeks with multiple deadlines across different subjects. There will be weeks where deadlines for applying for graduate jobs clash with revision time, or where you've got to do a class presentation and three of your friends inconveniently all have something to celebrate at the same time.

Finding the tools that help you manage your time and energy early on in your university journey could prove invaluable. For some students, having a tight structure with each hour of the week mapped out on a planner is exactly what they need to manage their time well and stay on track, but for other students this would be absolutely unworkable because that's just not who they are. In Chapter 4 we covered some time management techniques for organising your studies and learning. Here, we will focus on two key areas that students struggle with most when it comes to self-leadership: prioritisation and procrastination.

THE TIME MANAGEMENT MATRIX

Stephen Covey set out something called the Eisenhower *time management matrix* in his book *The 7 Habits of Highly Effective People* (2020), which we've experienced students finding helpful when it comes to thinking about their own approach to time. The matrix gets you to think about tasks in terms of importance versus urgency, and this gives us a simple 2×2 matrix, as shown in Figure 6.4.

- Top left (quadrant one) includes important and urgent tasks, all the things you have to do. These are often deadline driven, such as handing in assignments, sitting exams and covering your shifts at work.
- Bottom left (quadrant three) contains tasks that are urgent but not important. These are things which have an immediate demand on your time, but which don't hold much value in the long term. This could be getting involved with your flatmates' crises, dealing with superfluous emails and texts, and other similar interruptions.
- Bottom right (quadrant four) holds tasks that aren't urgent or important. This is all our typical procrastination activity – scrolling through social media, falling down a YouTube rabbit hole, vegging out on the sofa all afternoon. Now, there are times when these activities can tip over into being important – when you need a break, or to build up relationships in your social networks – but when they are chronic procrastination activities they belong squarely in this quadrant.
- Finally, top right (quadrant two) contains activities which are important but not urgent. Ah, the magic quadrant! Here are all the things that really do pay off in the long term regarding your success. Doing that extra chapter of reading, going to that skills development workshop the Careers Centre is offering, creating a **LinkedIn profile**, being committed to going along to your society or club meetings. They all live here.

	URGENT	NOT URGENT
IMPORTANT	Q1 • Computing project • 2-5 Shift at work	Q2 • Internship application • Call Sister
NOT IMPORTANT	Q3 • Email tutor • Clean room	Q4 • Movie night • Post on Instagram

FIGURE 6.4: The time management matrix with some examples, adapted from Stephen Covey, *The 7 Habits of Highly Effective People*, 1989

Covey calls the things that go into quadrant two 'big rocks', with the analogy outlined in Figure 6.5 being that if you don't put the big rocks in first, all the space gets quickly filled up with the little rocks of less important stuff that takes up all your time. So, you need to be clear about what your big rocks are. Everyone's set of rocks will look a little different, but they should represent something that you attribute purpose and importance to.

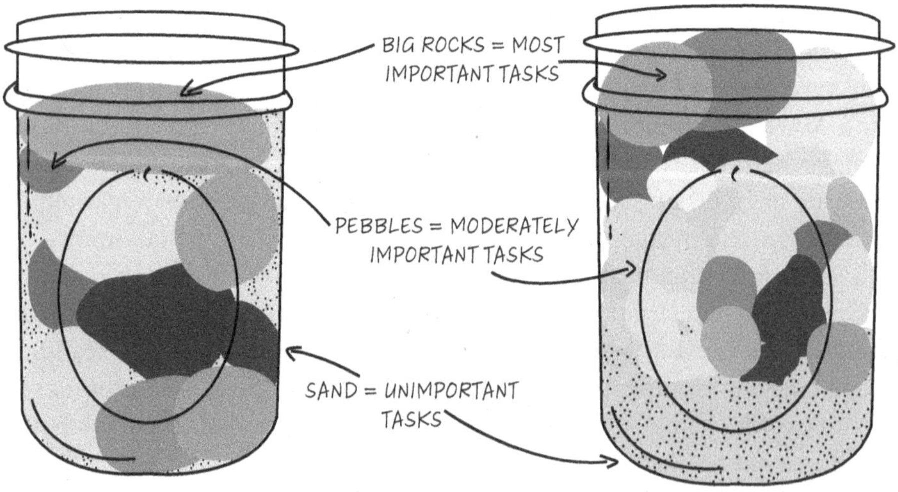

FIGURE 6.5: Conceptualisation of fitting in the 'big rocks' first

ACTIVITY 6.3

Time management matrix

- In the time management matrix, add in your own activities into each of the four boxes. You'll need to think about each in terms of its urgency and importance to place it in the best quadrant.

	URGENT	NOT URGENT
IMPORTANT	Q1	Q2
NOT IMPORTANT	Q3	Q4

The important but not urgent quadrant tends to hold our longer-term goals – the ones we need a bit of grit and self-motivation to achieve. What can we do to spend less time in quadrants one, three and four, and more time in quadrant two?

Well, in terms of quadrant one (the important and urgent one) we can focus on doing these now with minimal delay and fuss, but in the longer term aim to tackle some of these tasks earlier before they become urgent. For quadrant three (other people's crises and interruptions) we can practise pushing back on these and not getting too sucked in. For quadrant four (procrastination activities) we can learn techniques to reduce these. And for magic quadrant two there is one thing above all else that we can do to spend more time here: planning.

PLANNING AND PROCRASTINATION

Planning is another key skill of the effective self-leader – the ability to protect time for those important but non-urgent tasks. Good planning *prevents* them from becoming urgent.

Planning is not rocket science – it requires a bit of effort and being able to think backwards (see Chapter 4). Planning, however, has an enemy – well practised and deadly – which just can't wait to sabotage those beautifully crafted schedules. Meet procrastination.

Procrastination is the action of delaying or postponing something. Almost everyone procrastinates to some degree, although our reasons why will vary. It might be because we are lacking motivation or interest in the task. It might be because we are overwhelmed by what needs to be done and don't know how or where to start. There are lots of different reasons. We also have lots of different time sponges that we gravitate to while we procrastinate: our favourite website, social media platform, TV show or computer game. It's a good idea to think about what your common causes of procrastination are, and what are your go-to time sponges. That way you can be more conscious of when you feel yourself tempted to fall into a procrastination trap.

Procrastination is a habit, which means that you won't just break it overnight.

TACKLING PROCRASTINATION

- Complete any tasks that may act as distractions (eg organising your desk) before studying – but don't let it take over the session!
- Make up your own rewards: promise yourself a treat if you've completed a certain task by a certain time. You can use a reward chart for this, as outlined in Chapter 1.
- Ask someone to check up on you: external accountability can be really helpful to keep you on track.
- Identify the unpleasant consequences of not doing the task.
- Aim to complete the most difficult or unpleasant task first to get it out of the way and allow you to spend the rest of the time tackling the easier or more enjoyable tasks.
- Break the task into small, manageable chunks, and start with those so you feel like you're achieving things – this might make the whole task seem less overwhelming.
- Keep a schedule and to-do list so that you can't conveniently forget about unpleasant or overwhelming tasks.

> *'Do not wait; the time will never be 'just right'. Start where you stand, and work with whatever tools you may have at your command, and better tools will be found as you go along.' George Herbert*

FOCUS AND ATTENTION

Staying focused on a task involves being able to direct your attention. Let's dig a bit deeper into how attention works. There are two types of attention.

1. **Passive attention** – involuntary and reactive (this happens when you hear a loud noise, for example).
2. **Active attention** – deliberate and conscious effort.

You're not going to make much headway into your university career if you rely on being surprised by a loud noise to get any work done, so instead you need to get good at switching on your active attention. To do this you must follow several stages:

1. alertness – if you are going to pay attention to something, you must be aware of it;
2. selectivity – choosing what to pay attention to;
3. previewing – deciding on the different options you could take and choosing which is best;
4. self-monitoring – keeping your focus on the task and not getting distracted.

You are more likely to find active attention if you're also tuned into your energy management. This is being aware about how your energy tends to ebb and flow over the course of a day. You'll get the best rewards if you line up your work that requires the deepest focus with when you have the most energy. There's no point forcing yourself to try and focus on work at 11pm if you are not a night owl and are going to have a natural surge of energy at 7am tomorrow morning – best to get a good sleep and surf your energy wave when you wake up.

Another way to make active attention easier is to avoid the temptation to multi-task. Although we may think we are good at it, our brains tend to be very bad at multi-tasking. When you flip between tasks, we have a **cognitive switching penalty** – our brains waste time and energy moving from one thing to another, like trying to lift the needle from a record, switching vinyl and dropping it in the right place on the new track. It takes effort.

Switching between tasks also leaves us with **attention residue.** You may think you are now focused on reading your lecture notes and not your phone, but part of your brain will still be thinking about the thing on your phone you just came out of. Of course, some students might have brains that are wired to function this way and they are only able to focus their attention on something for very short bursts of time. It might be that you need lots of variation in order to stay engaged. If this is the case, you might need to experiment to find what works best for you and how you can hold active attention for longer.

To reduce this switching penalty and increase your active attention, a good strategy is to remove distractions.

- Remove distractions if you can: Having your phone or laptop switched on and within your line of sight can be very distracting. If you do have your phone or laptop on you during study, it can be useful to use 'blocker' apps to encourage you to stay focused, such as Forest for your phone, and FocusMe for your computer's web browser.
- If you are working alongside other people, it can be all too easy to get distracted by them. Reflect on whether you work best with others or if you often get too distracted by them.
- Take effective breaks. Try to avoid low-impact breaks that you don't really enjoy – we often take these involuntarily when we are tired, bored or unfocused. These low-impact breaks often include aimlessly scrolling the news or social media. Instead, aim (and plan) for **high-impact breaks** – something really enjoyable and purposeful.
- Try the **Pomodoro technique** to see if it works well for you. This is a time management method that uses a timer to break down work into smaller intervals, usually 25 minutes, separated by short breaks. There are several apps that can help you with this technique, including Be Focused (iOS), Focus Booster (web) and Goodtime productivity timer (Android).

When it comes to time management, which is such an important part of self-leadership, you really have to do a bit of trial and error to find the set of tools which work for you. We promise you, it's worth the investment.

ACTIVITY 6.4

Time and energy management action planning

Having read this section on time and energy management, answer the questions below to help you reflect on your own time and energy management and think about how you can manage your time and energy efficiently.

- Write down two times in the day when your mental energy and ability to concentrate are the highest.

- Write down a time in the day when you most struggle to concentrate.

- What activities are best done in times when you struggle to concentrate?

- When are you most likely to procrastinate?

- What small steps can you take when you feel like you are procrastinating in starting a piece of coursework?

- What would a 'high-impact' break be for you?

6.5 HOW TO LEAD OTHERS: IDENTIFYING YOUR LEADERSHIP STYLE

So far in this chapter we've thought about self-leadership – how you present yourself to the world – and we've looked at reflection, motivation, grit and resilience, and time and energy management. These are skills which you can refine and polish throughout your university journey and beyond. Once you have got the basics down for these skills, also think about looking outwards. Are you ready to lead others?

The research around leadership has largely moved away from who leaders are (what traits they might have) to what leaders do (what behaviours they exhibit). This is good news for us because it signifies that leading others is a skill that can be learnt rather than a fixed quality that you either have or don't have. Take a moment to think of good leaders you might know. Perhaps it's someone you've worked with or someone who's been in position of responsibility, like a coach or manager? Perhaps they're a well-known figure with a leadership role in a social movement, politics, business or charity? Whoever you have in your mind right now, think about what it is they *do* that makes them a good leader.

ACTIVITY 6.5

Thinking about good leadership

- Think of four people you would classify as being a good leader. Write down what it is that they do that makes them so.

Leader 1 ____________________

Leader 2 ____________________

Leader 3 ____________________

Leader 4 ____________________

The list of reasons you're producing might well be a mixture of skills and behaviours. When we asked a group of students this question, they listed things like communication, listening skills, having empathy for others, being true to their values and being inclusive. But the list could be much longer. Leaders today are faced with a set of complex problems which cannot be easily solved by individuals but rely on collaboration and teamwork.

EMERGENT, SHARED AND AUTHENTIC LEADERSHIP

You can imagine modern leadership as like being in a yacht race. The yacht has a nominal leader (the captain/skipper), but they can't possibly be responsible for achieving the goal (winning the race) themselves. The environment they're leading in is very complex and unpredictable; the sea and wind conditions are changeable, and they can't know what the other yachts will do. They have a vision (to navigate to the finish line) but they don't know how exactly they will get there and when they suddenly might have to tack and change course. Instead, they have to work in tandem with a skilled crew who each know their role in the team and have autonomy for making quick decisions. In essence, the leadership responsibility sits not just with the captain but is shared by the entire crew.

According to Kouzes and Posner (2023), modern leaders aim to do the following.

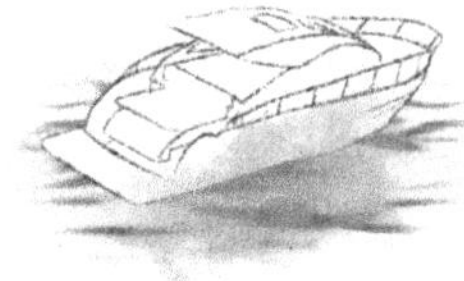

- Have a vision: And are able to communicate it clearly to the team.
- Empower others: Give people autonomy to make decisions and complete tasks.
- Role model the way: Create an example for others to follow.
- Recognise others' contributions: Acknowledge effort and celebrate accomplishments.
- Challenge the status quo: Not be afraid to make change and do things differently.

The crew on the racing yacht can demonstrate something called **emergent leadership**. This is the idea that anyone can step up and be a leader when the conditions are right. There will be instances where you will be well placed to exercise leadership – perhaps you're the only person in the group who has experience in this situation, or perhaps you have a skillset that suits the particular task but also other times when you are not necessarily the best person to lead the team.

At university, there will be lots of times where you can step up as an emergent leader. It might be that you are in a tutorial and you feel invested in the topic and want to lead the conversation. It might be that you're a member of a band and are good at bringing the musicians together, even if you're not the defined leader. It might be that you're confident at speaking in public and are happy to represent your fellow students in making suggestions for improving the course to a lecturer. All of these are examples of emergent leadership.

A step up from emergent leadership is the idea of dispensing with a single leader entirely. What if we see leadership not as coming from a person, but as being a process that can be shared by many people at once? This is the concept of **shared leadership** and might be something you encounter in your team experiences at university. For shared leadership to work, each team member must be committed to the team's goal and take responsibility for their part in getting there. Team members need to be able to support one another and appreciate each other's strengths and contributions. Often new teams will struggle to implement effective shared leadership unless there is good communication in place and team members are equally motivated.

Another useful way to lead, whether that is in an emergent or shared way, is to do so authentically. Bill George, a professor at Harvard Business School, set out his notion of **authentic leadership** (George, 2003). He believed that the most effective leaders were simply themselves: they had a good level of self-awareness and knew their strengths and weaknesses. Being authentic was most likely to generate a high degree of trust from the team and strengthen team bonds.

Bill George set out some of the key elements of being an authentic leader.

1. Purpose: You need to know '*what is the purpose of my leadership?*' This is tied closely to passion and can be very personal.
2. Heart: Authentic leaders genuinely care about the people they work with and what they do. They have a high degree of emotional intelligence, which is when leaders have a natural empathy and compassion for those they lead. Put simply, they 'get' people.
3. Values: They know what really matters to them, eg honesty, treating people with respect. Personal values become a sort of leadership compass and will help leaders make the right choices in difficult situations. Consistency is very important here. Can a leader stick to their values and speak up when they see things that aren't right?
4. Relationships: Building a culture of openness and trust is key. Leaders need to spend time with those they lead, getting to know them as people.
5. Self-discipline: Authentic leaders set high standards for themselves and others, and display grit.

So, we've thought about the concept of emergent leadership, shared leadership and being an authentic leader. Let's now also think about what your natural leadership style might be.

DiSC STYLES

There are many different models you can use to help you reflect on your preferred leadership style, but the one we use most often with students is something called a **DiSC profile**. This is based on the work of William Marston in the 1920s and 30s (who alongside inspiring DiSC also invented the lie detector machine and the character of Wonder Woman!). A DiSC profile helps you understand your preferred work style and way of interacting with others.

The theory sets out four main styles: Dominance, Influence, Steadiness and Conscientiousness, as outlined in Figure 6.6. There's no one best style for leadership – effective leaders can have any style. You will be able to exhibit elements of the four styles while being part of a team; however, you will also have a 'default setting' – a home base as it were, where you feel most comfortable.

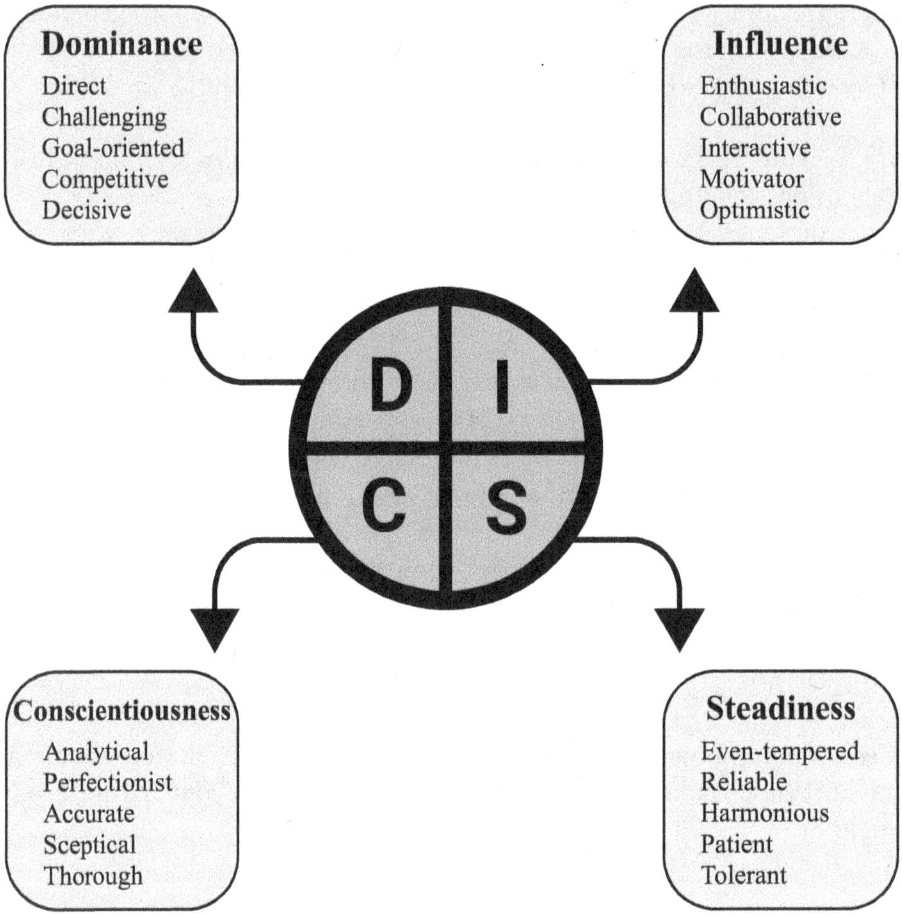

FIGURE 6.6: An overview of the four DiSC styles

Which of the four styles do you think you most relate to? You may well be a blend of more than one style, and indeed as well as D, I, S and C, the DiSC model also has styles that reflect these crossover points – DI, IS, SC, CD. Think about which segment you might fit best into. If you know your own style preference, you can then begin to think about how you interact with people who have a style that might be very different to your own. This will allow you to begin to adapt your behaviour when you lead people with differing styles in order to be the most effective leader.

ACTIVITY 6.6

Identify your DiSC style

- Put a dot on the wheel in Figure 6.7 which you think represents your DiSC style most of the time when you're in a team. If it's towards the centre of the wheel it's a mild preference towards that style. and if it's towards the outside of the wheel it's a strong preference towards that style.

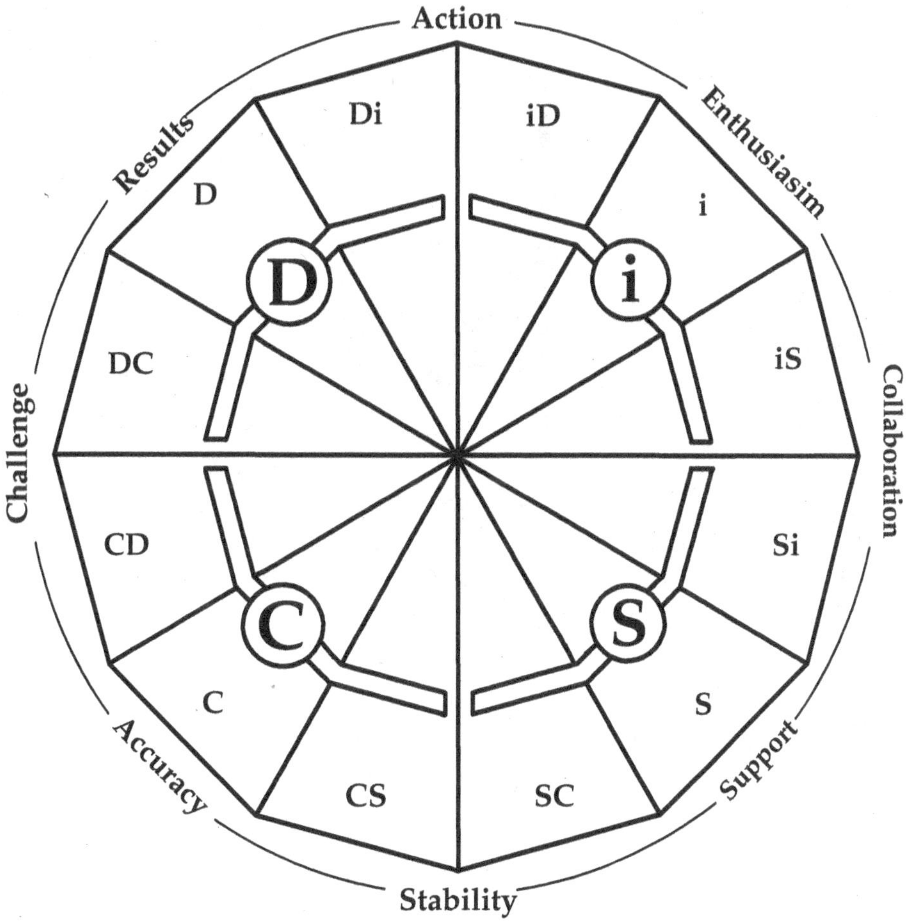

FIGURE 6.7: The DiSC wheel

You can think about teams as having inputs, processes and outputs. As a leader in a university student setting, the likelihood is that you won't have control of many of the inputs. For example, if you're put into a group to carry out a project for your module, the task might be set by the lecturer, the people might be assigned to the group and the class culture is already established. To be effective and produce a high-quality output, what you do have control over is all the processes – things like how the group is led, how communication is handled, how the group makes decisions and how well the group is bonded. As a leader, this is where you can make an impact. You have influence over the leadership style you use, the communication methods you suggest and model, inclusive decision making and setting up a trusting team culture. Figure 6.8 gives an overview of this process.

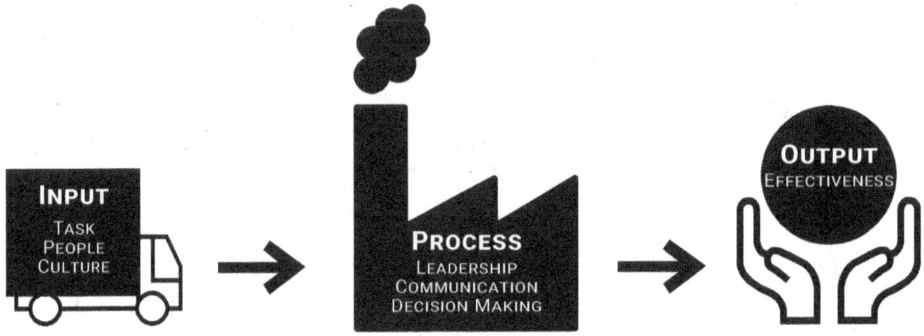

FIGURE 6.8: Team working conceptualised as a process

To set yourself up for success as a leader, we recommend using a leadership checklist. It's not exhaustive, but it covers some of the key aspects that are important for effective leadership. Next time you take on a leadership role, refer back to it and see if you can put these elements in place.

LEADERSHIP CHECKLIST

1. Do you know what your role is? Aside from being the leader, do you know why you're the leader? What leadership style are you modelling?
2. Do you understand what the team is trying to do? Do you have a clear idea of what the team is hoping to achieve? Are you able to explain this simply to others?
3. Does everyone feel valued? Teams perform better when members feel that their contributions are seen and appreciated. What are you doing to let people know this?

4. Are people happy to give and receive constructive feedback? How do you know this? If you can develop a team culture where people have a growth mindset and see feedback as a positive, then you will have a more effective team. And, if possible, make sure as the leader that you also seek feedback on your own performance.
5. Do you have discrete tasks, and do they feel significant? Do the team members have clear tasks to complete, that they can have some autonomy over, and do they know how their task links to the overall team goal? As the leader, you can help make clear linkages between tasks and overall outputs.
6. Are people working to their strengths? If people can use their skills and work on tasks they enjoy and are good at, the outputs will be stronger.
7. Do you have regular team meetings? At these meetings does everyone have a say? As leader, you can make sure that people are asked for their opinion, and it can help if you are sometimes the last to speak – seek everyone else's opinions before you share yours.
8. Do you celebrate success? It can help create a stronger team if you recognise and celebrate your milestones on the way to your objective.
9. Do you ask for help? As a leader you won't be able to know every answer and solve every problem. There will be lots of times when you are unsure. In these moments, are you able to ask for help from those around you or others outside of the team?

6.6 HOW TO BE AN EFFECTIVE FOLLOWER

In your university career you will be a part of a number of groups and teams. You can think of the difference in these terms: a group is a collective of people with a shared interest, whereas a team has a shared goal and needs to work together to achieve it. Groups can therefore switch over to become a team. For example, if you live in a shared flat you might be a group with a shared interest in being university students, but when you work together to clean the flat before an inspection you've just stepped over to become a team! You will also likely experience group work as part of your university classes. You might also experience group or teamwork as part of sports clubs or societies or volunteer activities you undertake. No matter the circumstance, the chances are that you will be in a team on multiple occasions, and crucially in those teams you will be a follower more often than a leader. How can you become a truly effective follower?

One way to look at your contribution to a team or group is to think about both how engaged you are and also how good you are at thinking critically (for more on critical thinking, see Chapter 7). This can form the basis of a simple model, as shown in Figure 6.9, and we can look at five types of follower (Kelley, 1988).

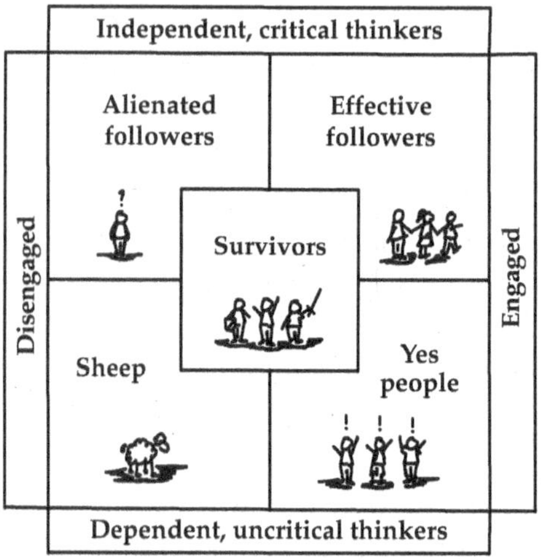

FIGURE 6.9: Follower types, adapted from the model of Kelley (1988)

At the bottom left corner, we have people who do not engage particularly in the group, and who show little critical thinking. Kelley called them 'sheep'. Sharing a lack of critical thinking, but this time being more active and engaged in the group activities are 'yes people'. These followers tend to agree with what the leader says and don't challenge or criticise. At the top left of our model, we have 'alienated followers' who are very good at challenging in terms of being excellent critical thinkers, but they are disengaged from the team and tend to only make negative contributions. These followers can be energy-suckers and tricky to work alongside. Somewhere in the middle of it all are the 'survivors' who are moderately engaged and moderately critical, and tend to see which way the group is going before jumping in. They are followers who hedge their bets and do just enough. However, the top right of the model is the place we all should be aiming for: the effective follower.

Effective followers are active and engaged in the group activity but also are confident enough to challenge the views of the leader and other team members. They think critically but from a place of being committed to the team's vision and wanting to make things better. They see themselves as having a valuable contribution to make and are motivated to perform well. When you join a team, you almost have an active choice as to what kind of follower you are going to be. To be an effective follower takes energy and effort – it's hard to be at the top right of the model all the time. Over the course of your week, perhaps you can pinpoint examples of when you were in all five areas of the model. Perhaps in your tutorial you were feeling tired and took a backseat, relying on others to do all the talking for you. In other words, you chose to be a sheep. Perhaps in your presentation group you gave lots of encouragement to your team but didn't make any suggestions as to how the layout of the graph on the slide could be improved. This was you choosing to be a yes person. Perhaps in your part-time job in a coffee shop you spent your shift pointing out everything you didn't like about working there to your colleague. This was you being an alienated follower. The point is you need to *choose* to be an effective follower and work at combining engagement and constructive criticism. If you're aware of the effective follower role, you'll get better at reflecting on the difference it made to the team when you chose to adopt it. This topic is explored in more detail in Chapter 8 when we look at how to be an effective team member in an under-performing team.

ACTIVITY 6.7

Followership

- Think of examples of when you've been at different places on the effective follower diagram. Most people won't be effective followers all the time, and there might be occasions where you choose to be a 'sheep' or 'yes person' or even an alienated follower. Note down any examples you have, as well as times when you think you've taken on the role of effective follower.

PRACTITIONER INSIGHT

Filip Nemecek, PhD student and tutor, University of Oxford

Effective followership is just as important as effective leadership in lectures and tutorials. Effective followers aren't only passive memorisers of information, but people who actively engage with the information they receive, ask questions, and share their own ideas and opinions about what they've been taught. In doing so, they develop abilities such as critical thinking, communication skills and the ability to make and defend their arguments in front of others.

From my experience as a tutor on multiple university courses, I know that having active followers in a tutorial also helps other students, as it gives them the opportunity to hear a greater range of opinions and encourages them to be active themselves. It also enables me as the tutor to assess how effective I am in leading and how I can improve, and whether students understand the course content.

Being able to follow is an important skill in academia, as academic work increasingly relies on collaboration. Answering the many complex issues that face

→

us today requires the input of different people, each of whom may add a different perspective and contribution based on their own unique experiences and abilities. As a research assistant on multiple projects which I undertook alongside my PhD studies, I have always strived to be an effective follower by taking the initiative in suggesting innovative solutions to problems that I've been asked to solve. Not only did this lead to better results; it also gave me a stronger feeling of achievement, contribution and using my full potential.

CHAPTER SUMMARY

This chapter addressed one of the most common challenges experienced by university students – how to stay on top of things by exhibiting good self-leadership. Hopefully you're now aware that you are a self-leader in progress and have more of an understanding of the component parts: reflection, self-motivation, resilience and grit, time and energy management, leading others and effective followership. You should now have a model you can use to reflect; a list of your most important values; a model to help you think about your beliefs; a time management matrix you've used to categorise your tasks; some key actions for managing your time and energy; and an identified leadership style. Put all of these in your toolbox and you can draw on them throughout your student life in order to be the best self-leader you can.

TOP TIPS AND NEXT STEPS

- Practise reflecting on your experiences with a view to deriving learning that will help you in future situations.
- Keep your resilience levels topped up by cultivating a supportive network, looking for a sense of purpose in what you do and keeping a growth mindset.
- Be prepared to take on a leadership role when the situation supports it, and think about how would you describe yourself as a leader and as a follower.
- Find a place to store your six top values where you will see them regularly, for example a note in your phone or a postcard on your desk. Think about which of your values will help you most in self-leadership.

- When you get new tasks to do this week, categorise them in your mind in terms of Covey's time management matrix and decide which quadrant you'd place them in.
- When you next find yourself working alongside someone, think about where you would place them on the DiSC wheel.

CHAPTER 7

YOUR RESEARCH MINDSET

CHALLENGES WE EXPLORE IN THIS CHAPTER

As a student, it can be challenging to gain confidence in receiving, analysing and producing knowledge in higher education. These skills will be a vital part of your university journey and will support your further learning and career development after university. It also is one of the most enjoyable parts of learning, whether you are completing discourse analysis, conducting experiments in the lab, embarking on field studies or holding interviews. Producing new knowledge and developing your **research mindset** should be an enjoyable, exciting and sometimes scary part of your university life.

This chapter explores a research mindset; fundamentally it looks at the way that you approach knowledge as a university student. Engaging a research mindset means that you will no longer simply be receiving information; you will be generating knowledge too. This, like many things at university, can be a daunting prospect but it also offers exciting opportunities.

To begin with, we think about your role as a scholar, understanding how you will join an academic conversation at university. Building on this, we look at creativity and the role of this at university before analysing what critical thinking is and how you can engage with it. These skills are also vital, especially as generative AI and technology is changing how we engage with information. We move on to examine the fundamentals of research skills, focusing on academic **argumentation**, note-taking and readings.

INTENDED LEARNING OUTCOMES

By the end of this chapter, you should be able to:

- define creativity and understand its role in your university journey;
- apply System One and System Two thinking, and use Bloom's Taxonomy, in order to solve problems critically;

- understand academic argumentation and how to use it at university;
- identify a reading strategy to suit your study needs and organise your notes effectively.

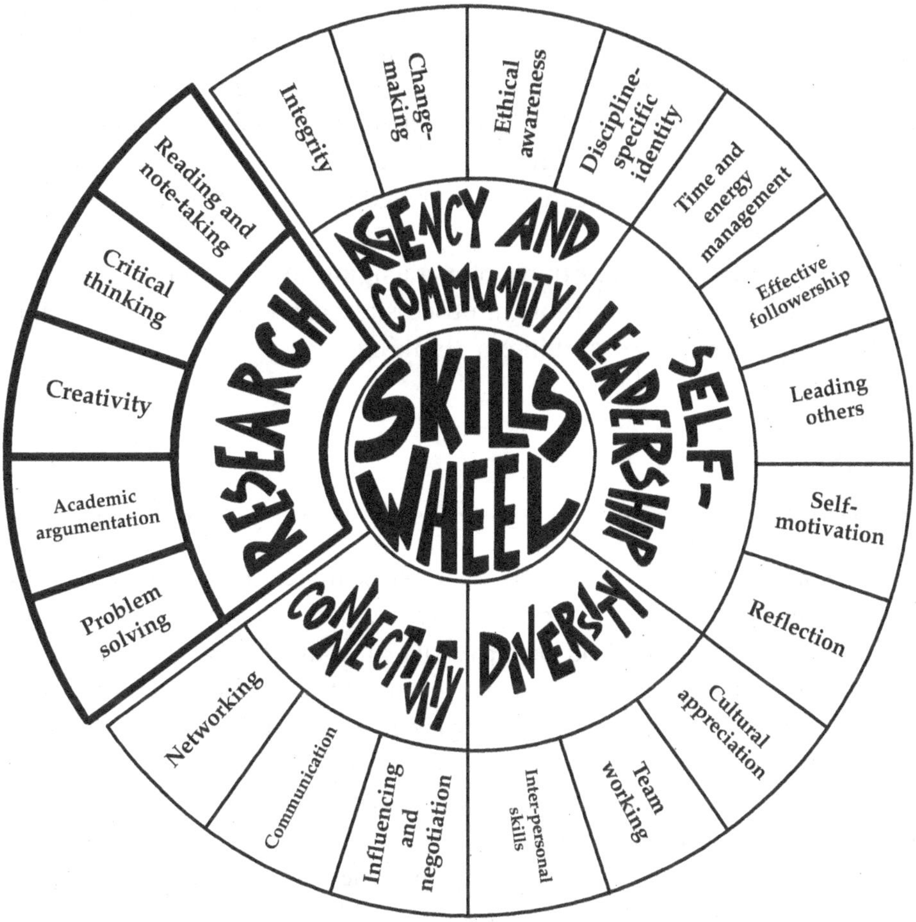

The attributes covered in this chapter are problem solving, academic argumentation, creativity, critical thinking and reading and note-taking.

7.1 ENGAGING YOUR RESEARCH MINDSET

We can understand research as an undertaking to systematically investigate a topic. Let's break this down and firstly explore the word 'systematically': this means that when we perform research, we are deliberately choosing to undertake this activity and to carry it out with a methodological and organised approach. The word 'investigate' refers to the approach which will include studying, analysing, and inspecting our field of knowledge.

In Chapter 2 we learnt that a mindset is an established group of assumptions, attitudes or beliefs. Thus, together we can see that a research mindset is the belief that we should systematically analyse and investigate information in an organised manner. Our research mindset means that when we receive information, whether this takes the form of primary results from a test we conducted in the lab, a transcript from an interview or a piece of text (such as a journal article), we do not simply accept this outcome as a given. Instead, we begin to question it, and this also means we endeavour to create new knowledge and contribute to the academic conversation.

Our research mindset is an example of **metacognition** or thinking about thinking. By gaining an awareness of our thought process, we can reflect on how we approach problems and be more purposeful in our thinking.

7.2 CREATIVITY

To many people, it may seem odd to start a research mindset chapter by looking at creativity. It would be easy to presume that creativity would be external to the rational and logic-focused world of university and, unless you were undertaking a fine arts or music degree, then you would not need to be concerned about it.

Yet, if we explore what creativity is we can see that it is fundamental to our research mindset: creativity enables us to become original thinkers, engage our critical thinking skills, and see new opportunities in our studies. Therefore, creativity helps us to become better scholars and to enjoy our time at university. We must have original thought in order to solve problems, whether that's understanding data from an experiment or interpreting a text for class.

Furthermore, creativity is a fundamental skill outside of your studies, whether this is pursuing hobbies and extra-curricular activities or getting ready for the workplace. Increasingly, employers are seeing creativity as a fundamental skill, one that they expect new graduates and interns to be able to demonstrate (World Economic Forum, 2020). Creativity is especially important as generative AI and workforces evolve increasingly quickly, meaning employees need to be accomplished problem-solvers to meet these demands (Li, 2022).

WHAT IS CREATIVITY?

Creativity can be quite difficult to define, but fundamentally it's the process of generating new concepts and ideas. If we look at the root word 'create', we can start to understand that creativity is about thinking in a new way. We think there are four factors that make up creativity.

1. Idea generation: thinking of new concepts or approaches.
2. Imagination: forming novel images outside of your current sphere of knowledge.
3. Originality: thinking independently.
4. New possibilities: exploring potential alternatives to current ideas and problems.

These four factors will be developed throughout your university journey, originality being fundamental to exploring the vast amount of data that you will process throughout your degree. You need imagination and idea generation to turn this information into new concepts and ideas, whether that be for experiments or essays. Throughout your degree you'll also be looking at new possibilities, exploring potential new solutions to problems both in and outside of your scholarly work. Creativity is fundamental to other skills too; for example, creativity is imperative for empathy, as without imagining another person's situation, we cannot empathise.

DIVERGENT AND CONVERGENT THINKING

Divergent and convergent thinking are approaches to creative problem-solving. The terms were coined in 1956 by J P Guilford.

- **Divergent thinking**, also known as imaginative or horizontal thinking, involves creating ideas and exploring possibilities.
- **Convergent thinking**, also known as logical or vertical thinking, involves analytically dissecting problems.

You will never be either a divergent or convergent thinker; these are simply two parts of the creative process. At the most basic level we can think of divergent thinking as coming up with new ideas and convergent thinking as analysing and thinking about what to do with them. Yet we don't commonly engage with divergent and convergent thinking this sequentially within our academic work; we constantly flip between the two. Tables 7.1 and 7.2 outline the characteristics of divergent thinking and convergent thinking, with examples.

TABLE 7.1: Divergent thinking

Divergent thinking	Example
Thinking of new possibilities	Designing an experiment
Originality	Using your experience to reflect upon a question in a new way
Seeing new problems	Creating your own essay question

TABLE 7.2: Convergent thinking

Convergent thinking	Example
Analytical problem-solving	Using theories and formulas to answer questions
Critical assessment	Reviewing a report or essay you wrote
Dissecting data	Evaluating and drawing conclusions from class readings

Now we know how creativity is defined and what convergent and divergent thinking refers to, let's move on to explore how you can develop your creativity in support of improving your research mindset. We can think of this as a five-step circular process, as outlined below.

DEVELOPING YOUR CREATIVITY SKILLS IN YOUR RESEARCH MINDSET

1. Mindfully think about creativity: Do not wait for creativity to just happen; actively think about the process and how you can schedule it into your week. Keep a notepad with you or use a note-taking app on your phone to jot down any ideas that come to mind.
2. Do not aim for perfection: When you are being creative it is really easy to be disheartened by overthinking what you are creating. Creativity, like all other skills, is something that is developed with practice. If you aim for it to be perfect on the first attempt, you are likely to limit your creative process.

3. Collaborate with others on creative ideas: A great way to improve your creative skills and your confidence in this area is to work with others. Of course, you will have limited scope to do this on assessed coursework. However, you can try to find ways to integrate collaboration and creativity into co-curricular or extra-curricular activities.
4. Start with small steps: Rather than setting out huge blocks of time (that you probably do not have) to develop your creative skills, think how you can introduce small steps. This could be as simple as actively thinking about a new way to solve a problem or how you would undertake an experiment differently.
5. Reflect on your progress: Using the various measures we spoke about earlier in this book (such as the star chart in Chapter 2) reflect upon the progress you have made in your creative skills, which you can then use to further develop this area.

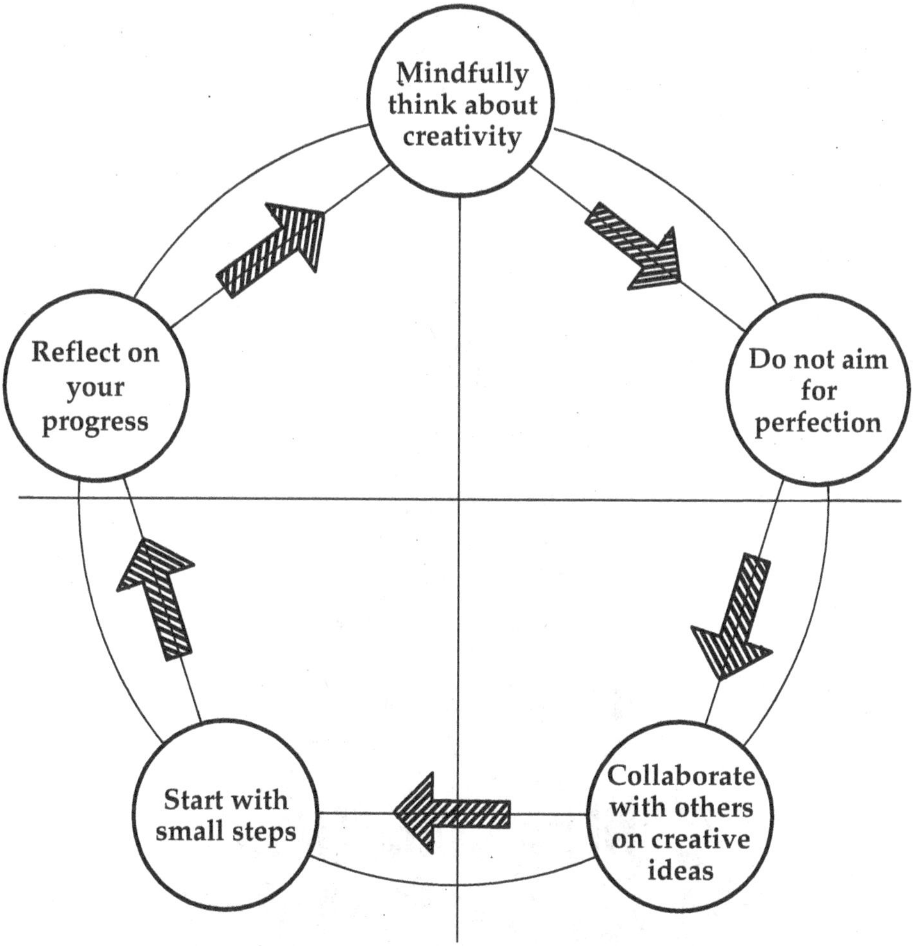

FIGURE 7.1: Developing your creativity skills

7.3 HOW TO SOLVE PROBLEMS AND THINK CRITICALLY

So far, we have covered what we mean by research mindset, and we have explored creativity. We'll now move on to look at critical thinking – a phrase you will hear many, many times during your university journey.

WHAT IS CRITICAL THINKING?

When we think of the word 'critical', we often associate it with the word 'argumentative' and in day-to-day life if someone was being critical, we'd often think that this was negative. Yet, critical thinking is a huge part of our research mindset and adopting a critical thinking approach will be fundamental to your success at university as well as understanding and evaluating the world. Here, critical does not mean negative; it means relevant, reasonable and clear-thinking. Furthermore, critical thinking is an active undertaking, which looks at reasons and implications within information.

BLOOM'S TAXONOMY

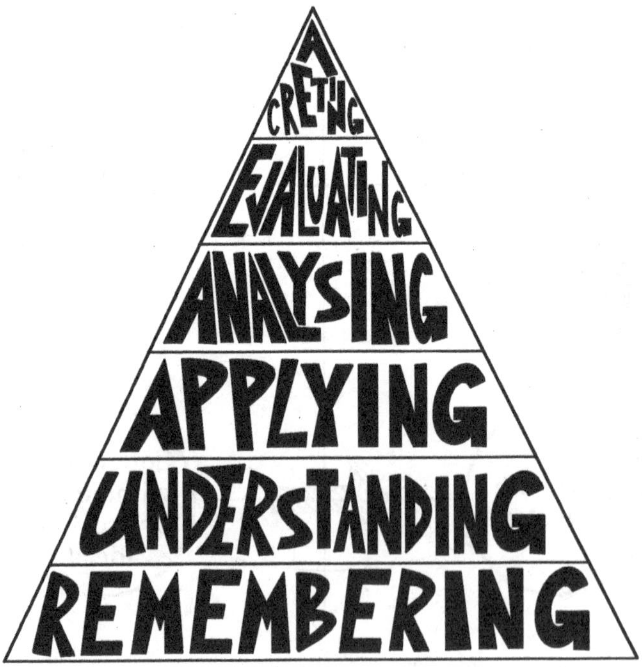

FIGURE 7.2: Bloom's Taxonomy.

At the bottom of the pyramid in Figure 7.2 is remembering. This is one of the simplest cognitive skills that we can engage with while learning, but it is absolutely crucial to the process. Here we have to be able to remember the information in order to use it later. Therefore, this step involves recalling, stating or even reproducing the information we share or that we read.

The next step is understanding this information. This means we can explain our new concepts and ideas, rather than simply recalling them. To appreciate the difference between remembering and understanding we can think of an actor learning a script: here the actor would simply remember the lines; they wouldn't necessarily appreciate the meaning behind them. Thus, understanding information means that we can identify it, paraphrase it, and even explain it.

Our next cognitive skill is applying this information. You can see that as we climb up the pyramid the cognitive skills become increasingly difficult, but we have to use the underlying skills in order to engage these new ones. When we apply information, we think about using it in a new way; for example, could you demonstrate or illustrate this information, or could you use this in a new setting?

The next skill which is fundamental to our research mindset is analysis. Here, we can distinguish between different parts of information. When analysing information, we can organise it, experiment with it and even criticise it.

The penultimate skill is evaluation: this allows us to begin to ask if we can justify or stand by a decision we make. We can appraise, argue, and judge information given to us. This is a complex cognitive skill that relies heavily upon application of the previous four levels of our pyramid. By evaluating the information, we fully appreciate and understand the nuances and complexity allowing us to decide whether we would come to the same conclusion as the author (if the data set was created by someone else) or be able to critically evaluate the conclusions drawn from the data set, asking how and why we arrived at those conclusions, if it was created by ourselves. We will look at evaluation information and evidence in more detail in the next section.

At the top of our pyramid is: creating. Here we can question if we can generate a new point of view, which is by far the most difficult skill in the pyramid and why it is located at the top. This is a skill that you'll spend your entire degree mastering but is a very exciting and rewarding prospect when you consider that you are creating new knowledge. This does not mean you are expected to come up with a new theory, model or ground-breaking experiment. Instead, this means that you are using your collective background, thinking about the experiences that you've had, the text and the information that you have read and received to create an original point of view. Only you have your experiences, and this means that you can successfully contribute to the academic conversation on your topic.

7.4 ARGUMENTATION

Argumentation in an academic sense is not about being confrontational; instead, it's about using evidence and reason to review information and present your own interpretation or thoughts. To argue is not the same as we might understand it in a colloquial sense, where it would be seen as a negative undertaking or even as a fight between people. Instead, **an argument** can be seen as a reasoned case put forward. Here, **evidence** is used to convince your audience (which may be other students in your class or your examiner) of a **hypothesis**. An easy way to see if you have an argument or not is to simply ask: '*Can someone disagree with this?*'.

For example, a statement would be '*London is the capital of England*', and most people would simply take this statement as fact. In comparison, an argument would be: '*London is the best city in England*'. This is a statement that many people would agree or disagree with. There would be multiple other questions people may ask, such as: '*What is the definition of 'best'?*', '*What evidence and quantifiers were used?*', '*Did you consider the cost of living, the quality of living, access to health care and good schools, opportunities for employment, social activities and transport links?*' With this second statement, you would need to make a case as to why you held this opinion and ensure that you are qualifying the statement. While you may present a very strong case for London being the best city, the person you are speaking to may have heard an even stronger argument that Birmingham is in fact the best city in England and, while they understand your evidence, they do not come to the same conclusions as you.

What is important to remember though is that while the facts or data that you will use will need to be correct (in our example, the definition of a city), you will often be marked for your skills in creating an argument, whether you are arguing that platinum is the best catalyst or the printing press was the primary cause of the Protestant Reformation. With this starting point of argumentation at the heart of our research mindset, we will further unpick the skills and attributes you will need in order to develop this mindset and succeed at university.

JOINING THE ACADEMIC CONVERSATION

In order to develop your argumentation skills, you can think about joining a large conversation. As a student you are expected to contribute to the academic community, which means not only learning the facts but interpreting them using a research mindset. In order to do so, you need to develop your academic voice.

We often see students face two main challenges when establishing their academic voice: the first is that they do not commonly engage with the current debates on the topics they are writing or speaking about; instead, the piece reads more like a blog or even a newspaper column highlighting the opinion of the student. The second issue is that their work often relies solely on the existing material and has little analysis by the student; it reads like a commentary. Table 7.3 summarises the characteristics of opinion and commentary-based writing.

TABLE 7.3: The characteristics of opinion and commentary-based writing.

Opinion-based writing	Commentary-based writing
Lacks evidence	Lacks analysis
Is not aware of current research on the topic	Has a large portion of quotes and paraphrasing
Uses a lot of emotive and hyperbolic language	Does not link data together
Shows biases	Shows no originality

To overcome either of these issues, when establishing your academic voice think of joining a conversation on your topic matter. You are asked to respond to the existing things said in this conversation while adding your own thoughts.

To make this clearer we could think of a regular conversation Rebecca may have about ordering a pizza.

Alex *I think the best pizza is pepperoni, with a stuffed crust.*
Shruti *I also think the best pizza has a stuffed crust. I know pepperoni is meant to be tasty and adds salt, but I don't eat meat, so I like lots of vegetables on pizza.*

Response 1: If Rebecca used her voice like an opinion piece:
Rebecca *(covering her ears so as not to hear any of this conversation): I would like a pineapple pizza.*

Response 2: If Rebecca commented instead of contributing:
Rebecca *Both Alex and Shruti like stuffed crust pizza. Alex likes pepperoni but Shruti likes vegetables.*

Response 3: If Rebecca listened to the thoughts of others and contributed her own opinion in response:

Rebecca *We all like stuffed crust so we should order one of those. I like spicy pizzas so maybe we could order a spicy vegetable one? And Alex, if you would prefer something else, maybe you could order a small pepperoni pizza?*

Of course, in academic conversation (either in class or formal writing assignments) we would be engaging in far more complex topics and writing more formally (and not discussing pizza quite so much).

But continuing with the pizza example, we can look how this translates to our opinion and commentor problems.

Opinion: The best pizza is pineapple; I like pineapple on pizza as it makes it sweet and taste nice. In addition to this, pineapple is aesthetically pleasing and contains vitamin C.

Commentator: Initial research indicated that pepperoni is the best pizza topping; more recent studies conclude that anchovies are the best topping.

Conversation: Both deep pan and stuffed crust theories share key features in their priorities for pizza topping. The deep pan theory highlights that the best pizza toppings are anchovies due to the high salt content, allowing contrast to the sweetness of the tomato sauce. Similarly, the stuffed crust theory highlights that a salty topping is an excellent choice for a pizza topping but favours cured meats rather than anchovies. While I can understand that this contrast may be tasty to many palates, both choices can be controversial – firstly because doctors recommend us to regulate our salt intake (Kalbs, 2021) and secondly because many consumers of pizzas are vegetarians. Instead, this paper argues that pineapple is the best pizza topping due to three reasons: firstly, it has an appealing sweet taste; secondly, its colourful nature makes the pizza more appealing (see Jacobs, 2022), and finally it contains vitamin C (Toronto, 2010). Please note that these are fake citations.

STUDENT INSIGHT

Lily Bates, biochemistry, third year

When starting university, I found it challenging to voice opinions or present arguments in my work. I felt like I was not qualified to have opinions about my subject. However, forming ideas is important for learning and growing as a student.

A helpful strategy I have found for developing ideas in my coursework is organising my notes across different readings by concepts and subtopics. Then, when writing about a particular topic, you have notes from multiple sources in one place, making it easier to weave different pieces of evidence and information into your argument.

Asking questions is another great way to start, such as staying after lectures, emailing lecturers and tutors, and speaking up during tutorials. Developing an inquisitive attitude towards your work helps you start thinking critically about your subject, which makes it easier to develop your ideas, voice your arguments and participate in the academic conversation.

ARGUMENTATION IN PRACTICE

When you approach your academic assignments, you will need to evidence your argumentation skills. When writing essays in school, often pupils are taught to write a general introduction, then give one side of the argument, then the other side of the argument, and then in the conclusion you can specify which side of the argument you agree with and why.

At the university level, we want you to lead and develop your writing around an argument instead. At the start of the essay, in your introduction, you include a '**thesis statement**', which is a summary of your own argument or opinion. This is a single statement which summarises your argument (note that an argument is different to a summary). As we have discussed, an argument is something that can be agreed or disagreed with. You will use evidence, either original research you have completed (in a lab, fieldwork or archival) or from existing published academic works. Here every section of your paper should be directly related to evidencing how and why your thesis statement is true. Of course, you are encouraged to show any limitations your arguments may have, but there should not be evidence in your paper which is not connected to this.

An example thesis statement would be: *This paper will argue that pineapple is the best pizza topping.*

The following is an example of a summary not a thesis statement: *This paper will explore the best pizza toppings.* You can quickly tell this is not a thesis statement because you cannot argue or disagree with it.

Once you have your thesis statement, you can split your essay up into sections which convey the different points you want to make. Each section includes evidence and clearly links back to your thesis statement. Each section tries to answer these questions:

- What are you arguing in this section?
- How are you going to prove this?
- How does this link back to your larger, overarching argument?

In the conclusion, there is not new evidence or arguments – it summarises what you have laid out earlier.

The introduction comprises an engaging opening, some scene-setting and context, and the important thesis statement (presenting your own views). Academic work has often been described as 'the worst crime novel' – we know exactly what is going to happen from the start. You lay out the methods or the roadmap you'll be taking us through.

In your conclusion, you restate your argument or the methods you used, and you can talk about the implication or broader themes your essay draws upon.

ACTIVITY 7.1

Reverse analysing an article

- For this activity you will need to choose an article or paper you have come across at school or university that you found particularly clear and easy to read. Go through it and try to summarise each paragraph or section into a single sentence. As you work through it, you will be creating a summary of the document's structure, which helps show you what the author did to build their article or paper.

PRACTITIONER INSIGHT

Dr Sharon Leahy, Associate Dean (Education), University of St Andrews

A research mindset focuses on embracing a questioning outlook on phenomena in the world. Students can struggle initially to develop this mentality, but be assured that it will come if you commit to engaging with other's work on the topics that interest you. It is essential to read as broadly as possible around the subject matter. As you engage more deeply in each topic you will begin to question others' research approach. Consider how they have devised and tackled the research questions that they pose, how they have scrutinised their data and whose work they have drawn on to discuss and critically analyse their work. Think about how their work corresponds to and deviates from others' work. Where are the potential gaps in the research, what questions have still to be answered? A research mindset is enhanced by conversation and debate with your peers and others in the field. Healthy debate and discussion are essential for a critical mind to grow. I always strive to turn my students into scholars as they progress through their programmes of study. A student is an individual who is here to learn and absorb knowledge; a scholar is an individual who is no longer passive, but plays an active role in creating knowledge. As a student progresses through their degree, they learn the skills and approaches that allow a scholarly research mindset to develop.

7.5 DEVELOPING YOUR RESEARCH SKILLS: READING AND NOTE-TAKING

READING

There is a distinction between how you read for pleasure and how you're going to begin to critically engage with academic material. When you read at university, you're not simply taking in the information; you're thinking about joining academic conversations. You join this conversation by thinking about how and why you're reading any material, questioning who produced it and what methods were used to produce it.

When reading for pleasure, often you'll accept the information, but when you're in your research mindset you want to start thinking about the following.

- Do I believe this?
- How does this link to other texts/lectures?
- Would I come to the same conclusions as this author did?

This can be nerve-wracking when you are starting your university journey. It can seem very daunting to think about questioning something that an established academic has produced. This is when you must think about engaging in academic conversation and, consequently, thinking about how you can engage with texts.

Therefore, in order to engage your research mindset when undertaking academic reading, you need to be prepared before you are reading. You must be present and active when you are reading and think about the text once you are finished. This section will help you do just that.

WHAT ARE YOU READING?

Before you begin reading, it is important to note what type of text you are engaging with. This will impact the way you read and use the text. Here, we will look only at non-fiction texts; however, some subjects, such as film studies or literature, will also use fiction-based sources. We will return to when and how to reference in Chapter 10.

ACADEMIC TEXTS: OKAY TO REFERENCE!

An academic text is one that:

1. is **peer reviewed** (text that has been critically reviewed by other experts in that field);
2. written by an expert, or several experts, in the field;
3. includes citations and a full bibliography;
4. has a scholarly writing style and technical language.

TABLE 7.4: Examples of academic texts

Article in journal	A single text looking in specific detail at a single subject in a thematic journal. Example: Brooks, S K (2020) The Psychological Impact of Quarantine and How to Reduce It: Rapid Review of the Evidence. *The Lancet*, 395: 912–20.
Book or monograph	A detailed overview of a topic, often including multiple angles and research projects. Example: Virág, C (2017) *The Emotions in Early Chinese Philosophy*. Oxford: Oxford University Press.
Edited volume	Multiple authors contributing chapters to a book, usually on a single topic. Example: Cornelio, J et al (eds) (2022) *Routledge International Handbook of Religion in Global Society*. Abingdon: Routledge.

ALMOST-ACADEMIC TEXTS: REFERENCE WITH CAUTION!

These texts are ones that are related to academia but do not go through the same peer-review process. If you do reference these texts, ensure that this is acceptable in your discipline (everyone does this slightly differently) and that it is a reliable source.

TABLE 7.5: Examples of almost-academic texts

Textbook	An introduction to a topic, often written by an academic in this field. Example: Scott et al (2022) *Biological Science: Exploring the Science of Life*. Oxford: Oxford University Press.
Policy documents or reports	Written by practitioners in the field about a broader topic, either for a specialised or general audience. These are often funded by a particular body or organisation. Example: UK Government (2022) *Keepers of Time: Ancient and Native Woodland and Trees Policy in England*. London: Department for Environment, Food & Rural Affairs.
Theses and dissertations	Completed by postgraduate research students, these will normally be in-depth explorations of a very specific topic for an academic audience. Example: Yeboah, M A (2008) *Gender and Livelihoods: Mapping the Economic Strategies of Porters in Accra, Ghana*. PhD thesis. Morgantown, WV: West Virginia University.

NON-ACADEMIC TEXTS: DON'T REFERENCE!

It is good practice not to reference non-academic texts in university work. On occasion you may engage with them; for example, if you were completing a discourse analysis on the public perception of climate change you may quote newspaper articles to show how the information was broadcast. You would not use the newspaper article to back up findings and evidence. If you are planning on using a non-academic text, speak with your lecturer/supervisor first.

TABLE 7.6: Examples of non-academic texts

Online encyclopaedia	Overview of topics; often these can be edited by the general public. Example: Wikipedia.
Newspaper	A periodical (usually daily) publication sharing recent events and opinions. Often news sources will start from a specific political opinion. It's important to note that some newspapers are more credible than others. Examples: *The Times*, *The Guardian*, *The Independent* (in the UK).
Webpage	A HTML document on a vast number of topics displayed on a web browser. Examples: blog sites, company websites etc.

Now that we've covered the different kinds of text you will be engaging with at university, it's time to move on to look at strategies for coping with (often) long reading lists that you'll be given for your modules at university.

STRATEGY FOR READING

When engaging your research mindset and approaching academic reading, it's important to do this systematically.

One of the most common questions students ask is: how much should they read to prepare for an exam, to complete a piece of coursework, or to simply get ready for a tutorial? I'm sure they're all quite frustrated that there is no simple answer for this and it's a little bit like asking how long a piece of string is. As we discussed at the start of this section, you're not simply reading for pleasure, but rather extracting information that you can later analyse and dissect. Therefore, when trying to decide how much to read you can ask three key questions.

1. What is the key information I need to understand?
2. What am I trying to learn from each text?
3. What am I going to use the reading for?

Considering the first question, the key bits of information you need to understand will most likely be outlined in your intended learning outcomes in your module guide and lectures; therefore, it is extremely important to familiarise yourself with and think about these. Moreover, considering the second question, you should aim to clarify the purpose for which you are reading the texts before beginning the exercise; for instance, you may be looking at a particular author's take on the information.

For example, perhaps you have an upcoming lecture. Firstly, you need to read enough to gain a baseline understanding of the information on which the lecture will be based. This might be where your core textbook is essential, and you may not need to read anything else in order to understand the topic. However, you will most likely be required to move on to more advanced readings, such as book chapters and articles, to engage in the different debates within the topic. You will need to read more widely to obtain a cross-section of opinion and interpretation within the subject area. If you think back to the academic conversation, you need to read enough to know who the main voices are in the conversation that you are reading about.

Once you have answered these two questions, you can move on to the third question: what are you going to use the reading for? If you are preparing for a tutorial or a class, it's likely that you'll need to read less than if you are completing an assignment. If you are preparing for an exam or coursework, you need to make sure that you have read enough to understand the topic, can create the argument for your piece of work, and can evidence every point that you're making in that argument.

Hopefully, this can be a starting point for you to understand how much reading you need to undertake. This will vary depending on what discipline you are studying and which module you are undertaking.

When choosing what to read, you should start with the reading list provided by your lecturer. Most reading lists will have a core or essential section; these quite often include textbooks or any readings you will be discussing in class. They often contain an additional 'recommended' or 'suggested' section, which are a great starting point for preparing for exams or assignments. Your module leaders will be able to advise you on the most important items on your reading list. You should focus on what they have outlined as essential reading for classes, and then pick additional readings that will be useful for enhancing your understanding for key tasks such as coursework or exams. When choosing your additional reading, you can skim-read the introduction or look at abstracts to decide whether the sources will be useful, reflecting back on the three previously outlined questions.

A good general rule is to aim for quality not quantity when engaging with academic reading. It is far more important that you understand and can critically engage with the text that you're reading, rather than reading vast amounts that you will forget within a few days or not commit to understanding at all.

Academic reading, especially reading lists, can be extremely daunting, and it's normal to feel apprehensive when engaging with it. Asking yourself why you're reading this, and how you're going to use it, can be a good starting point to overcome this apprehension. Time and practice will also be vital in choosing what to read and how you will use it. It's vital when you do read that you do this strategically. We will outline a system of how to do this in Figure 7.3.

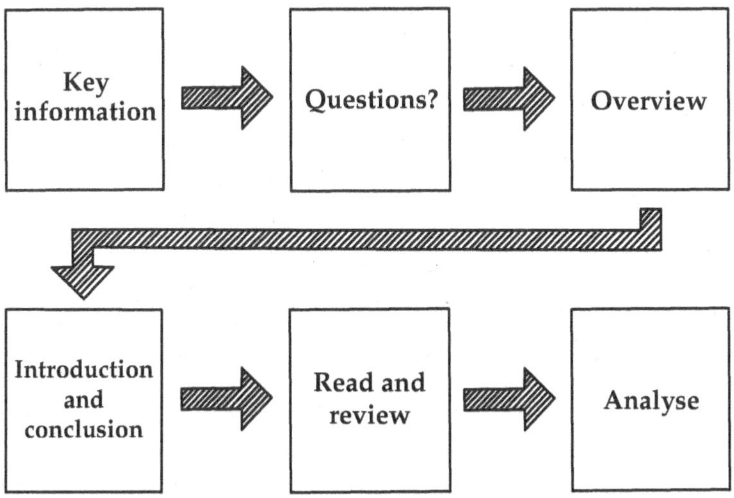

FIGURE 7.3: Strategic reading flowchart

- Stage 1, key information: Think about *what* you are reading. Why was it written? Is it an academic text? Almost all sources shared on your academic reading list will be peer reviewed, but if you are branching out and identifying your own sources, you'll need to be able to judge their credibility.
- Stage 2, questions: Think about *why* you are reading this text. What is your purpose? What questions are you trying to answer? It may be that you are preparing for an assignment or an exam and therefore you may have a research question in mind, or it may be that you want to get a greater depth of knowledge on a subject and so may have a broader question.
- Stage 3, overview: Skim read the entire text. Quickly engage with the text, so you have an idea or an overview about what it's going to say. One method of doing this is to read both the introduction and conclusion and, subsequently, look for the topic sentence in all the subtitles throughout the article. A topic sentence is a sentence that introduces a new paragraph or idea; these are typically at the start of a paragraph, although they are not always found here.
- Stage 4, introduction and conclusion: Go back to the introduction and start thinking about the purpose of the paper. What questions are the authors trying to address here? You are then able to look at the methods of how they are going to fulfil this purpose and, finally, what is the central argument of this chapter or article and what do the authors want you to take away? Then, review the conclusion, thinking again about the purpose, method and argument of the article.
- Stage 5, read and review: Read the text from start to end, focusing on the questions you outlined. If you are struggling with the text, you may want to skim-read certain paragraphs or sections and then go back through it and try to read it more thoroughly, looking for any keywords.
- Stage 6, analyse: Bring this reading together and analyse the text. You should have been reflecting on your questions throughout the reading process, but here you might want to go back to them and make some more detailed notes. Analysing an article or chapter is the most difficult part of academic reading to begin with. If you are struggling, you may want to simplify this and think about one good element of the article and one bad element of the article. An example of a good thing could be the way that the authors have used certain data or an experimental report. A bad thing could be something that you don't understand or a point that seems to contradict a principle that you may have previously learnt or read about.

Being mindful and strategic in your academic reading will make the process much simpler. Academic reading takes time and practice. In addition to applying the outlined strategy, you can think of reading as a three-step process: i) before you begin reading, think about what the key questions are and why you are reading it; ii) during the reading process, make sure you are selective and are really sticking to what is relevant to your questions; and iii) once you have completed your reading, ensure that you're reviewing it, analysing the text and thinking about what you have and have not understood.

MAKING NOTES

An essential way to engage your research mindset and study successfully is to create an effective note-taking strategy. We take notes for numerous reasons.

1. Active learning: avoiding passive reading to engage with the text. This involves making notes when engaging your active learning principles by deciding what information to include in your notes, what to paraphrase, what to highlight and what you might not need to know right now. This helps you to understand the text and improve your memory.
2. Citing and referencing: keeps track of where the information is from, in order for you to reference it later in assignments.
3. Develops your writing: by paraphrasing your own thoughts, you are developing your writing skills.
4. Motivation and concentration: taking notes can keep you focused and help your motivation as they provide evidence of the work you have completed.

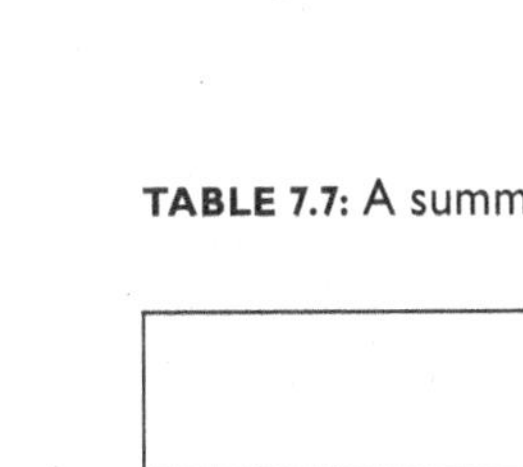

When studying, you take notes for different reasons, and different types of notes suit different tasks. Thinking about the purpose of your notes should impact how you create them. At university you are likely to take notes for three main reasons, as outlined in Table 7.7.

TABLE 7.7: A summary of the three main reasons for note-taking

	Lectures and reading	**Essays, reports and assessments**	**Revision**
Frequency:	Daily/weekly note-taking.	Created when preparing for assessment.	Created throughout the semester and during revision periods.

→

TABLE 7.7: *(Cont.)*

	Lectures and reading	**Essays, reports and assessments**	**Revision**
May focus on:	Focus on key points from class and set readings. May also focus on understanding information.	Focus on the detailed topic you are producing your assessment on. This could include detailed analysis and evaluation of a topic.	Focus on how topics are interlinked and the core themes from class.
Guided by:	May be guided by questions lecturers have set ahead of a seminar, lecture or workshop.	Guided by an assessment question.	May be guided by possible exam questions.
Main use:	It may include any preparatory and reflective work for/ from classes.	Will be used to write your essay/report/ assessment. Will need to include citations/references to keep track of sources.	Especially important for open-book exams and for highlighting topics you need to focus on revising.

ORGANISING NOTES

In order to have effective notes, it's important to have a system of organisation that is easy to navigate. Therefore, you should aim to have a system in place that works well for you, so that you can quickly and easily find notes that you previously made. For example, you might take paper notes during classes, but when you're working on assessments you use electronic notes. The simplest way to do this is to try to create a system early on in your degree, but if you're already part-way through it's never too late to introduce an organised system.

Think how you will organise your notes.

- Paper or electronic?
- If electronic, what software will you use (notes app, MS Word, Notion)?
- How will you organise these? – if paper, will you be using notebooks or paper and folders? If electronic, what sort of filing system will you have?

How you're going to save and organise your notes is important to decide at the outset. For example, if you're choosing to take notes electronically then we'd recommend getting a folder and naming system in place. It sounds obvious, but having all notes relevant to one module in one place, neatly filed away with filenames that are descriptive and/or numbered, will help you locate the notes you need and quickly. If you're taking notes using a notepad, then consider buying different folders/notebooks for each different module. You could also buy some index/page tabs to further help you locate key pages of notes (like those relevant to an assignment).

HOW TO MAKE NOTES

Creating good notes does not mean that you need to write down all the points from the lecture or reading that you are working from! Usually if you are copying down large chunks of information, this means that you are on autopilot and, as we learnt in Chapter 4, we want to engage in active learning. As you are applying your research mindset, you want to evaluate the information and decide what is important to you by asking why you're taking notes and any questions you have in mind for these notes. Therefore, being selective is key, otherwise you'll spend your time just writing down huge chunks of information and not really listening to the lecture or thinking about what you are reading or reviewing. This will take time and practice, but eventually you will have more confidence and think about what phrases or words are particularly important for the purpose of the notes.

KEY FEATURES OF NOTE-TAKING

Here are some of the key features of note-taking which should help you keep your notes organised.

SOURCE

When taking effective notes, it is always important to include your source. It's easy to write down half the source, such as the author or the general edition name rather than the specific details, telling yourself that you can look up the full source later if you need to. But if you do this, there's a high likelihood in the future that you won't be able to retrace your steps easily and could fall foul of **plagiarism** rules (see Chapter 10). Make sure that you write down all the information you need about the source. It will save you time in the long run!

YOUR PURPOSE AND QUESTIONS

As we've discussed throughout this chapter, it is also really important to focus on why you were listening to that lecture, reading the chapter or researching a topic; think about the specific purpose and questions you have. Writing these questions at the top of your page will keep your notes focused and help you avoid taking notes that you don't need or will never use. Irrelevant notes will only distract you later on. If you are worried about needing more information at a later date, just write down the key words and phrases (as well as the source) so you can locate the details later if you need to.

CLARITY

Making your notes clear and organised will be far more helpful when returning to them at a later date. You need to think of this at both micro and macro levels. We've already discussed the macro-level thinking about how and where you're going to save your notes and what system you're going to use, but you also need to think about this at the micro level. The micro level involves thinking about the actual note-taking: things like the use of headings and subtitles, leaving white space on the page, and ensuring that if you were to come back and read them a later date you would understand all the abbreviations and handwriting on that page. As there has been a large increase in open-book exams, this is especially important as you don't want to be in an exam and unable to read your notes. Similarly, preparing for an assessment could be very frustrating if you're not sure what you wrote. You could also consider using icons to indicate key points or notes that are relevant for revision/essays. Highlighters or different coloured pens could also come in handy if you are making notes by hand.

HIGHLIGHT QUOTATIONS AND PARAPHRASING

Finally, make sure that you are clearly indicating what are your own thoughts, or when you are using quotations and when you are paraphrasing. This means not only outlining your own critical analysis of the information, but also that you can reference and cite properly.

DIFFERENT TYPES OF NOTES

There are several different ways you could take notes – and it's likely you'll use more than one of these methods during your university journey.

LINEAR NOTES

Bullet points	• Most common way of taking notes. • Useful in lectures when receiving a lot of information. • Keep notes organised by using headings and subheadings.
Split page (Cornell method) (see Figure 7.4)	• Very effective for summarising large amount of information. • Useful in reviewing lectures and creating summaries for reading. • Promotes a research mindset, thinking about critical analysis and summarising information.

PATTERN NOTES

Tables	• Effective for comparisons. • Useful for summarising a large amount of information. • Useful for planning essays.
Mindmaps	• Great for making connections between topics. • Excellent way of planning or thinking about a topic. • Excellent tool for revision.

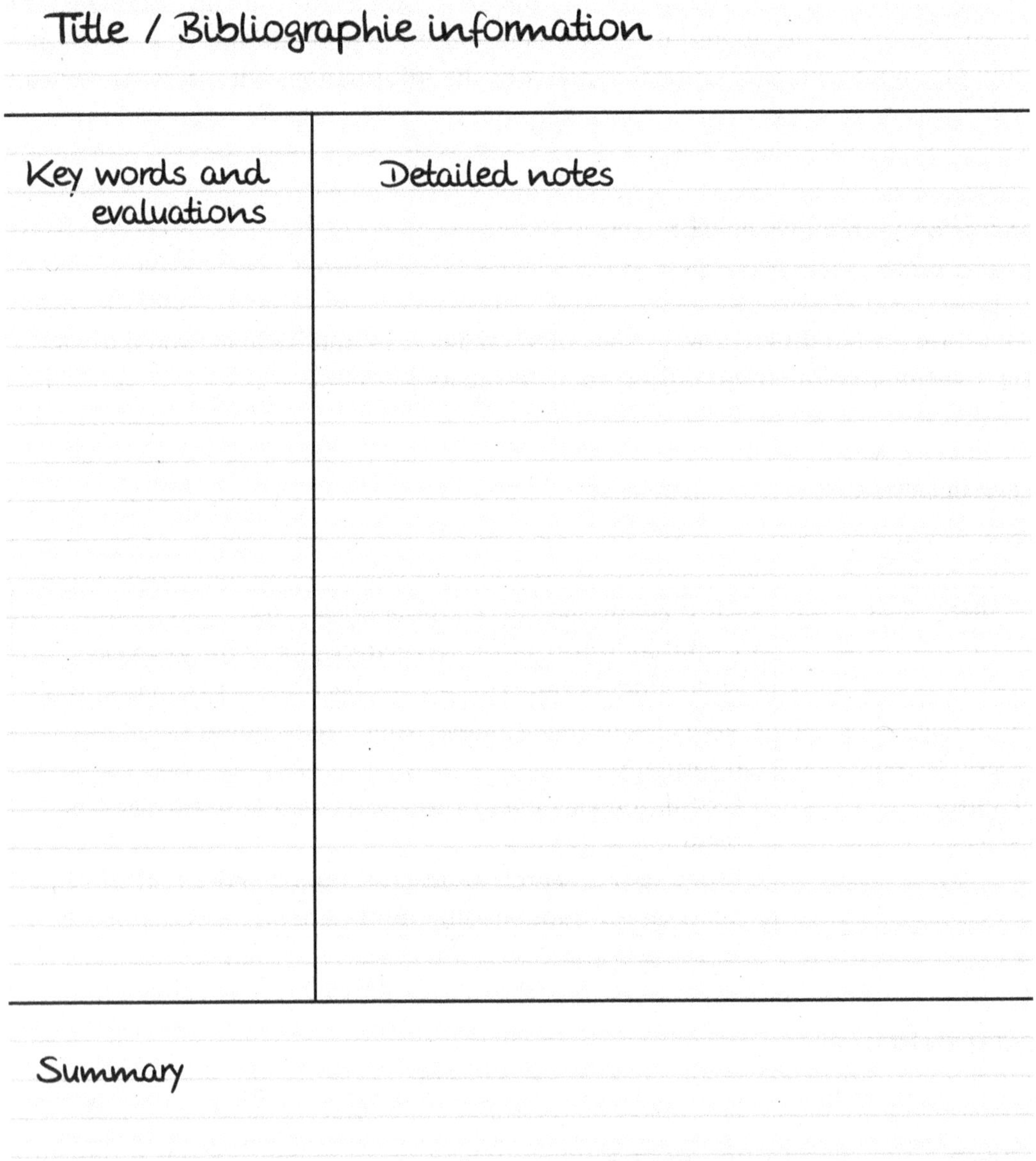

FIGURE 7.4: Split page note-taking

ACTIVITY 7.2

Devising a system for note-taking

It may be useful to reflect on how you have previously taken notes, for example while you were at school or college. Here you need to think about what worked well and what didn't work.

Step 1

- What types of notes did you previously take (you may wish to use the table above to guide this reflection)?
- What worked well with your previous note-taking? What would you like to continue doing?
- What didn't work as well? What would you like to do differently?

Step 2

- Identify changes you want to make to how you organise your notes.

Step 3

- Devise your own personal system for organising notes.
- If you are using a digital system, then use this time to set up your folders and decide on a naming convention for your files (you can do this in Microsoft Word software or on specialist note-taking apps such as Notion).
- If using paper/notebooks, obtain the things you need (notebooks, folders, highlighters, page tabs etc).

CHAPTER SUMMARY

This chapter explored how to establish your research mindset and why this will be useful in your university journey. We outlined that a research mindset involves systematically investigating a topic, and this is an example of metacognition, or being aware of how you think.

At the heart of this research mindset is the idea that you're joining an academic conversation. Here, you are encouraged to reflect upon your understanding of a topic, not simply as an opinion piece or as a commentary where you regurgitate what has already been said. Instead, we encourage you to know the current debate on the topic that you are studying and then add your own voice. The rest of the chapter explored how you could establish this research mindset and, thus, join the academic conversation through creativity, critical thinking and reflection, as well as the ability to take clear and thoughtful notes which aid your analytical observations.

TOP TIPS AND NEXT STEPS

- Engage in metacognition – thinking about your thinking has a lot of impact!
- A research mindset will take time and practice to develop – be patient and engage in practising critical thinking, creativity and recognising opportunities whenever you can.
- Reflect on the five-step process for developing your creativity and plan some small creative tasks into your week.
- Look through your last piece of coursework. Did you sit more on the opinion or commentary side of an academic conversation?
- Try to stay organised; if you don't manage your files, assignments and time well, you won't be able to engage in the research mindset.
- Thinking back to Bloom's Taxonomy, you have to be able to recall the information before you can start to critically analyse it. Therefore, you need to know the basics before you can engage in the research mindset.
- Reflect on the academic conversation in your field of study. What would the main debate be? Who would be the key academic be? (if you have not yet started university, you may need to complete your first few months of study to answer this).

CHAPTER 8
YOU AND DIVERSE UNIVERSITIES

CHALLENGES WE EXPLORE IN THIS CHAPTER

Universities are diverse places! This is brilliant – it's one of the main reasons universities are so interesting. Being able to share ideas with someone who approaches a topic differently to ourselves helps us develop our understanding of the world. Not only do diverse universities give students from a wide range of backgrounds the opportunity to study and increase their career options, but the more diverse our universities are, the more equal our society can become. Unfortunately, diversity has not always been celebrated in higher education. Historically, universities were highly discriminatory and exclusionary. The challenge is to reverse this, and there have been years of policy implementation and action to try and increase diversity in universities: for example, aiming to increase social mobility through contextual admissions and widening access programmes, as a student's educational opportunities are still strongly linked to their families' socioeconomic background (Sutton Trust, 2023); or trying to mitigate the BAME attainment gap, where BAME students collectively receive fewer first-class degrees compared to white students (Universities UK, 2019).

Yet the legacy of historic exclusion still exists, as does discrimination. This chapter highlights some of these legacies which, unfortunately, some of you will already be aware of, while highlighting why diverse universities are important. The second part of this chapter builds on this understanding to help you develop the skills to thrive in a diverse environment and communicate effectively with peers who may approach a topic differently to you.

INTENDED LEARNING OUTCOMES

By the end of this chapter, you should be able to:

- have an awareness of the history of, and lack of diversity in, universities;

→

- reflect on the importance of diversity and how it will impact your university experience;
- appreciate the importance of being an effective member in a diverse team;
- understand what emotional intelligence is and how to develop your own emotional intelligence.

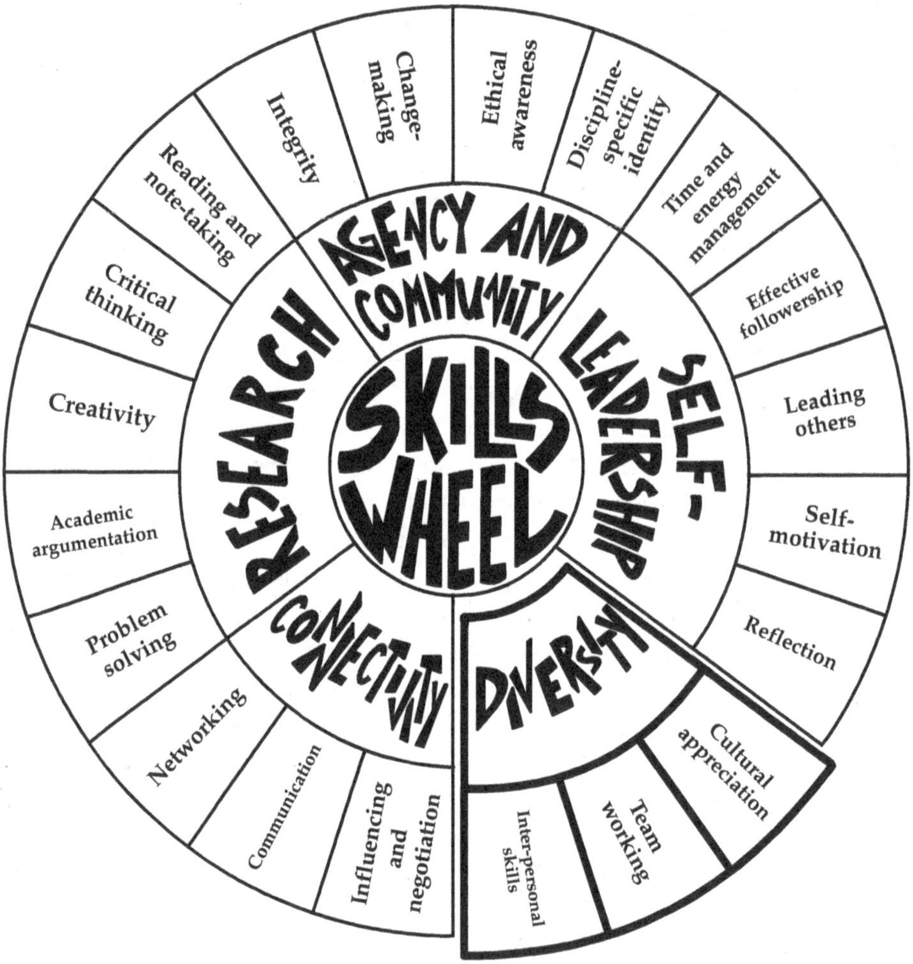

The attributes covered in this chapter are cultural appreciation, team working and interpersonal skills.

8.1 HOW DIVERSE ARE UNIVERSITIES?

If we look at the relationship between *diversity* and education, and the history of universities in general, and don't feel uncomfortable, then we probably aren't looking at the whole picture. In the past, universities have overtly enforced admission policies that were highly discriminatory and helped to create the knowledge that enforced a discriminatory social hierarchy. In other words, universities were not only discriminatory themselves by only letting a select group of students (and staff) attend based on their race, gender, religious beliefs etc, but the 'knowledge' they researched and subsequently taught helped to create and perpetuate ideas in society where some individuals were seen to be of a lower status than others. The universities often then financially benefited from these ideas of society (Bhambra et al, 2018).

A notable example of this is the relationship between **colonialism**, race and higher education. Historically, many British universities produced incorrect information which argued that people of colour were of a lower social status than white people. This provided ethical grounds for the oppression of millions of colonised subjects (Bhambra et al, 2018).

It would be easy to be so frustrated by this situation that you want to disengage with higher education altogether. This would be a valid response; universities have caused great harm. But we should also acknowledge that, today, universities can provide a method to help eradicate, or at least lessen, the social injustices that exist in our society. One of the most notable ways is education on these injustices. To begin this chapter, we will start to look at some of these injustices that exist at a university level. However, we are only scraping the surface of this complicated and expansive topic.

WHAT IS DIVERSITY?

To further explore diversity at universities and your own experience within this, we need to unpack what diversity is.

ACTIVITY 8.1

Defining diversity

- How would you define diversity? Try and write a broad definition encompassing your thoughts.

There are many ways of defining diversity, and it's likely you thought about the definition regarding the inclusion of people from different backgrounds, possibly including different identities such as race, gender, sexuality, religion, disability or socioeconomic class. There are so many different ways of approaching the topic of diversity; the definition we use in this book is: the purposeful inclusion of individuals who have multiple and different backgrounds and identities.

At your university you may see that diversity is often included in EDI: equality, diversity and inclusion. EDI recognises that diversity is only one factor to consider in making universities fairer places; it is important to also look at how diversity is put into practice.

When looking at different identities within diverse universities, it is important to understand these identities not as singular factors but as interconnected categories. This means using intersectionality to understand diversity. The Combahee River Collective, a black, feminist, socialist organisation, pioneered the idea of interlocking systems of oppression and a wider understanding of identity politics (The Combahee River Collective Statement, 1977).

Building upon this, Kimberlé Crenshaw coined the term intersectionality, which highlights the multiple strands of prejudice or privilege faced by individuals. It looks at the multifaceted factors that make up identities, which cut across gender, national identity, class, sexuality, neurodiversity, race and other categories. Some of these categories or characteristics are identified and protected by law, while others are self-identified (Crenshaw, 2022). Many of these characteristics are invisible, adding further complexity to intersectionality.

Simply put, intersectionality encourages us to look at how multiple discrimination is simultaneously taking place. We can understand this further by looking at how intersectionality plays out in practice. Take the gender pay gap, for example, which is '*the difference between average hourly earnings ... of men and women as a proportion of men's average hourly earnings*' (Office for National Statistics, 2023). Examining the pay gap by looking only at gender does not give us a full understanding of the problem, as other factors such as race, socio-economic status or immigration status reinforce the pay (and other) inequalities.

Here, we can look at inequalities at the most basic level: a difference in treatment or circumstance, also known as disparity. If someone is being treated unequally in comparison to another person, they have a different experience to others. For example, if there are ten children in a class, and only nine are given a chocolate bar, this would represent inequality, as the tenth child wouldn't have been treated the same. Beyond this there are structural inequalities, which are rules, procedures, policies and beliefs in a society or organisation which marginalise individuals or communities. For example, if a school is only reachable by a one-mile walk over inaccessible ground, only able-bodied students are able to attend. Many complicated structural inequalities exist and contain barriers that are difficult to see at a surface level. Here, it's important to note the difference between equality, where everyone is treated in the same way, and equity, where everyone is given the same opportunity. Not everyone starts from the same point or has the same background (for example, due to disability or neurodiversity), so reasonable adjustments are often made at university to ensure that every student has a fair chance of success.

REFLECTING ON PRIVILEGE

When exploring topics within diversity, we can think about how certain categories are treated in a privileged way in society compared to others. Many readers will already have a great understanding of these terms, especially as the term 'privilege', or to 'check your privilege', is increasingly used in the media and popular culture, including

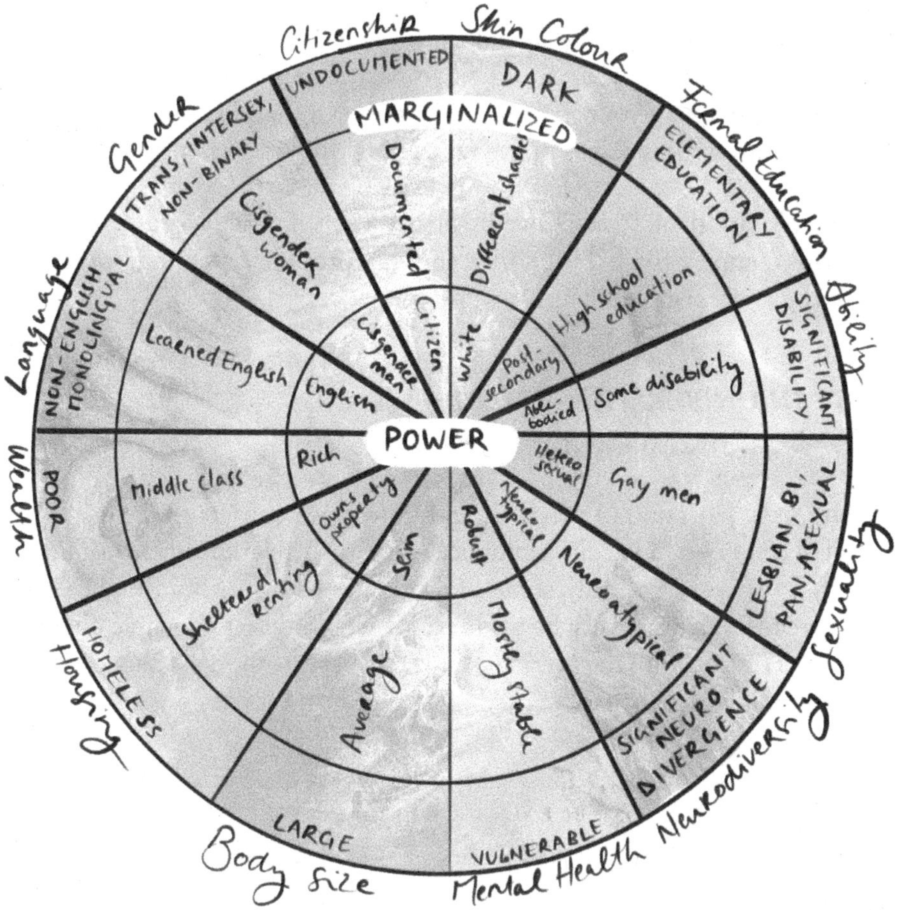

FIGURE 8.1: The wheel of power/privilege

national newspapers exploring the term, and the hashtag #CheckYourPrivilege has been used on Instagram over 59,000 times.

This is the idea of understanding how your own identity and background is likely to give you more advantages in society. Sylvia Duckworth has created a visual representation of the wheel of power/privilege, based on the work of the Canadian Council for Refugees, to help us understand how privilege impacts the power a person may have based on their identity and/or background. Of course, there are many other categories that could have been added to the wheel, but this is an excellent starting point to visualise the issue. Those identities which are on the outside of the wheel are more likely to be marginalised or excluded with those categories.

ACTIVITY 8.2

Understanding your privilege

- Now you have the opportunity to reflect on your own privilege. Use the wheel in Figure 8.1 to map where you would sit in each category in order to 'check your privilege'. Being aware of your societal 'advantages' or 'disadvantages' is an important exercise in self-awareness as you strive for a more diverse and fair society.

This brief exploration of the definition of diversity has only begun to scrape the surface on this complex topic. Hopefully, this can provide a starting point to explore diversity in the context of your university experience.

DIVERSITY IN UNIVERSITIES

Building on our exploration of privilege and power, we can now take a look at three key areas of diversity – gender, class and race – and their relationships with universities. Here we offer a snapshot of only some of the issues of diversity in higher education, which many readers may already be aware of. It would take this whole chapter, if not this whole book, to cover all the myriad of diversity issues; this snapshot aims therefore to provide a starting point to reflect on diversity and universities.

GENDER

Gender provides an interesting snapshot into diversity in universities. We could look at the many different ways that gender and education intersect, but we can start with the proportion of female students in universities. The University of London became the first university in the UK to admit female students, allowing them to sit the gender exam in 1868 (Carter, 2018). In the 1960s, only 25 per cent of full-time students at UK universities were female, but in 2015 they were 55 per cent, although they are still in the minority in many of the science subjects (Whilletts, 2017, pp 49–50). This is also reflected in the cross-section of senior academic staff, where women and, sadly even more so, women of colour are in the minority (Byrne and Clarke, 2020, p 42).

Further culture shifts in society mean that there is an increased number of openly trans and non-binary students attending university. While there is very little research outlining their experience at university, what does exist shows a mixed experience of trans and non-binary students: on the one hand, there is anxiety over inclusive spaces, deadnaming (referring to a person by the name they were given at birth, prior to transitioning), outing (the practice of revealing the sexual or gender identity of a person) and general lack of representation; on the other hand, a sense of community, especially through LGBTQIA + societies, was noted as a positive (Smith et al, 2022). So, while universities have shifted from an only *cisgender*, male space, there is still an imbalance.

SOCIOECONOMIC CLASS

We can also get a snapshot of diversity at universities through the lens of socioeconomic class. Traditionally, education in the UK has been highly interlinked with the class system, universities being designed for, and delivered to, upper-class and upper-middle-class (male) students. Therefore, university staff also mirrored this group. Since the 1960s, participation of more middle-class and working-class students has greatly increased, with university being seen as one of the primary ways to increase your opportunities (Byrne and Clarke, 2020, p 121).

It is increasingly difficult to use the three-tiered socioeconomic class system (in Britain) to explore this area, as identities and lives are far more complex than these three categories in reality. However, one way to explore the exclusion or inclusion of students based on socioeconomic class is to look at the proportion of students attending university from state or private education (free or fee-paying schools). Despite a general consensus that this is no longer acceptable, with millions of pounds spent by universities, the government and charities on *widening participation* projects, privately educated students are still disproportionately enrolled in universities, especially the 'elite' universities such as Oxford and Cambridge. In comparison, looking through the lens of intersectional analysis, there are very low participation rates among young working-class men in UK universities (Byrne and Clarke, 2020, p 42).

Charities such as the Sutton Trust (2023) and The Access Project (2023) are dedicated to addressing this imbalance and making universities accessible to everyone. Most universities have dedicated teams working to expand inclusion, and many now give contextual offers based on an individual's previous education experience or background.

RACE

The final snapshot of diversity at universities that we will consider is race. The relationship between race and education has increasingly been in the media, especially around the Rhodes Must Fall movement (discussed below) and wider efforts to decolonise the curriculum. But this is not a new topic; sadly, inequalities in UK society are mirrored in universities, and this is evidenced in many areas such as the BAME attainment gap.

> *A student's race and ethnicity can significantly affect their degree outcomes. Of the disparities that exist within higher education, the gap between the likelihood of White students and students from Black, Asian or Minority Ethnic (BAME) backgrounds getting a first- or upper-second-class degree (13 per cent) is among the starkest.*
>
> (Universities UK, 2019, p 1)

Further evidence of this inequality is the racialised bullying and abuse staff and students have faced at universities (Tomlinson, 2019, p 221).

When considering race and diversity in higher education, we need to think about two things:

1. how a student's race impacts their experience at university;
2. how race affected the creation and role of universities.

One of the pivotal points in the campaign to decolonise the curriculum is the Rhodes Must Fall movement, which started as a protest in March 2015 at the University of Cape Town, targeting the statue of British imperialist Cecil Rhodes (Rhodes Must Fall Oxford, 2018) at a time of increased awareness of racial injustice in the media. The campaign received global attention and subsequently propelled other movements to decolonise universities, both the physical spaces and the content of what is taught. In the UK, other campaigns created by the National Union of Students include 'Why is my Curriculum White?' and #LiberateMyDegree, seeking to address inequalities in the system by challenging the lack of diversity and the dominance of a Eurocentric, white-dominated approach in UK higher education.

We can understand decolonisation as the effort of removing the effects of colonisation. In a university setting, this can range from removing pictures that celebrate colonialists to considering what is important to teach and research. It's important to note that some scholars are moving away from the term 'decolonising', as they feel that university research is so embedded in a colonial history and mindset (O'Connor and Robbins, 2024).

This snapshot provides just a quick overview into some areas of diversity. Yet there are other areas we could have explored, such as how universities have been designed to support neurotypical rather than neurodiverse students. Or the relationship between religion and higher education and the impact this has on universities today, or even how universities offer limited provision for disabled students in terms of accessibility, or the experience of mature students in higher education.

From this surface exploration of diversity at universities, coupled with your own experience and knowledge of the higher education system, it's very easy to be disheartened. But although there is a long way to go, progress *is* being made: from policy changes, admission procedures and university strategies to the knowledge being produced. The same universities that generated the falsehoods that generated inequality (as well as hundreds of sites that didn't) are now producing and distributing knowledge to try and end this discrimination (Connell, 2019, p 170). Arguably, the largest driving force to end this discrimination (especially the ones that are not easy to see) are students themselves, who are rightly fighting to enable an end to inequalities at university and in wider society.

8.2 CONTRIBUTING TO A DIVERSE UNIVERSITY

We have established that universities are diverse places, and there is a long way to go to combat discrimination within universities (both in terms of student experience and the institutions themselves). The good news is that universities are becoming more diverse. This diversity leads to a more equal society and helps to overcome stereotypes, and diverse teams are better at solving problems and bringing different perspectives and opinions (Reynolds and Lewis, 2017). This makes for an interesting and exciting university experience. Here we can consider the ways in which you can contribute to this diverse university. As with any of the skills we explore in this book, it's likely there will be some that you are more confident and experienced in than others.

STUDENT INSIGHT

Jingxuan Jin, international relations and management, second year

Diversity in a team can bring a pool of creativity, new perspectives and innovation, as everyone has different experiences and comes from diverse backgrounds. Personally, I have come to appreciate that, although working in a diverse team can mean it is challenging to navigate our differences, each person brings something unique to the table. I believe that it is essential to embrace plurality and celebrate these differences and be curious about them. In addition, I consider that we must be willing to learn from each other and encourage inclusivity to achieve a respectful team dynamic. Finally, while it might sound cliché, clear communication and interaction with your team members is always the cornerstone of success in any diverse team setting. It's not just about conveying information; it's about fostering mutual understanding, building relationships and being flexible to create a sense of belonging for everyone in the team. In brief, my top tips would consist of respect, communication and always keeping an open mind!

As we have briefly delved into how universities are diverse, we can now explore how to navigate this diversity actively and positively, starting with **unconscious bias**.

UNCONSCIOUS BIAS

When YouTube added a video upload feature to their mobile app, the developers were confused as up to 10 per cent of the videos were uploaded upside down. They had no idea why this was happening so frequently. Finally, the team realised that it was not a misunderstanding on the user's part or poor design of the app, but an unconscious bias. The developers had designed the app for right-hand users, not realising that left-hand users would turn the phone to landscape in the opposite direction and therefore the videos would be upside down (Agarwal, 2020, p 9).

When thinking about the student experience in a diverse university, it is important to consider your own approach to being a student. One important way of doing this is to explore unconscious bias. An unconscious bias, also known as an implicit bias, is an unintentional mindset towards an individual or a group of people that affects your decision making.

In order to understand this topic in more detail we can use Pragya Agarwal's book *Sway: Unravelling Unconscious Bias*. Agarwal explains that implicit or unconscious bias exists without our conscious knowledge. These beliefs are different to explicit bias, which are thought on a conscious level; an example of explicit bias would be hate speech (Agarwal, 2020, p 4). This distinction is important, as not all prejudice and discrimination is a result of unconscious bias. Agarwal highlights that, unfortunately, unconscious bias is very common:

> *Each of us form and carry unconscious biases of some sort. It's not only the behaviour of bigoted, racist or sexist people but of everyone, including you and me. So really the answer is to go to the roots, to understand the processes that shape us, to be aware, to acknowledge that we are all biased – to a certain degree – and that we all discriminate. We judge, we exclude people, we stereotype. Sometimes that's a little tough to comprehend.*
>
> (Agarwal, 2020, p 13)

You may have witnessed other people's unconscious bias (or even your own) while at university. This often occurs when we look at who is seen as a stereotypical student or staff member. As we explored earlier in this chapter, universities have traditionally been exclusionary places, created for privileged, white, upper-class, young, cis men. Although there has been great progress in recent years, these archaic standards can shape present-day biases.

Unfortunately, students may experience biases (most likely unconscious and *explicit bias*, when an individual is aware of their prejudice towards an individual or group) in every segment of the power and privilege wheel we explored earlier in Section 8.1. These biases are also faced by university staff; for example, female lecturers are more likely to receive negative feedback in their students' reviews compared to their male colleagues, with women being viewed as less qualified and seen more as a 'teacher' than a 'lecturer' (Mitchell and Martin, 2018). Looking at this through an intersectional lens, ethnicity, race and even physical attractiveness also impact the feedback (Boring et al, 2016).

We can return to Agarwal to explore how to tackle unconscious bias; she argues that *implicit biases*, when an individual is unaware of their prejudice towards an individual or group, can be helped by learning control techniques that turn automatic responses into acceptable reactions (Agarwal, 2020, p 13). Therefore, she encourages us to reflect on our own attitudes as well as addressing systemic inequalities. This means taking time when making big decisions – in the workplace, this may be hiring a new employee; in the social side of university this may be choosing people to study or even live with, so we do not rely on unknown bias (Agarwal, 2020, p 14). Overall, she argues for a prejudice-breaking approach, rooted in the idea that forming a stereotype is a habit and therefore requires an active intervention to break it (Agarwal, 2020, p 8).

ALLYSHIP

ACTIVITY 8.3

Defining an ally

- How would you define an ally? Write down your definition.

One way to help support other people facing bias, whether implicit or conscious, is to be an effective ally.

We can understand allyship as an individual using their own influence and privileges to help amplify the voice of an underrepresented or marginalised group. The EDI team at the University of Kent (2023) share that there are two types of ally.

1. Effective ally: takes action to promote change.
2. Performative ally: often speaks about change but will only undertake action when it is convenient for them.

The notion of performative allyship, which takes place at surface level has, rightly, come under a lot of scrutiny. An example of this is a large corporation posting for LGBTQIA+ awareness and changing their social media picture to include the rainbow flag, but then not having policies that support LGBTQIA+ staff members.

We can take the following steps to become effective allies.

- Listening: This is at the heart of effective allyship, and means intentionally engaging with others to gain greater empathy for, and understanding of, the problems they face. It can be easy to assume what the issues are, but engaging in **active listening** can overcome this assumption. Part of listening is also taking on board feedback and changing your behaviour accordingly.
- Educating yourself: Take ownership of your education, in order for you to be informed of key issues. This will help to avoid stereotypes about, and categorisation of, different **groups** of individuals.
- Taking action: Take action to tackle discrimination, even if it's inconvenient. You can do this by acknowledging your privilege (as we explored in Activity 8.2) and by making sure that you are not the centre of the conversation.
- Being courageous: Speaking up can be daunting, and it's easy to worry about saying or doing the wrong thing. Remember that doing nothing is still a decision!

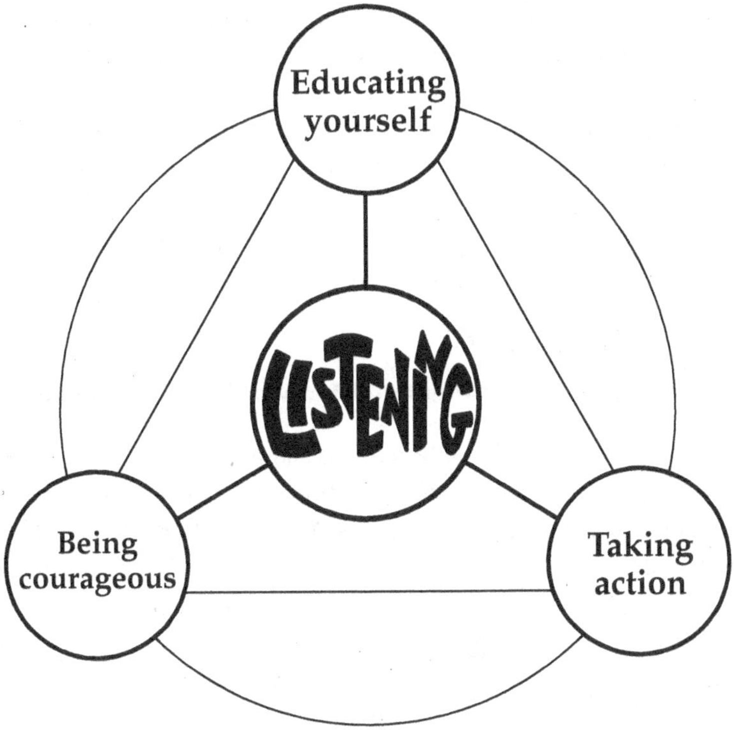

FIGURE 8.2: Becoming an effective ally

Building on this exploration of diversity and universities, we will look into building practical skills to help you thrive during your degree.

8.3 APPRECIATING CULTURAL DIFFERENCES

Already in this chapter we've looked at how valuable diversity can be and the benefits it offers to individuals, groups and universities. Part of this tapestry of diversity is the range of cultural differences people carry. You can think of culture as being the unwritten rules that bind a group of people together. Cultural researcher Geert Hofstede explained it as follows:

> *All people share a common human nature. Our shared human nature is intensely social: we are group animals. But the unwritten rules of how we do these things differ from one human group to another. 'Culture' is what we call these unwritten rules about how to be a good member of the group.*
>
> (Hofstede, 2022)

Cultural differences can be seen across big and small groups of people; at its most expansive we can think about cultural differences across entire countries or religions or genders. The idea that culture is built on 'unwritten' rules suggests that we might find it hard to understand cultures we aren't part of and to know how best to interact with people from different cultures to our own, or how best to integrate with a new culture if we want to join one.

PRACTITIONER INSIGHT

Lauren Henderson, Access Manager, University of St Andrews

I have seen students' different cultural backgrounds have a large impact on their university experience, and especially how they approach learning. For example, having the confidence to engage in class, to speak up or to ask for help. Sometimes students don't want to ask for extra support, as it is not their culture to do so. These cultural differences also impact the way students communicate; for example, often students find at university they are being asked to write in a very different style to what they have been used to. It can be daunting to navigate a new academic culture. However, there are many benefits to engaging in a diverse university too, especially meeting and learning from other students from around the world.

It's likely that you're part of multiple cultures already. You might associate with a national culture, a culture associated with your religion or beliefs, a culture associated with a particular team or club you are part of, or an organisation you work for, and you are soon to be part of an academic culture too. Reflect on one of the cultures you are part of, and complete Activity 8.4.

ACTIVITY 8.4

Describing your culture

Pick one of the cultures you identify as being part of and take a few minutes to think about how you would describe that culture to someone who didn't belong to it.

- What words would you use?
- What traditions, behaviours and signifiers go towards being part of that culture?
- Write the culture in the centre circle and the descriptors in the outside circles.

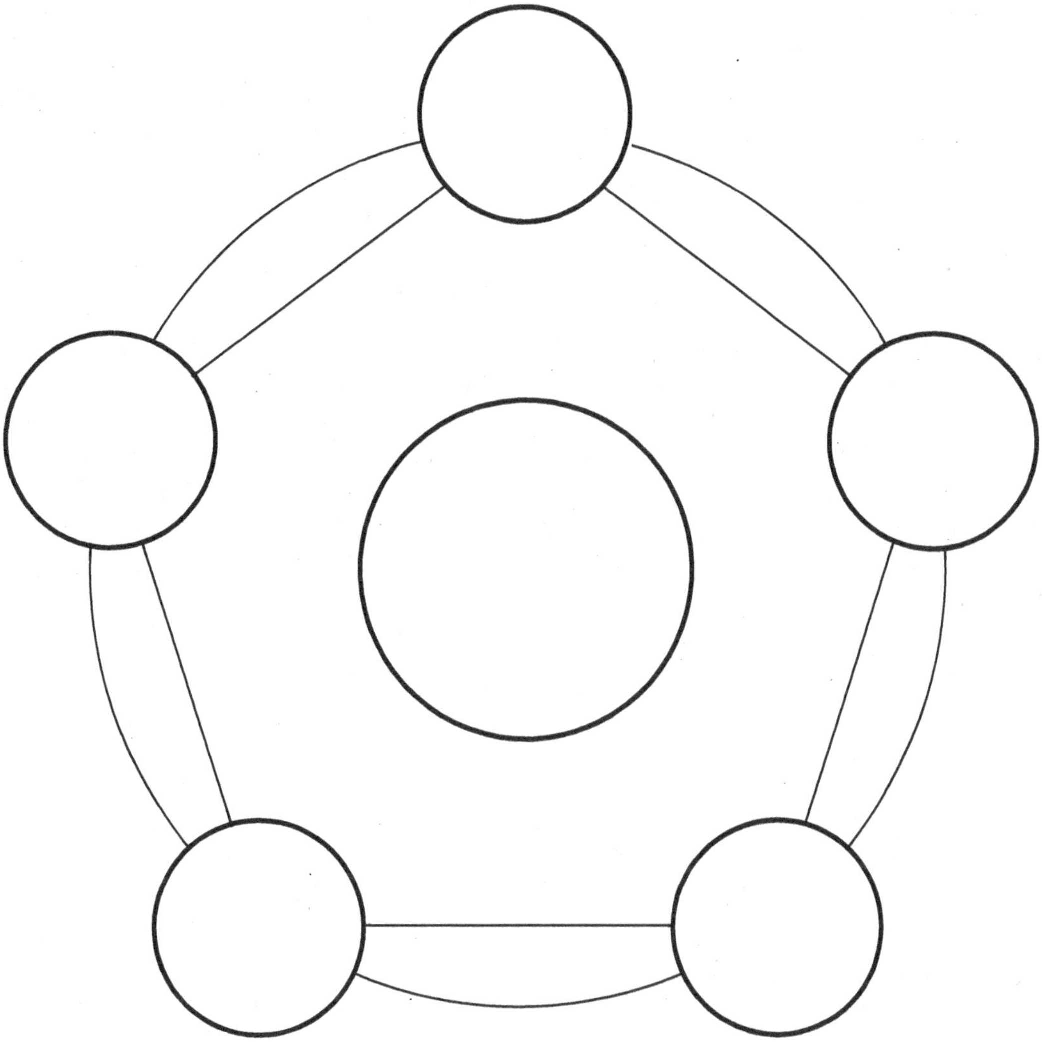

Being aware of and able to work well with people from different cultures is an important part of being successful at university and is a brilliant graduate skill to develop. In a British Council report (2013) examining different kinds of cultural skills, they found that employers valued these intercultural skills as much as formal qualifications. The cultural skills they highlighted are:

- respectful;
- multi-lingual;
- flexible;
- builds trust;
- accepts different cultures;
- understands different cultures;

- adjusts communication;
- aware of own culture;
- tolerates ambiguity;
- adapts to different cultures;
- works in diverse teams;
- continuous learner;
- open to new ideas;
- listens and observes.

At university, you will probably find yourself working in groups of students with different national cultures. These can impact how individuals approach group work and shape their contributions to the team. Erin Meyer wrote a book in 2014 called *The Culture Map* (Meyer, 2014), which aimed to show how national cultures differ, particularly in relation to workplace environments. She identified eight dimensions to map national cultures against – things you might do in a typical project team. These were:

1. communicating;
2. evaluating;
3. persuading;
4. leading;
5. deciding;
6. trusting;
7. disagreeing;
8. scheduling.

Meyer found that there were pronounced differences between national cultures on these dimensions. It's worth saying at this point that there are of course many individual differences between people within a single national culture with regard to these areas. Not every person from Scotland has the same approach to leadership; nor does everyone from Finland communicate in the same way or every Brazilian show the same leadership style! However, in general the research showed significant differences between cultures. For example, some cultures tended to avoid confrontation, whereas others were much more comfortable with it. Some cultures liked to make decisions as a group, whereas others looked towards a leader to make a decision. Some cultures took a very flexible approach to timekeeping and scheduling, and others did not.

When we encounter people in our university groups who exhibit different preferences to us in terms of group approach and behaviour, it's valuable to keep in mind that this difference might be explained by their cultural experience, to accept this, and crucially to appreciate and value the diversity this brings to the group. While you work within the 'unwritten rules' you're familiar with, others are unaware of them – they have their own set – and no set has more value than the other. Each set has a contribution to make. Appreciating cultures, and having an openness and curiosity to learn about them, truly helps you become a global scholar.

One culture that you are becoming a member of is academic culture. As a university student, you will begin to learn a whole host of unwritten rules about how to communicate, collaborate and engage with your subject discipline. The more you study your subject, the deeper into the culture you go and the more the culture forms part of your identity.

Different cultures can favour different ways of communicating and as a student you will have to work with a diverse range of people; we can now explore this in further detail by looking at working in diverse teams.

8.4 DIVERSE TEAMS

In many ways, saying a 'diverse' team is pointless. All teams are diverse by their nature. If you have more than one person working together, they are going to have different backgrounds, identities and ideas. While some teams may be more overtly diverse than others, having an awareness of diversity and how to actively contribute to a diverse setting (as we have explored so far in this chapter) will be essential to being successful in teamwork.

When we think of teamwork in a university setting, we often think of an assignment given by a lecturer where your class is divided into teams and asked to complete a project. There is a strong possibility you will encounter this type of teamwork at university, but you may also experience other types, such as sports teams where you train and play with your teammates, student societies where you work with your peers towards a shared goal at university, or living in shared accommodation where you may work together to clean your communal fridge. It's likely that in the majority of these teams you will not choose who you are working with, from lecturers assigning members into a group assignment to playing with other people who are interested in playing the same sport as you. When we don't choose our teams, it can make working with others more challenging, especially when other members of the team have different commitment levels compared to ourselves. Understanding how to engage in a team effectively can make this experience easier.

The ability to work with others is not only an essential skill for university study and day-to-day life, but also for employment opportunities. Teamwork is consistently one of the most common competencies in job descriptions (Hartley and Dawson, 2010).

It's likely you have already had a lot of teamwork experience in school, college or work, and it's useful to reflect on these experiences to improve and develop your skills.

ACTIVITY 8.5

Reflecting on teamwork

- First, think about teams you have been in that worked well, in terms of how well everyone got on with each other and how successful the team was in achieving its goals/outcomes, etc. Why do you think it worked well?

- Now reflect on a team that you didn't enjoy working in. Why didn't you enjoy this experience? Was there poor communication? A lack of trust? Were the tasks not divided equally?

EFFECTIVE TEAMWORK

There are numerous answers you could suggest for what makes a good team, and this was explored in some depth in Chapter 6. Social scientists, psychologists and practitioners (Harvard Business School, 2004; Seethamraju and Borman, 2009; Hartley and Dawson, 2010) have completed extensive research on what makes a successful team. Hartley, and Dawson (2010). have identified key characteristics for a successful team:

1. a common purpose;
2. all team members committing to a common goal;
3. team members having the ability to complete the required tasks;
4. team members being motivated;
5. having a mixture of expertise and backgrounds.

While factors one to four may seem like common knowledge, factor five (having a mixture of expertise and backgrounds) is not something many people would automatically highlight as a key to successful teamwork. However, having a diverse group means teams are better problem-solvers and are more likely to use critical reasoning (Hartley and Dawson, 2010, p 13). When working in diverse teams, we have to ensure that this enhances our team and we don't fall into the trap of forming cliques.

Cliques can form when people join together as they identify with others based on one or more factors, such as gender, race, geography (such as hometowns) or experiences (such as taking the same classes). We can explore this more by looking at team dynamics.

An exemplary team might look like one where communication flows – all team members communicate equally with everyone.

However, a team in practice might have a lot of undercurrents to communication. There might be people who communicate frequently and well but other team members who don't communicate at all – when it would be beneficial to the team if they did so. It is easy for sub-groups to form, which can restrict the flow of information more widely. Leaders emerge, who take care to connect team members and share information and communication, but so might cliques, which can be a real issue for the productivity of some teams.

Imagine a team where sub-groups have formed, and some members are quite isolated with limited communication from others. What advice would you give to this team? One of the best ways for this team to move forward would be to try and dissolve the sub-groups, coming back together into a singular team.

To unpick this a little further, imagine students were placed in groups for a teamwork activity in class. Three out of the five students attended prestigious private schools before attending university, and they formed an in-group as they had similar experiences and felt they could approach the task well together. The other two group members felt left out, and the team did not work effectively together.

Two actions the team could undertake to reduce the sub-groups are:

1. focus on common goals;
2. increase contact across the team, to help reduce the assumptions of others.

Think back to the team activity you reflected upon in Activity 8.3. Were there sub-groups? Did you make assumptions about others in the group? You can use these reflections to help improve your teamwork in the future.

BEING AN EFFECTIVE TEAM MEMBER IN AN UNDER-PERFORMING TEAM

As we learnt in Chapter 6, being an effective team member is a very pro-active choice. Whenever you join a new team or group, there are things you can do to help the team operate to its full potential and collaborate well. Of course, teams and groups in an academic context often go wrong instead of going right. Many of the students we speak to do not enjoy their experience of teamwork. Some of the common issues they describe include followers who don't want to collaborate but shoulder all of the work themselves, the 'sheep' follower who does nothing, the team breaking off into sub-groups who don't communicate well, the leader who is dominant and controlling, and the endless meetings where no decisions get made. Well, the good news is that being part of a team that doesn't go well is an excellent way to develop your skills – you can talk about this stuff in job interviews for days! However, that does not make things feel any better in the moment. For that, you have to step up and be a super-hero effective team member. Here's what you can do.

SETTING THE CULTURE

When you first meet your team, you can absolutely help set the culture that you want to establish. A smile and eye contact and introducing yourself go such a long way! You can be the person that suggests going round the group to introduce each other. Remembering people's names and preferred pronouns (he, she, they) and using them can really make people feel part of the team.

KEEPING COMMUNICATION FLOWING

If the team isn't communicating well, you can be the person who makes a point of connecting people and sharing information. If you're part of a big team, there's a tendency that cliques and sub-teams will form. Keep people linked by asking for updates and finding a way to share them. Encourage the team to decide the most effective way to communicate – it might be by setting up a WhatsApp group, an Microsoft Teams site or Google doc.

INCLUSIVE DECISION MAKING

When it comes to making decisions, be the effective follower who is interested in the opinions of others. Make a point of asking for others' thoughts. You could suggest forums where people can share their ideas in a simple and accessible format, for example adding them to an online document. This also hopefully gets around the scenario where everyone says '*I don't mind*' because they don't want to cause any conflict. Another hallmark of an effective team member is where they summarise and record what decisions have actually been made and who in the team is going to do them.

GENERATING TEAM BONDS

Anything you can do to make the team feel more like they are a team is an act of an exceptional team worker. It could be that you suggest that the team has a meal together or takes a team photo. It could be getting the team to acknowledge they are a team (this can be as simple as saying '*we're a team*' from time to time) or helping the team to reflect on what has gone well or not so well. Celebrating team success or a job done well is another way to make the team glue together better and ultimately perform better.

DEALING WITH CONFLICT EARLY

This is a tricky one, but the number one issue we see in student teams that break down is that conflict wasn't addressed when the issue first arose, and the team becomes more and more dysfunctional. To be an effective team member you can try to help resolve conflict when it first arises rather than turning a blind eye and hoping it goes away on its own. It very rarely does. One thing that can help you navigate through conflict is learning about the five **core concerns**, the five key elements that people normally want met when they interact with others, which you can learn about in Chapter 9.

SUPPORTING YOUR LEADER

An effective team member stays in close touch with their leader and offers support when needed. It may even be that an effective follower stands ready to become leader if it makes sense in the situation. Often in university teams, leadership is split among the wider team. In this scenario, the effective follower takes on their share of leadership responsibility.

GETTING ON WITH IT

The most effective teams are ones which actually get on and produce outputs. As an effective team member, you can help make this happen by role modelling some excellent planning skills and a lack of procrastination. You can encourage the team to collaborate on setting some goals and creating a plan to keep on track.

SWITCHING ON YOUR RESILIENCE AND GRIT

Finally, the effective team member is ready for the road to teamwork success to not be a smooth one. Expect some hiccups and things not going to plan. You are aware of the importance of reflecting on your own beliefs and challenging faulty thinking, as well as being gritty and recognising that your team project might well require some effort and perseverance. You will also have a sense of perspective: this teamwork experience is part of the marathon of your university career. Some teams just won't work well and even all your best efforts, trying to implement all these suggested steps, won't change that. When this happens, it's something that you have to accept and move on from. Each team experience will teach you something useful that you can reflect on and use your learning for next time. You will be part of some terrible teams, and hopefully some excellent ones too. You will become a better follower as a result of both.

Teamwork will be an essential part of your university degree, and thinking about how you will work well with others, especially those who approach a task differently to you, will be key to having a successful experience in a diverse university setting. We will now move on to look at developing interpersonal skills, which are crucial to working well in teams but also in engaging more widely with a diverse university.

8.5 HOW TO CULTIVATE STRONG INTERPERSONAL SKILLS

Interpersonal skills are the skills or abilities we need to communicate with other people. These skills help us to undertake teamwork, listen and respond to others, navigate conflict and have successful relationships. Interpersonal skills are especially important in diverse environments, such as universities, where different backgrounds and values may lead to different communication styles. For example, we need to be aware if someone has different cultural references to us or a different understanding of the topic. These interpersonal skills are also vital to being an ally, as we explored earlier in the chapter.

EMOTIONAL INTELLIGENCE

At the heart of interpersonal skills is emotional intelligence. To explore this topic, with a focus on interpersonal relationships, you can study Daniel Goleman's book *Emotional Intelligence.*

An emotion is a feeling that arises as a response to our mood or circumstance. Emotions are how we navigate life; they are central to how we respond to, and understand, situations, as well as to how we communicate with other people and learn new things. Therefore, emotions are crucial to developing strong interpersonal skills as well as how we see the world.

For example, if you heard a loud unexpected noise, it might make you feel (momentarily) scared. However, we need to learn to manage our emotions, or they can cloud or impair our judgement. When you heard that loud noise, you would probably begin to rationalise it: is it building work outside? Or a neighbour making noise? If we didn't manage this emotion, we could find it hard to rationalise situations and, therefore, to navigate them.

In order to deal with emotions and respond to them effectively, we need to develop strong emotional intelligence. We can understand emotional intelligence as '*the capacity to be aware of, control, and express one's emotions, and to handle interpersonal relationships judiciously and empathetically*' (Goleman, 2020, p 115).

Goleman explains that there are five parts to emotional intelligence:

1. self-awareness;
2. managing emotions;
3. self-motivation;
4. empathy;
5. handling relationships.

People with high levels of emotional intelligence can calmly and effectively manage difficult situations, navigate change and have a strong sense of self-awareness. There is also research that shows students who have high emotional intelligence (in comparison to high IQ) are more likely to be successful in their academic work (Goleman, 2020). The great news is that you can develop your emotional intelligence! With practice and time, you can become more aware of your own and others' emotions, and learn how to navigate them. A well-developed emotional intelligence is helpful in a diverse university setting in order to be sensitive to different approaches to ideas you will encounter when studying. One way to develop your emotional intelligence is to think about three Rs: reflection, relating and responsibility.

- **Reflection:** It's important to reflect on our own emotions so that you can identify what you are feeling and why. You can also reflect on how your emotions impacted your actions, and if you would do something differently next time. Adding regular reflection into your week can greatly improve your emotional intelligence. You can remind yourself about reflection in Chapter 6.
- **Relating:** Relating to others and their emotions is fundamental to emotional intelligence. Here, you can develop your emotional intelligence by thinking about empathy: this means ensuring that you are not only listening to other people but also thinking about their perspective. You can practise doing this in your day-to-day life, ensuring you don't assume what someone is thinking, but actively engaging them in conversation (we further explore communication in Chapter 9). You will have to develop greater empathy skills to relate to individuals you have less in common with.
- **Responsibility:** To develop your emotional intelligence skills, you need to take responsibility for your emotions. It can be easy to entirely blame your emotions on external factors, such as someone else's actions or things that are out of your control. Taking responsibility for your emotions means acknowledging them and reflecting on why you are feeling this way. You will be impacted by other people and situations, but if you take responsibility for your emotions and corresponding actions, you can start to think about your next actions.

SHARING FEEDBACK AND CRITICISM

We can further explore interpersonal skills and emotional intelligence by looking at sharing feedback and criticism. This may be highlighting micro-aggressions you have witnessed, asking your lab partner to carry out a process differently during an experiment or sharing feedback with a colleague on their project.

Anecdotally, it seems that many people aren't that great at giving criticism, as we often fall into two camps. The first is wanting to avoid conflict, so staying silent. This often means the issue isn't solved and one person is left feeling frustrated and resentful, while another person may not know there is an issue at all. The second camp involves being too blunt with our criticism and focusing on our own feelings of annoyance, rather than trying to find a solution. This second situation can often happen as a result of the first, as if a person stays quiet, they can become resentful and then bluntly share their criticism.

There are some steps you can take when sharing feedback. The first thing you can do is ask the question: am I giving feedback or sharing how I am feeling? Expressing your feelings is not bad, but if you are going to do this, you might not find this framework helpful. When thinking about the best ways to give feedback, we can return to Goleman (2020), who offers us a framework for delivering an 'artful critique'. This delivery has four steps.

1. Be specific.
2. Offer a solution.
3. Do it face to face.
4. Show empathy.

BE SPECIFIC

If you are feeling very angry, this one can be tricky, so it's good to think in advance what you are going to say and enter the situation calmly. It is more useful to label the actions rather that the person, so that the other person does not feel attacked.

OFFER A SOLUTION

By offering a solution to the problem (but not commanding them what to do), the person you are speaking to can begin to see a plan or option to overcome the problem rather than feeling powerless or overwhelmed.

It's important to listen to the person's idea on the solution too (maybe it's something they have already tried, and it didn't work).

DO IT FACE TO FACE

It can be tempting to craft the perfect message to text or email, but a lot of communication comes from non-verbal cues. This is the inflection and tone in our voice, our body language and facial expression.

When having a challenging conversation, it's best to speak in person, even if you are feeling nervous. This means you can communicate more clearly and confirm any ambiguity immediately.

SHOW EMPATHY

No one likes to be told they are doing something wrong or upsetting someone. It's important to think about how the person you are speaking to will be feeling. This can make it more difficult to share feedback, but you are more likely to get a positive response.

Strong interpersonal skills are essential to thriving in a diverse university setting, helping you to navigate your relationships and your studies.

CHAPTER SUMMARY

This chapter started by looking at a brief history of diversity and higher education. Here, we considered key factors in diversity such as inequalities, power and privilege, before taking a snapshot of some of the diversity issues universities face today. We built on this short exploration by looking at how students can engage in diverse universities, beginning by learning about unconscious bias and allyship. We then moved on to look at practical skills, exploring other cultures, what teamwork is and how to work well in a diverse team. Next, we explored how to build strong interpersonal skills, with a focus on emotional intelligence, considering how to express our emotions and handle relationships empathetically.

TOP TIPS AND NEXT STEPS

- Reflect on diversity in universities and how the histories of universities shape stereotypes today.
- Reflect on your own biases and take time when making big decisions.
- Follow the four steps to be an effective ally.
- When working in a team, focus on the common goal to avoid cliques forming.
- Use Goleman's framework when you need to share feedback or criticism, using the three Rs: Reflection, Relating and Responsibility to develop your emotional intelligence and interpersonal skills.

CHAPTER 9
YOUR CONNECTIVITY

CHALLENGES WE EXPLORE IN THIS CHAPTER

As a university student today, you have to deal with the challenge of learning while the world is changing quickly around you. The interconnectedness of the world can be a real positive, but it can also be daunting to work out how to manage all the opportunities you'll have for forming connections as a student. In this chapter we engage with these challenges by looking at how you can build connections through having a global network and learning to network effectively. Next, we look at how you can develop connections through communicating well, specifically through writing and presentations. Finally, we think about influencing and **negotiation**, and recognise the importance of being able to do these respectfully in order to strengthen connections while appreciating the differing opinions of others.

INTENDED LEARNING OUTCOMES

By the end of this chapter, you should be able to:

- recognise the importance of being able to form connections as a student;
- appreciate the significance of creating global networks and the part you can play in international communities;
- identify and adopt strategies for communicating clearly;
- value and identify the benefits of being able to influence and negotiate respectfully.

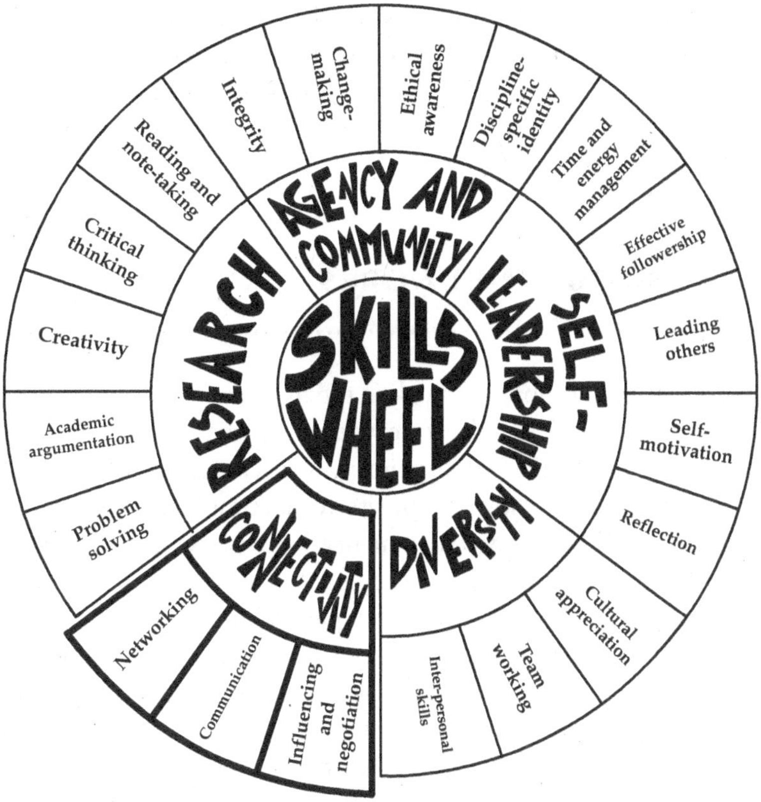

The attributes covered in this chapter are networking, communication, and influencing and negotiation.

9.1 STUDYING IN A CHANGING WORLD

You are part of a world that is changing fast. Being a student, and the knowledge required for your university journey, is becoming increasingly reliant on access to more and more technology. It's something that can open our world up, yet also draw us closer together by increasing our connections. It also exposes gaps and barriers with respect to access to equipment and infrastructure – some parts of the world are better resourced than others, and some people have greater privilege.

This interconnectedness, this dependency that global citizens have on one another, means that students today can see themselves as belonging not just to their own university cohort, but to a worldwide cohort of students and scholars. You are part of an academic system where knowledge is shared between universities, and collaboration is necessary to push forward our understanding of the world and how it works.

As a university student, practical skills that will help you to cultivate your connectivity include being able to form networks, communicate clearly and be able to influence and negotiate. It will also help if you can appreciate cultural differences, as covered in Chapter 8. We will start with thinking about how you can generate connectivity through building networks.

9.2 CREATING GLOBAL NETWORKS

In many ways, creating a global network is much the same as creating any network; you are part of an interconnected group with a shared interest. You can both add value into a network and take value from it. You can think of it a bit like a bank account – you need to make some deposits to accumulate interest and add value, which you can then withdraw when you need to. Networks can share ideas and information, and spread knowledge. At the heart of networks is people, and to get the most from a network it helps to get to know people and have them get to know you.

When you start university, you might not know many other people there. By the time you leave university you will likely know many more. These connections can form part of your network. They might be other students, members of staff and people who have taught you, and perhaps others from the community, friends of friends, or even people you connect with online. You can see how you can form many different kinds of overlapping networks. For example, you might have a friendship network who you socialise with, a social network of people you follow or like on social media, an academic network of people who study the same discipline as you, or other networks centred around work or specialist interests. Student societies and clubs are a great way of forming a network and practising the skills of networking, as can tapping into organised mentoring or buddying schemes your university might offer. Many provide opportunities for students to meet and connect with alumni, which can be a very valuable way to help grow your network.

When it comes to developing global connectivity, you can consciously try to build a network that reaches beyond your immediate classmates, university and country. This might mean reaching out and making connections and introductions in a deliberate way, and you can do this both online and in person. You might find that you are increasingly part of online networks. For example, you might connect to others through chatting via social network posts, commenting on an online article or discussion or taking part in a webinar.

One place to start online networking is through creating a LinkedIn profile. You can create a profile that gives others some information about you, for example your education history, what you're studying, your skills profile and what you're interested in. In turn, you can connect with others who might have something in common with you – perhaps you attend the same university or they work in a field you're interested in. This is a quick and easy way to build a global network, albeit one focused on professional advancement. As people in your network post information, updates and job vacancies, you can learn more about them and their connections, and so your network grows. You can also add to the network (putting value into it) by posting your own updates and comments. Cumulatively, you develop a deeper understanding of the professional world around you. You can also use other social media platforms to curate online networks. The most valuable networks are where you hear viewpoints and opinions different from your own and accumulate knowledge from a diverse range of sources.

FIGURE 9.1: Networking can help you grow your contacts exponentially – you meet people who know people, who know people, who know people etc

Say if your degree subject is psychology, and you want to create a global network using social media to help you deepen your understanding of the subject. You could include:

- other people from your university studying psychology;
- some of your psychology lecturers;
- other psychology departments from different universities around the world;
- psychology journals and publications;
- the student group associated with the professional body of psychology in different countries;
- your university's alumni group.

From there you can add other accredited accounts and people to your network as you see posts and replies. It is important to be mindful of the line between personal and professional when you're growing your social media networks. If you're using these platforms as a showcase for your professional self to enhance your employability, keep your personal accounts separate.

As well as developing a network online, you can also develop networks in person. If you are studying in person, you will likely have various opportunities to develop an academic network in person while you're a student. As well as interacting with students and teachers on your course, or colleagues if you do a work placement as part of your studies, you might get a chance to meet guest speakers or visiting lecturers from other universities. You might even get the opportunity to study part of your course overseas – many universities provide opportunities for students to undertake some of their studies abroad such as global exchange programmes, study abroad schemes, internships and placements. You might also get the opportunity to attend a **conference** or event associated with your subject. Most academic subjects have conferences associated with them, with an undergraduate element or even an entire conference for undergraduates. These can be excellent opportunities for connecting with people and building your academic network.

Students we work with often get nervous at the thought of having to network with people in person, or don't know how to approach it. If you're at an event where there is the opportunity to network with others, it can certainly feel intimidating to have to approach a stranger and make conversation with them – even more so if they are a lecturer or someone you admire. Here are some networking tips you can use to help you feel more comfortable.

- **Don't think of it as exploitative:** Students often say that networking feels as if you're using people or taking advantage of them; that you're ingratiating yourself with someone in the hope that you can exploit the relationship in the future. That certainly doesn't sound good! Instead, see networking as lots of people looking for ways in which they can help each other, now or in the future, and trying to find out a bit more about each other so they can figure out how best they can help. That's a much more positive and relaxing way to frame it. By networking with others, you are trying to be helpful.
- **Don't always take:** It's generally not a good idea to directly ask someone you've just met for something. You might not even know what it is you want at this stage. See your networking interaction as an opportunity for you to give: you have a unique perspective because of all the things that make you an individual and others might find that very valuable to hear about.
- **Look at the floor:** Not because you are shy, but because this can help you work out who to speak to. Sometimes it can be intimidating to walk up to a group of people and introduce yourself, so look at the floor to see what clues you can get

from people's feet. Wait, stick with it! When you're in a room full of people, you can split them up into four simple categories – singles, pairs, trios and bigger groups. In my experience, it's best to ignore the big groups unless you already know someone. Focus on the singles, pairs and trios. Now, the pairs and trios will be either open to receiving someone else to talk to, or closed – they're just fine having a conversation between themselves. This is where the feet come in. If people's feet (and bodies) are pointing towards each other, that's an indication that it is a closed group. If they're pointing away from each other, that's an indication that it is a group that is open and you can join. So, the people you want to go chat to are either single, in an open pair or in an open trio. Out of the three, go for a single person – they probably don't know anyone either and are keen to find a buddy to chat to.

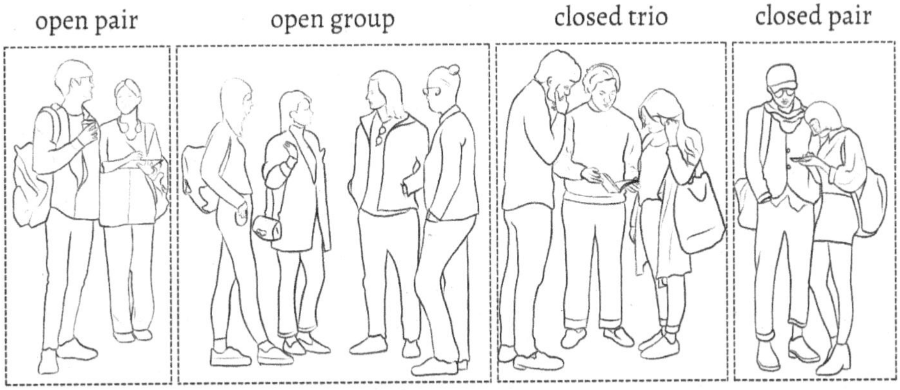

FIGURE 9.2: Different groups at networking events

- **Start strong:** When you meet someone for the first time, it sounds obvious but don't forget to say your name! You don't have to over-complicate things, but it can really help if you smile, say hello, introduce yourself, and perhaps say a sentence or two about who you are and why you are there. It's really important to make a strong first impression. Also, focus on the person you are talking to. There's nothing worse than the person you are talking to scanning the room to find someone else they want to talk to more. Don't be that person!
- **Be curious:** It can be hard to think of things to say when you meet someone you don't know. The good news is that people tend to like talking about themselves, especially academics if you're building your academic network! So it's good to be curious and ask people questions about their role, interest or subject (not their personal life). A really good tip is to start in the present, then go backwards, then

go forwards. What this means is to begin by asking some questions about the here and now:

- What brings you here today?
- Who else have you met?
- Have you tried the sandwiches?

Anything that is rooted in the present is a good and easy place to start. Next, you can go backwards in time a bit: you can ask the person a bit about their career or student journey:

- How did you become interested in your subject?
- How long have you been associated with your university?
- What made you decide on this career area?

This tends to be the area people enjoy talking about. Lastly, you can travel forwards: you might want to ask them what they would like to do next or what advancements in the subject they're most excited about:

- How do you think your sector will change?
- Is there anything else you'd like to accomplish in your career?
- How is technology impacting what you do?

This can be where you can learn some helpful information and build your knowledge.

- **Be polite:** This goes hand-in-hand with being curious. It's important to be polite in the moment and in the follow-up. Depending on who you met and what you spoke about, you might want to follow up with a short email the next day to thank them for their time and say how much you enjoyed meeting them.
- **Ask for their advice:** You already know not to ask directly for something (like a favour or a job), but people tend to be generous if you ask them for advice, especially as a university student looking to build a global network. In fact, you could simply say '*what advice would you give to a university student looking to build a global network?*' You'd likely get some excellent responses.
- **Add them, don't hog them:** Finally, remember that at a networking event the aim is to meet several different people and it's important to let the person you're talking to have time to circulate and meet others. You're looking to add them to your global network, not hog them for the entire event, so once you've had a chat you can simply say '*I know you'll be keen to meet others today, so I won't take up too much of your time*' and thank them for talking to you.

ACTIVITY 9.1

Building a network

- Take some time to think of questions that might work in the 'be curious' section. Build a list of some ice-breaking questions or questions that focus on past, present and future.

We'll now continue to think about developing a global mindset by turning our attention to communication skills and how we can aim to communicate our messages clearly.

9.3 HOW TO COMMUNICATE CLEARLY

Part of having global networks and a global mindset is being able to communicate in a way that is clear to others. Our communication these days takes place verbally, in writing, sometimes in other visual formats like animation or video, and can be in person or digital. A lot of what we are trying to say can sometimes be muffled or distorted by obstacles like different languages, cultural references or a general lack of clarity. To be an effective student, working and studying in a global space, you need to be aware of your communication skills and how you might want to strengthen them.

In all of our forms of communication, we can think of there being a sender and a receiver. In instances of successful communication, the receiver understands the message in the way the sender intended. In 1947, Claude E. Shannon, a research mathematician working for Bell Labs, created a theory of communication designed to facilitate the transmission of information over telephone lines. Later, Warren Weaver added the component of feedback to Shannon's linear model, making it circular. Although originally intended to be used by engineers dealing with information that was void of meaning, the Shannon–Weaver Model, shown in Figure 9.3, is still one of the most popular interpersonal communication models used today (Shannon and Weaver, 1949).

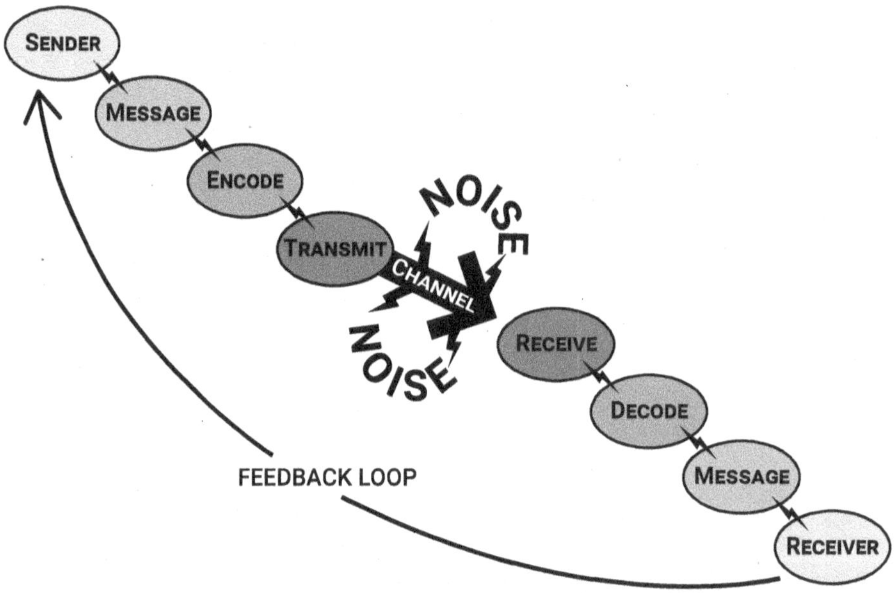

FIGURE 9.3: Shannon–Weaver model of communication

In the model, we see the sender at one side and the receiver at the other. There are various stages within the model: message – encode – transmit on the sender's side and receive – decode – message on the receiver's side. Linking the two is a feedback loop – the ability of the sender and receiver to check that the message has been correctly received. It's easier to have a strong feedback loop in place when communication takes place face to face and it's easy to check understanding. This tends to be missing in written communication and online interactions.

In his 2024 book, *Supercommunicators*, Charles Duhigg talks about the importance of listeners being able to prove that they're listening (Duhigg, 2024). A simple but powerful technique for doing this is to 'loop for understanding'. To do this, the receiver asks questions, summarises what they heard and then asks the sender if their summary is accurate. By using your own words to summarise and not simply repeating back what the sender has said word for word, Duhigg says that you are showing that you are engaged and working to understand the sender's meaning, which can reduce the likelihood of confusion and conflict. The 'looping' part means that you go round the 'question – summarise – check' cycle until there is agreement.

A feedback loop is helpful because at each step of the model there is noise. Not literal noise, although it can be tricky to communicate well in din, but metaphorical noise. Ask yourself what might cause this noise in conversations you have? It could be speaking in jargon, cultural references that your receiver doesn't understand, technical issues in online meetings, being native speakers of different languages, or transmitting really complicated sentences and complex ideas that are hard to take in. You can think about noise through the following categories.

BARRIERS TO GOOD COMMUNICATION

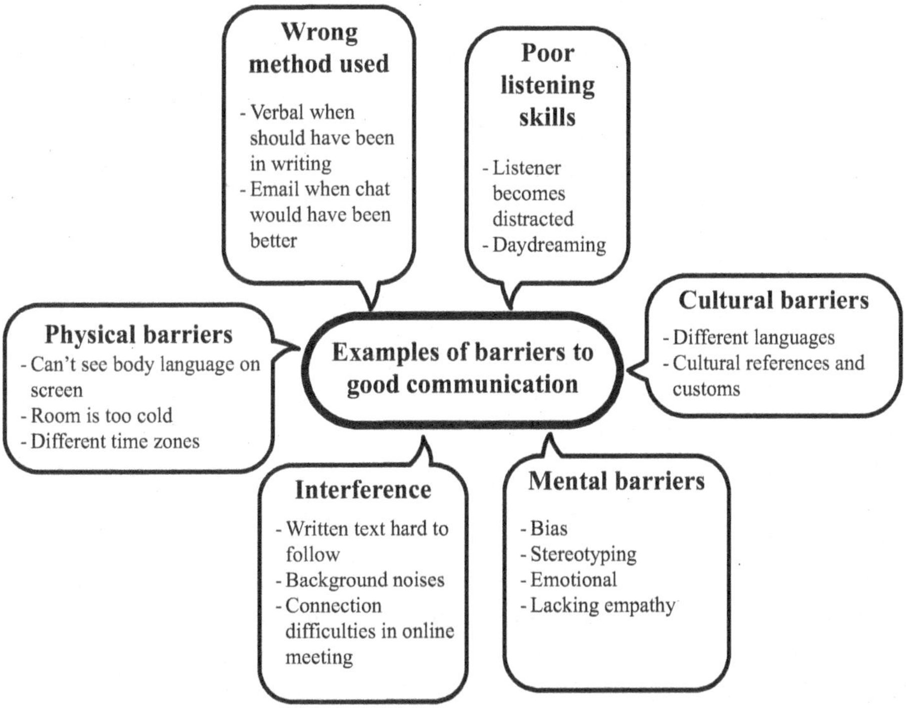

FIGURE 9.4: Categories of barriers to good communication with some associated examples

ACTIVITY 9.2

Understanding barriers in communication

- Think of examples where communication did not go well. Perhaps there was a misunderstanding, or you couldn't send or receive the message correctly.
- Pick out two or three examples and think about which barriers were involved. Record this in Table 9.1.
- Think about how you might be able to lower or remove these barriers if the situation were to happen again.

TABLE 9.1: Examples of barriers in communication

Example	Barriers	Ideas for improvement
Attempted to make plans for the group project while walking to lecture	*Interference (hard to keep track while walking)*	*Make sure group project discussions happen sitting still*

As a university student, you will likely come across all of these barriers as you send and receive messages. To improve your communication there are a couple of 'easy wins' you can implement. First of all, it pays off to plan your communication before you begin. Figure out what you want to say and why you want to say it. Think about who you are communicating with and what they need to know. This will help you pick the right communication method, whether it's verbal, written or an alternative. No matter the method, try to seek feedback in terms of checking if your recipient has understood the message.

In terms of overcoming barriers as a recipient, think about not just how you can listen but how you can *actively* listen. Active listening is where you apply the active attention we spoke about in Chapter 6 towards the person who is communicating with you. Focus on what they say. Give them your full attention and don't let yourself be distracted by derailing thoughts. Show them you are actively listening via your body language (eye contact, nod, smile). Give them feedback that you understand what they are saying by summarising or asking questions to clarify your understanding.

Withhold judgement on what they are say while they are speaking; don't interrupt or be busy thinking of counter-arguments – really listen to what they are saying. You can practise active listening in a tutorial, lecture or in any conversation.

INDIVIDUAL DIFFERENCES IN COMMUNICATION

While we have been looking at some general communication barriers that everyone will have to consider, there are also many individual barriers and differences in communication styles. There is a wide variation in how people communicate and how comfortable people feel with different communication methods. People who are neurodiverse might communicate in a different way to neurotypical people. A study by Crompton et al (2020) found that neurotypical people communicated effectively with each other, and also that neurodiverse people (in this case people with autism) communicated equally effectively with each other. Yet, when neurotypical people and people with autism interacted with one another there tended to be less effective communication. The findings suggest that people with autism have a communication difference to neurotypical people but not a communication deficit.

If you are communicating with a wide range of people, you can assume that you will encounter neurodiversity as well as 'neurotypicalness'. Techniques for communicating well with neurodivergent people are the same as those for communicating well with neurotypical people – don't go in with assumptions, keep your language clear and simple, and avoid euphemisms, ambiguity, sarcasm and colloquialisms. If someone has disclosed that that they are neurodivergent, you can ask them if there is anything that might help you both get the most out of your interaction.

STUDENT INSIGHT

John McNealy, medieval history and Middle East studies, second year

When I engage with people, I focus on telling them the truth. I emphasise my delivery and tone to make sure that my words land correctly. I try to take a positive tone, so that the information is received well. I want to keep the frame of mind positive. By keeping my tone encouraging and helpful, even when delivering bad news, I can keep the person I am communicating with engaged with me. If I am hostile or negative in my tone, I shut down any chance for collaboration with the person I am interacting with.

This positive tone is useful across all forms of communication. Whether in emails, face to face or online meetings, I use a positive tone. This helps me ensure that even when delivering criticism, the dialogue continues and doesn't just shut down and both parties can continue to engage and learn. I believe that this positive tone drives fluid and constructive communication across platforms and would encourage anybody to use it.

WRITTEN COMMUNICATION

At university, communicating in writing will be a common requirement. This could be informal communication such as using email or Microsoft Teams to message teaching staff or fellow students, or more formal communication such as completing an essay or report for an assignment. In the global workplace, email is still a core communication method, despite being over 50 years old, although trends indicate it may soon be overtaken by real-time messaging apps (Spiceworks Ziff Davis, 2022). Let's look at how you can structure an effective message.

EMAILS AND MESSAGING

When emailing and messaging your aim is to convey your message clearly and efficiently to your recipient. If you are communicating with a staff member, you want to be respectful and polite, and recognise that they're likely busy people with limited time to read and reply. It's therefore good to keep things brief and simple. (As an aside, you can show respect and politeness by using their correct title, eg Prof, Dr, Mr, Ms, Mx etc.)

Journalists use a technique called the **'inverted pyramid'** when they write their stories, and you can adapt this for emails too (see Figure 9.5 for an example). Simply, you make sure you put the most important information first. This is the critical information that you absolutely need the recipient to read and that will attract their attention. Next, you add the important information to help them understand the message; they are not mind-readers, so provide context and avoid jargon. Finally, there is a call to action – be clear about what you would like them to do – is it to provide you with some kind of information, convey a decision, consider a request you have made? In addition to this, your email subject line should be descriptive – it should give your reader a head start before they open the email about what is coming.

In messaging rather than emailing (such as using the messenger feature in Microsoft Teams), the communication is briefer still. The aim here is to use simple, clear language and limit it to the most important information. It should be accurate, complete in terms of all the necessary information and not overly complex.

Dear Dr Ruadh,

THE FIRST TIME YOU ARE WRITING TO AN ACADEMIC MAKE SURE YOU USE THEIR FULL TITLE E.G., DR, PROF, MS, MR ETC. TO GIVE THEM ACADEMIC RESPECT

I wonder if you might be able to provide me with a reference for my application to be a University Ambassador to assist with Visiting Days.

THIS IS THE 'HEADLINE' OF YOUR EMAIL... IT CLEARLY LAYS OUT THE MOST IMPORTANT PART OF THE MESSAGE

The application requires both an academic and personal reference, and I was hoping you might be able to contribute the former to verify the information about my grades, attendance and engagement with my academic studies.

THE NEXT PARAGRAPHS PROVIDE MORE CONTEXT AND USEFUL INFORMATION BUT SHOULD BE SUCCINCT AND TO THE POINT

I am a member of your EM1002 tutorial group and gave a presentation last week on healthcare inequalities. Strong presentation skills are an essential competency of the role, along with excellent interpersonal skills and good time management. I hope I have demonstrated these to you through my engagement with the tutorials.

The role itself is to conduct tours for prospective students of the University campus and to tell them about the student experience. You can find out more information via the job advert.

THERE MAY BE ADDITIONAL INFORMATION YOU CAN SIGNPOST TO, BUT NOT WRITE ABOUT AT LENGTH IN THE EMAIL

The reference letters are to be sent to ambassadorapplications@myuni.ac.uk by 2 November, and I'd be grateful if you could let me know if you'd be willing to provide one?

THIS IS THE CALL TO ACTION. END WITH A CLEAR SENSE OF WHAT YOU'D LIKE TO HAPPEN

I'd be happy to answer any questions you might have, and thank you sincerely for your time.

MAKE SURE THAT YOU ARE POLITE AND ACKNOWLEDGE TAKING UP THEIR TIME

Kind regards,
Kelso Brodie
Student Number: 1062345

BE CLEAR ABOUT WHO YOU ARE AND MAKE IT EASY FOR THEM TO FIND YOUR DETAILS

FIGURE 9.5: Example of an email using an inverted pyramid structure

COMMUNICATION THROUGH PRESENTATIONS

At university, there's a high likelihood that you'll be asked to communicate via giving a presentation at some point in your programme. A three-part structure (introduction – main body – conclusion) works well for presentations, both in person and online. The main difference between presentations versus written communication is that while a reader can re-read and go over sections of text to aid their understanding, a listener only has one shot to take in and process the information. Therefore, presentations need to be simpler than written text and more repetitive. Presentations are designed to disseminate information in a digestible format to a group. They can be for a local audience or, indeed, a global one.

When giving a presentation, like in other forms of communication, you should think about who your audience is: how familiar will they be with your topic, how many of them will there be, how varied they will be? This information will impact how you want to communicate with them. Nancy Duarte, a communication expert, did a popular TED talk called 'The secret structure of great talks' (Duarte, 2012). She talks about the impact of a story when communicating ideas and moving back and forth between the status quo and what could be.

In a bid to help the audience understand and process your argument, you can use your body language in an in-person presentation in a way you obviously can't with written communication. Here are six things to think about in terms of body language and other non-verbal communication when you're presenting.

1. **Make some eye contact:** Drawing your audience in to your presentation is important and making eye contact is a powerful way to connect with the people listening to you. Of course, you don't want to terrify your audience by staring them out – aim to hold their gaze for no more than a second or two before looking away. Some people find it difficult or uncomfortable to make eye contact, so a good tip is to look directly over the audiences' heads instead – it still looks to them as if you're directing your focus towards them.

2. **Keep your hands in a box:** Not a literal box, but it can help to create an imaginary one between your waist and your shoulders. It can be very effective to use hand gestures to emphasise your key points, but take care to not distract by waving your hands about liberally or breaking out of your imaginary box too often.
3. **Move your body:** Just like using hand gestures to emphasise a point, you can also use your whole body. Say you have three main points to your presentation. You can physically take a step each time you get to a new point to help the audience follow your direction. Some presenters like to pace the floor as they talk, and this can keep the audience

engaged as they work to watch you, but it can also create interference and detract from getting your words heard.

4. **Take a breath and use pauses:** One of the most common pitfalls presenters make is talking too quickly for the audience to have time to listen and process the information. Non-verbal punctuation, such as a well-placed pause, can be extremely effective in giving the audience time to catch up. A short pause (just a second or two) immediately before or after a key point can help make the information land in a much more meaningful way. It also helps you look like you're in control and that your presentation isn't a runaway train that you're struggling to keep up with.
5. **Break out of PowerPoint prison:** You might have heard of the phrase 'death by PowerPoint' – coined to reflect the mind-numbing situation you might have been in when a presenter has too many dense, boring or irrelevant text-heavy slides that they read verbatim. Using presentation software such as MS PowerPoint can be a great addition in terms of giving your presentation structure and using text or visuals to make your message easier to understand and process. However, think about what you can do to break out of PowerPoint prison – the default setting of lots of black text bullet points on a white background with a title at the top of the slide. You can experiment with different layouts and colours (while keeping within accessibility guidelines). PowerPoint now comes with a 'designer' menu option to help you create more engaging slides.
6. **Use images to add to your message:** Humans are visual creatures and as the saying goes, a picture is worth a thousand words. You can use images in a way that truly complements your message. We've been to lots of presentations that feature texts and images on the same slide, with the presenter talking to it. This creates a huge cognitive processing load! The audience has to read the slide text at the same time as listening to, and processing, what the presenter is saying and interpreting the image at the same time. It's like trying to read a book and listen to a podcast while watching a YouTube video all at the same time. Some of the most effective presentations fill the entire slide with a single image. This way the audience can take in the image while the presenter's words add value to it. Try it next time you have to give a presentation.

In short, to communicate effectively when presenting, keep your message simple, use a structure, repeat your main points, and use your voice and body language to help engage the audience. Engaging your audience is key – if the audience isn't paying attention and following your points, your message will be lost. There are several things you can do to increase audience engagement, and we can start thinking about these in Activity 9.3.

ACTIVITY 9.3

Making presentations engaging

Think about the very best presentations you've experienced. Perhaps you felt enthusiastic about what you were learning, or found it entertaining, or felt connected to the presenter. Reflect on what it was that made the presentation engaging for you and mark down which of the following elements were the most important:

- what they said;
- how they said it;
- body language;
- presentation structure;
- use of visuals/props;
- audience participation.

Here are some more ideas that you can employ to increase the level of audience engagement in your presentation.

- **Introduce a memorable fact, statistic or quote:** Even more so, if you use one that might be considered somewhat controversial it will stimulate thought and discussion in your audience.
- **Get the audience moving:** It might not be appropriate to get the audience out of their seats, but you might want to get the audience to do something in the first minute or two of your presentation – if you can set the mood that sitting back and zoning out is not an option, then you are on the way to an engaging presentation! For example, you could ask the audience to raise their hands if they agree with a statement or if they have prior knowledge of a topic.
- **Help the audience set the direction of the presentation:** The audience will feel engaged if they have some autonomy over what they are learning. Is there a way you can give the audience a choice about what they are learning or how you structure the presentation? We have used live polls in a presentation before to ask

the audience what they wanted us to focus on. Another option might be to embed Q&A sessions at points of the presentation so you can give more airtime to the parts the audience is invested in.

- **Ask a question:** You can also ask the audience questions – it doesn't have to be them always asking you! Requiring the audience to think and critically engage with your presentation as you go can deepen their learning and help them be engaged.
- **Break it up:** People have short attention spans, so anything you can do to break up big chunks of presentation delivered in the same format is a good thing. You can ask the audience to break for short discussions with their neighbours, pause for people to do a short activity, play a video clip or even have a short comfort break.
- **Ditch the script:** It can be comforting to have your entire presentation written down on a script that you can then read aloud, but this can prevent you from fully connecting with your audience. While there are some circumstances where you might choose to go with a full script, there might be other times where you feel more comfortable with no script at all, or by using some cue cards with the main bullet points to give you a basic structure. Experiment with what works for you and see if it makes a difference to how well you can engage your audience.

PRACTITIONER INSIGHT

Dr Amanda Martindale, senior lecturer in sport and performance psychology, University of Edinburgh

Giving a good presentation doesn't have to be a stressful experience. It can be fun once you get the hang of it. You don't need to be perfect to succeed. When presenting to a diverse audience, it can be hard to please everyone in the room. You don't have to tell them all you know about your topic – instead you only need to concentrate on a few main points.

It is natural to feel a bit afraid of the limelight and to worry that you might not be heard or understood, but there are lots of coping strategies that can help: prepare well, breathing/relaxation, positive mental attitude, keep well hydrated, contingency planning (eg having a backup).

Finally, Three Steps to Success:

1. *Ask yourself some questions prior to planning/writing the presentation. For example: Who will I be speaking to? (What audience?)*

Why will they be there? (Their needs?)

What will I be trying to get across? (Message/style)

2. *Know your material.*

Practise/revise as necessary.

Include a timed rehearsal.

The best predictor of self-confidence is perceived readiness...

3. *Remember that people want you to succeed!*

ONLINE PRESENTATIONS

In our global, interconnected community, the likelihood is that you won't always have everyone you want to communicate with in the same physical space. For communication to have a global reach, you will need to make use of online presentations. The same rules apply in online presentations as in in-person ones, although your body language will be more constrained, and people will find it harder to pick up on cues you might be giving. For online presentations you will find that you might have to give verbal cues more than visual ones – for example, explicitly asking if people have questions because you can't tell if they're making eye contact with you. On the plus side, giving an online presentation allows you to make use of the interactive features of online platforms like Microsoft Teams. For example, you can make your presentation more interactive by using features like polls or encouraging people to write comments in the chat box or use emojis to share how they're feeling. You can also make your presentation more accessible by enabling the audience to view live subtitling.

Some key things to consider when getting ready to do an online presentation include the following.

INTRODUCTIONS AND ROLES

For an in-person presentation, the audience can usually identify who the presenter is going to be – they're the person standing at the front of the room looking like they're just about to do a presentation. The audience can also say hello to each other and take part in some chit-chat before the presentation begins. These elements can be lost in the online space. You might want to think about if/how you replicate this: do you encourage people to introduce themselves via the chat function or answer an ice-breaker question as you wait for people to arrive? Do you take a few additional moments at the start to introduce yourself as the presenter and explain any other roles?

AN EQUAL SPACE

There can be something quite equalising about giving an online presentation. Everyone has the same-sized little box on a screen, and status, hierarchy and power dynamics can be less visible. I've heard students say that they feel more empowered to participate in the online space than an in-person environment. Can you leverage this dynamic to help you make your presentation effective and engaging? Perhaps the audience will be willing to interact via the chat function or in group discussions?

GROUND-RULES AND ETIQUETTE

In the online environment, the audience isn't constrained by the same social rules that an in-person audience is. In an in-person environment we are likely to pay attention to the speaker because to do otherwise would look rude to the people around us. These rules can fall away in the online space and bad behaviour can take their place! People might let their attention drift and multi-task or drop in and out of your presentation. You can address this at the beginning by flagging good presentation etiquette, but you might also want to realistically plan for the fact that your audience might not be 100 per cent focused on you and use summaries and handouts strategically.

BE VISIBLE

It's important to get the basics right. As a presenter you should be visible with your camera on and at eye height. Think about how your camera frames you – you don't want to be a tiny object in a huge space: make sure your face and features are clearly visible. Think about lighting too; you don't want to be in shadow or silhouetted. Have a good light source in front of you. Most online meeting software gives you the option to set a background image if you don't want to show the room you're presenting in. When you're speaking, try to look directly into camera when you can to simulate making eye contact. Finally, if you stand rather than sit when presenting (and raise your camera accordingly), you will likely find that you speak with a bit more authority. While you are visible your audience might not be. It can be disconcerting to present to lots of turned-off cameras so be prepared for this.

KNOWING THE KIT

When we first started doing online presentations, we had some disasters! Most of these stemmed from not fully knowing how the online set-up worked. We weren't sure how to share our screens without sharing our notes, we weren't sure how to mute people who had left their microphones on and were creating distracting background noise, and we weren't sure how to run interactive features like polls and whiteboards. It didn't take long for us to figure out the importance of practice and to learn how the kit worked. Take some time and implement some rehearsal ahead of your presentation. It's also useful to plan for the tech failing. What will you do if you can't share your slides as you intended or an interactive feature doesn't work? One additional element that online presentations give you is the ability for the audience to engage with collaborative tools such as creating a Padlet together, or writing on a virtual whiteboard, or moving between breakout rooms.

TEAM UP WITH AN ASSISTANT

A lot can happen at once in an online presentation. You might be trying to give your presentation while also keeping an eye on comments in the chat box, while being distracted by cameras being switched on or off, or virtual hands being raised or lowered. If you have a large audience or you are planning on having a very interactive presentation, it can be helpful to have an assistant to help marshal them at points.

Being able to communicate clearly, no matter if that's through verbal communication or written, in person or online, helps you interact with your global network and navigate cultural differences. Different cultures have different communication styles and preferences, so clarity and simplicity give you the best chance of reaching across the greatest number of these.

9.4 HOW TO INFLUENCE AND NEGOTIATE

What is the first thing that you imagine when you think about **influencing** and negotiating? Perhaps you think about important peace treaties or lucrative business deals. Maybe you think of smartly dressed people speaking in jargon, with lots of complicated documents. If we were to delve further, you may think of someone selling a used car and trying to get the best deal. Or if you think only about influencing, you may think of someone trying to sell you something aspirational on social media.

In these thoughts, you might not consider yourself to be an influencer or negotiator. But we all engage in negotiations on a regular basis, from choosing which restaurant to eat at with friends to persuading a young child to eat their vegetables, or asking someone to undertake a challenging project at work. Influencing and negotiating are part of our personal, professional and academic lives and, therefore, developing our skills in this area will enhance our ability to communicate with the people we connect with.

ACTIVITY 9.4

Unpacking negotiations

- Describe a recent negotiation you have witnessed. (This could be in a film or TV programme.)
- What features made you identify this as a negotiation rather than a simple conversation?

From UN summits and corporate boardrooms to kitchen-table discussions, **negotiation** can be understood as a conversation in which there is a difference of opinion, which is aimed at reaching an agreement. **Influence** is at the heart of negotiation. It can be understood as the ability to persuade or affect the thoughts or behaviours of an individual or group.

When looking at the definition of negotiation it's important to note that it is not necessarily about getting a desired outcome or aiming to 'win', but to reach an agreement, which is often a compromise in negotiations. If you enter a conversation with the aim of a specific outcome, and want to beat the other person, it's likely you will enter into an argument. Being able to properly hear and respect others with opinions different to your own is an important part of negotiation.

Of course, in negotiations both parties will have a firm limit; there are 'non-negotiables'. In a business transaction this may be the minimum price for which they are willing to sell something; when choosing a restaurant this may be a certain type of cuisine you don't like. So, we can see this in practice as the difference between '*I don't want to go to a seafood restaurant*' to '*The only place I will eat is Nando's*'. The first is the start of a negotiation; the second is a statement which people can either reject or accept.

Building on our exploration of interpersonal skills in Chapter 8, emotions are vital in negotiations. We can't switch off our emotions, so they will be present in all our conversations. Even more so, negotiations can often intensify our emotions; therefore, it's important not to ignore them. But, as there are so many different emotions, it's near impossible to guess what other people's emotions are.

So, in order to navigate emotions, we can think of core concerns. This is a concept created by Roger Fisher and Daniel Shapiro in their book *Beyond Reason: Using Emotions as You Negotiate* (2005). They highlight five core concerns that all humans have, which impact our emotions:

1. appreciation;
2. autonomy;
3. affiliation;
4. status;
5. role.

Negotiations are especially important when you are coming from different approaches, which is likely in a diverse university setting. We will now look at each of these core concerns in turn.

APPRECIATION

Appreciation is about being valued by the other parties in the conversation. Fisher and Shapiro (2005) argue that cooperation between individuals increases significantly when there is a feeling of mutual appreciation. Therefore, it can be damaging to diminish or reject someone's point of view and, even more so, to insult them. It's also important to make sure your own ideas are appreciated by making sure that you advocate for them and explain why they may work. This does not mean you have to accept every idea (nor expect your own ideas to be automatically accepted) but to treat every idea with respect, and of course to treat each other with respect.

AUTONOMY

Autonomy is having the freedom to make a decision without someone imposing a choice upon you. If you intrude on someone's autonomy, you are telling them what to do. The clichéd line in negotiations of 'take it or leave it' is a very good example of what not to do. Fisher and Shapiro (2005) highlight that this line can actually be very damaging to negotiations, and often the other party will 'leave it'. This is because the process of the negotiation is far more important than the content or 'deal' that is offered. An excellent idea can be suggested, but if it's not brought forward in the right way, it's likely it won't be accepted. This is because, as humans, we highly value the ability to choose.

AFFILIATION

An affiliation is the emotional connection between you and the other person/people in your group. This does not mean you are expected to become friends with the people you are negotiating with, but that you should think of yourself as being an active part of the team rather than as distinct. This means focusing on your similarities rather than differences. You are far more likely to reach an agreement if you take this approach. This can be problematic if you have a limited mindset about who you are affiliated with. In a diverse setting, you can be in danger of focusing on differences and thus forming in-groups with those who have a similar identity and background to you.

STATUS

Status highlights the power dynamic in negotiations. It can be upsetting when our status is not recognised, or we are treated as inferior to others. Sadly, you may have faced this yourself. Rebecca remembers an occasion when she was called '*just a student*' and so it was inferred that her opinion was worth less than the other members of the meeting. When establishing your own status, as well as others', it's important to respect each person's expertise and experience. Despite many characteristics being protected by law, an individual may be treated as inferior due to an element of their identity. For example, perhaps when a student society is organising a fundraising event, a mature student's ideas were discredited, as they were seen as out of touch. This would be a short-sighted assumption to make, which would remove status from the student and most likely limit new ideas.

ROLE

Our final core concern is having a fulfilling role and set of activities that you perform. When working in a team, such as completing group work, you undertake temporary responsibilities. Ideally, you find these fulfilling. Roles are satisfying when they:

1. have a recognisable purpose;
2. allow you to use your skills;
3. align with your values;
4. are meaningful.

When thinking about and implementing these five concerns, it's reassuring to know that you already know five things about a person, even if you have never met them before. If you know you are going to have to negotiate something, such as influencing the kitchen user to keep the fridge cleaner, you can run through the five concerns and think about how they may feel in each of these areas regarding the conversation and your own feelings. If you deal well with the five core concerns in negotiating discussions, you are likely to stimulate positive emotions and cooperation. However, if you don't then a conversation can be very difficult.

Although sometimes tricky, especially when using a framework to guide a conversation, it's important to be authentic when undertaking a negotiation. If you are systematically going through each of the five concerns like a tick-box exercise, then you can come across as insincere. In order to overcome this, it's important that your priority in a conversation is to actively listen; this means not planning what you are going to say next but waiting for their response. This can be facilitated by asking open questions. So, rather than asking: '*Would you like me to meet you at 7pm to work on the team project?*', you could ask: '*What time would you like to work on the team project?*' Of course, you will not always agree with their answer, but you can then discuss the best options.

When developing your influencing and negotiating skills, it's essential to reflect upon and evaluate your performance. If you have a successful negotiation, ask yourself:

1. What made it successful and why?
2. What behaviours can you take forward into future negotiations?

In contrast, if you feel the conversation could have gone better:

1. What made it unsuccessful and why?
2. What you could do differently in the future?

Like any of the skills we discuss in this book, influencing and negotiating, along with other interpersonal skills, take time to develop. In a diverse university, people will have different values and points of reference. The next chapter will highlight the importance of appreciating how you might use these skills of influencing and negotiation to create positive change in your communities.

CHAPTER SUMMARY

In this chapter we thought about the fact that you are living in an interconnected world and how challenging it can be to forge connections. We thought about how you can build a network of your own, and you now know the key skills involved in networking. Communication is a broad topic, but we looked at a model of communication and identified common barriers to good communication. We then thought about how best to communicate through writing and presentations, and also how to communicate well when influencing and negotiating, giving you some tips and guidance to take away and try. There are lots of extra resources out there to help you develop your networking, communication and negotiation skills – books, podcasts, videos and technology. Your university might well share or signpost you to them.

TOP TIPS AND NEXT STEPS

- Create a LinkedIn profile to connect with other students and professionals from around the world.
- Reflect on the circumstances in which you think you communicate well. What can you do to help replicate these circumstances in future?
- Which of the core concerns outlined in the section about negotiation do you think are most important to you?
- Review the last email you sent and consider what you would change if you used the inverted pyramid technique.
- Pay attention to the next presentation you're in about what the presenter does to engage the audience.

CHAPTER 10
YOU, AGENCY AND COMMUNITY

CHALLENGES WE EXPLORE IN THIS CHAPTER

In this final chapter of Part 2, we explore the topics of community and agency: thinking about how you can engage with, and contribute to, the groups that you will belong to as a student, both inside and outside your university. This is an essential, but often overlooked, part of university life. At times students can find it challenging to have a strong sense of belonging and connection while at university. The communities you join during your degree can have a huge positive impact on your university experience, giving you the opportunity to engage with new people, view your degree differently and develop a sense of belonging. Equally, developing your agency while engaging in these communities will likely mean that you are more successful and engaged in your learning while being able to navigate challenges more easily outside of your studies.

This chapter examines these themes in three sections: the first looks at the foundations of the topics of community and agency, exploring how they impact your life at university. In order to understand these topics more thoroughly, we also look at ethical awareness and integrity. The second section of the chapter looks more practically at agency and community in your academic studies, thinking about the identity of your discipline, referencing and academic conduct. The final section of the chapter considers agency and community beyond your academic studies and explores how you can become an agent of change more generally.

INTENDED LEARNING OUTCOMES

By the end of this chapter, you should be able to:

- identify what a community is, why they are important and how to engage with them;
- understand integrity and ethical awareness in the context of agency and how these will impact your university experience;

- appreciate your role as a student and the agency you have as part of many different academic communities. You should also be able to recognise yourself as an effective agent of change and learn how to contribute to your communities.

The attributes outlined in this chapter are integrity, change-making and ethical awareness and discipline-specific identity.

10.1 FOUNDATIONS: AGENCY, COMMUNITY AND INTEGRITY

WHAT IS COMMUNITY, AND WHY DOES IT MATTER?

A community is a group of people who live in the same place, or share the same characteristics or values. This may be a group of people you have known all your life, such as your family or neighbours, or an online community, such as fan page for your favourite book. It could be very local, such as the street that you live on, or it could be an international cause that you are part of. A community differs from a network in that networks tend to focus on one aspect of you; a community centres around you as a whole person.

When we are exploring community, we can consider it in two different ways. The first way involves seeing a community as a group of people who share commonalities. The second is a sense of community, that is, a feeling of belonging. The interesting thing about both these understandings of the word 'community' is that it's personal and can add a lot of meaning to our lives. How you regard your communities will shape the way you engage with your degree and your life at university in general. You will have the opportunity to engage with multiple communities, from those living near you to those studying the same thing or sharing the same passion in student clubs and societies.

Communities are very important to university life for two primary reasons.

1. First, they provide social connection. Feeling part of a community or communities is a key ingredient for a successful and happy degree. Your communities are where you will make new friends and will greatly help with the transition to settling into university. This is especially important if you have travelled a significant distance or are studying an online degree. Your peers will be undertaking the same programme as you and sharing many of the same experiences as you. The opportunity to reflect on your degree and experiences with peers will make your degree more rewarding and manageable.
2. Secondly, your communities are where you will gain a sense of belonging at university. This is vital for your happiness at university and research also shows that students who have a sense of belonging and identify with their university tend to have higher levels of academic achievement, be more engaged, be more self-confident and have higher levels of motivation (Pedler et al, 2022).

HOW DO YOU IDENTIFY YOUR COMMUNITY?

You may identify some communities straight away. It may be a community which centres around something you are very passionate about, or it may be one that you have never considered before.

How you identify your community is very personal: Some people will visualise a community at work, while others will visualise them in teams and hobbies. International causes or political parties may form a community. At university this will likely include subject(s) you study, any societies or clubs you have joined, and the people you live with. If you are a commuting student, you may feel that you belong to a community of other commuting students.

It's unlikely that you will value all communities equally, and these will shift according to your situation at a given time. Figure 10.1 illustrates examples of communities a student may be part of.

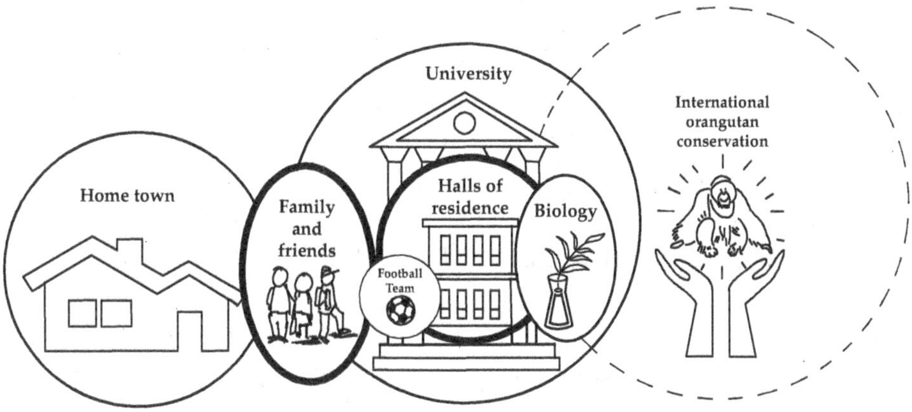

FIGURE 10.1: Examples of student communities

While this diagram does not include all of this person's communities, it does give an idea of the extent of some of them and how they intersect. The size of the circle shows how many people are in the community (not to scale), while the weight of the line shows how important that community is to the student; for example, the dotted line around international orangutan conservation is far fainter and a lesser part of this student's life compared to their halls of residence.

When you reflect on the image, is there anything surprising to you or any circles that you would also relate to?

ACTIVITY 10.1

Your communities

- Have a think about your own communities. Are they based on a shared place or interest? How important are those communities to you?
- Identify five (or more) communities that you feel part of?

1. 2. 3. 4. 5.

By outlining who your communities are, you not only have a better understanding of yourself and what is important to you, but you have a starting point for how to engage with them.

HOW TO ENGAGE IN YOUR COMMUNITIES

Engaging with your community means actively participating in it, from conversations with staff and other students to going to regular sports practices or volunteering at events (if you have time). You will automatically engage with some communities at university by default, for example your classes, while others may be optional, such as getting involved in societies or sports teams. It's okay to stagger the communities you join; you neither need to join lots of communities at once nor invest all of your time in them. Especially when you start university, the amount of new people and new opportunities you encounter can seem overwhelming. Sometimes taking a step back and thinking about your values (as we explored in Chapter 5) means you'll engage more meaningfully even if it's in fewer communities.

If you are not sure where to start, be intentional and think about your passions! Who do you like to spend time with? What do you like spending your time doing? What change would you like to see?

You can follow up that last question with: what change would you like to see in your particular community? You enter into a community when you start your degree. If there are changes you would like to see at your university, there will be opportunities to facilitate these changes, for example by being a student academic representative or helping to welcome new students during freshers' week.

The more you put into a community the more you are likely to get out of it, so it is worth investing time and energy into your communities to enhance your university experience. Remember you can also ask for help from within your community, for example asking friends for advice after a bad day, asking a neighbour to borrow something or seeking support from your university, such as booking an appointment with the careers service or mental health support service. One way of measuring the impact you have in a community is to consider how you could be an agent of change within it to foster positive development within that community, which we will explore in the final part of this chapter.

Building on this exploration of community, this chapter now looks at agency, reflecting on how you engage in these different communities.

STUDENT INSIGHT

Aurélie Coop, English and film studies, second year

The biggest way I have engaged with my academic community is through living in halls. It's allowed me to immediately find people that've encouraged me to get out there from the get-go. This led me to then get involved in my hall committee and later various university committees. I think I was very overwhelmed at the quantity of existing societies and clubs in my first few months as a student, which really paralysed me in figuring out where to even start. Halls gave me a starting point, and saying yes to any opportunity that arises from engaging in courses has cemented that engagement across all aspects of my uni life. Whether that's a mentorship programme or research opportunity, not feeling like you need to rush and do everything from the start, but putting yourself out there when the chance arises has been my way of engaging with my community.

10.2 AGENCY

Building upon this discussion of community, you can think about the way you choose to act within these communities, whether in your academic classes or friendship groups. To do this we can briefly explore the topic of agency.

Agency of an individual is the idea that a person is capable of formulating preferences and developing strategies to realise those preferences. In other words, you think about doing something and then make it happen. When you have agency, you believe you can make a difference. This covers small decisions, such as choosing what to have for breakfast, as well as bigger decisions, such as what to study at university. Our agency is impacted by other factors, from friends and family to logistics.

When looking at agency and being a student, we can focus specifically on learning agency, which refers to the '*feeling of ownership and sense of control that students have over their learning. Agentive learners are motivated not only to learn but also to take responsibility for managing the learning process*' (Larsen-Freeman et al, 2021, p 2). Simply put, learning agency is the belief that you can impact your own learning. This may sound obvious, but when we begin to reflect on this principle it can be easy to lose agency. It can be easy to think that your success is beyond your control and, instead, only impacted by those teaching you, your natural ability or previous experience.

While there will be many factors that are outside of your control and will impact your learning, you and your approach to studying will have the biggest impact. This is why we continue to return to this topic throughout the book, from looking at resilience and mindset throughout Part 1 of the book to autonomy and study skills in Chapter 4.

A panel on learning agency, from Oxford University Press, produced some interesting conclusions (Larsen-Freeman et al, 2021).

1. Students with a sense of agency are more likely to be engaged in their learning.
2. Students with a sense of agency have a growth mindset (as we explored in Chapter 2), which means they believe that they are control of their learning and the ability to improve.
3. Students who develop agency are not only more successful in their learning but are equipped to deal with other challenges outside of their studies.
4. Developing learning agency cannot happen alone and students need a to have meaningful interactions with their communities.

We return to look at how you can develop both your academic community and learning agency in Section 10.3, thinking about **discipline identity** and academic conduct.

This means thinking about how you are responsible for your own learning and your own behaviour. That is why, in this chapter, we look at agency and community, as well as ethical behaviour and integrity. In many ways, this is agency in action. We will start this exploration by looking at your understanding of ethical awareness and integrity.

ETHICAL AWARENESS AND INTEGRITY

Consider how you will approach your communities and agency through your ethical awareness and integrity.

ACTIVITY 10.2

Reflecting on ethical awareness and integrity

- What do the terms 'ethical awareness' and 'integrity' mean to you? Write your thoughts in the box below.

WHAT IS ETHICAL AWARENESS AND INTEGRITY?

Ethical awareness is the ability to recognise and consider ethical issues and principles in decision making and behaviour. It involves:

- being able to identify situations that may have ethical implications;
- understanding the values and principles that are relevant to those situations;
- being able to make informed decisions that are consistent with ethical standards.

Ethical awareness is important because it allows individuals to act in ways that are morally responsible and respectful of others. It helps individuals to recognise and avoid actions that may cause harm or violate the rights of others, and to act in ways that promote fairness, justice and the common good. Developing ethical awareness requires education and training in ethical principles, as well as exposure to real-world situations that challenge individuals to think critically about ethical issues. It also involves developing a habit of reflecting on one's own values and beliefs and being willing to engage in dialogue and debate with others about ethical issues. By cultivating ethical awareness, individuals can contribute to a more just and compassionate society.

Integrity is the quality of being honest, ethical and having strong moral principles. It involves:

- consistently adhering to a set of principles and values, even when it may be difficult or unpopular to do so;
- telling the truth;
- keeping promises;
- admitting mistakes;
- treating others with respect and fairness;
- taking responsibility for one's actions;
- being accountable for the consequences of actions.

In personal and professional contexts, integrity is highly valued because it builds trust and credibility with others. It is a key component of ethical behaviour and is often associated with leadership and success in various fields. Maintaining integrity requires ongoing self-reflection, a commitment to personal values and principles, and a willingness to learn and grow. It is important for individuals to be aware of the ethical implications of their actions and to strive to act in ways that are consistent with their values and principles. By doing so, individuals can build a reputation for honesty and reliability, and contribute to a culture of trust and respect in their communities and organisations.

ETHICAL AWARENESS, INTEGRITY AND ACADEMIC COMMUNITY

Your ethical awareness will guide your values, interests and agency. For example, you may wish to study biology as you are interested in wildlife conservation, or education, as you wish to be a teacher. Similarly, your ethical awareness may change how you spend your time outside of studying, from caring for others, volunteering and working, to joining teams and societies. Your integrity will not only influence what you choose to study but how you will approach your degree, including how you engage in research.

While at university, it's likely that you will encounter the terms 'ethics' and 'integrity' frequently, particularly in good academic practice contracts (as we will explore later in this chapter), but also when applying for ethical approval on research proposals or even studying these topics in your disciplines. At the core of both ethical awareness and integrity is understanding how your decisions will impact yourself and others; thus, it is difficult to explore agency and community without acknowledging ethics and integrity. You can think of these topics as your own code of conduct.

A practical way to explore integrity and ethical awareness is to consider artificial intelligence (AI). There are currently expansive debates (Hack and Knight, 2023) around the role of AI and integrity in universities, particularly involving applications which can generate text. The current focus is on whether students should be allowed to use this technology in assignments and whether it could be used to provide quick feedback on assessments (from a staff member's perspective). Universities appear to be divided on this topic. There are also much broader concerns surrounding AI. For example, can it replicate human language and research? This is a question you have the opportunity to reflect on yourself, as the previous section 'What is ethical awareness and integrity?' was written by ChatGPT, the only part of the book that is – did you notice?

Whatever the outcome of these questions, AI will undoubtedly change the way we create and engage with information. Therefore, it is important to understand your university's own guidelines on AI, and how you are allowed to use it, if you are allowed at all, in your degree. Beyond AI, it's important to understand the other rules that you will encounter in your academic community, especially the rules regarding **academic misconduct**.

10.3 AGENCY IN AN ACADEMIC COMMUNITY

This section unpacks your role as a student and your agency as part of different academic communities. To begin, we will consider discipline identity.

UNDERSTANDING DISCIPLINE IDENTITY AND THE LANGUAGE OF ACADEMIA

You can think of different academic subjects as having their own community and cultures. Just as with any other community and culture, it can be hard to pick up on all the nuances and rules, and it can take a long time to integrate and feel comfortable within it. You might have to study biology for years before you feel you can identify as being 'a biologist', or be a long way through your marketing degree before you can describe yourself as a 'marketer'.

This concept of 'discipline identity' is one that you can take steps to develop, mainly by spending time with people within the community. The more time you spend in your discipline, the more you'll absorb it, and this could be through observing and listening to experienced researchers and academics; reading articles, papers and textbooks about your subject area; talking about ideas and concepts in your subject with fellow students; and reviewing and learning from the feedback you get on your assignments.

ACTIVITY 10.3

Reflecting on your discipline identity

- Copy the table below and fill in each of the sections with your reflections on your academic discipline. You may wish to include two subjects if you are studying for a joint degree.

My discipline is:	
Words I associate with people in my discipline are....	Values I associate with people in my discipline are...

Research shows that the more you create a discipline identity, the more likely you are to engage in what's called '**deep learning**' and the more you cultivate a sense of belonging (Smyth et al, 2015, 2019). Deep learning is when students engage analytically with what they are learning and are able to build on their learning and connect ideas. They have a good understanding of what they are learning and are able to apply it in new contexts. This is what you should be striving for at university. Perhaps at school you engaged in more **surface learning**, which is where you might take on information as stand-alone facts, without questioning it or connecting it with other knowledge you have. If you've ever memorised a string of facts for an exam, regurgitated them and then forgotten all about them, this was likely surface learning.

As time goes on (and this could be years rather than weeks or months), you might find that you are beginning to build layers of more specialist knowledge. You might have a choice in your course about the subject matter of an essay topic, a field trip, a lab session or a module. The exact content you learn might be different from some of your fellow students on the same programme – you are beginning to build your own knowledge base in the subject and specialise in certain topics. This will also build your own learning agency and sense of belonging and community. As your subject knowledge deepens, you might also find that you write in a different way and analyse material differently because you understand the central issues and debates within your discipline. You might seek out research articles to read and deepen your understanding of a specific topic through doing a literature review, dissertation or even a PhD thesis. You will also become familiar with the beliefs, values and practices of your discipline. For example, some disciplines (eg some of the social sciences) tend to produce lone researchers who create outputs which they are the sole author of. Other disciplines (eg natural sciences) have a culture that is more about working in teams and creating co-authored works (Waldman et al, 2019).

As you become more and more specialist, you might find that a side-effect is that your discipline community becomes exclusionary. People who are not part of the culture might find it very difficult to understand the language and concepts you use. This exclusionary nature of academia can cause many people to experience imposter syndrome (Chapter 2) – where you feel you don't quite belong, or haven't truly earned your place, or that you are going to be 'found out' that you are lacking knowledge or the entitlement to be there. If you find that you are experiencing imposter syndrome, know that you are not alone. We have spoken to lots of students and staff, even experienced lecturers and professors who have felt this (and still do) from time to time. Feeling like an imposter is an unhelpful thought, and you might want to go back to Chapter 2 and refresh your knowledge on resilience.

In contrast to this exclusionary tendency, having a discipline identity connects you with others all over the world who are also part of your discipline and community. As well as the benefits that being part of a single discipline yield, the most exciting advances in research and advancing knowledge often come at the overlap of disciplines. Interdisciplinary collaboration is vital. To this end, some students and academics want to push for more openness within disciplines, such as open access to data and publications. There's value in resisting the urge to create an academic identity that is so narrow that it fails to be inclusive and open to opportunities and ideas from outside your specialism, especially as our relationship with knowledge changes quickly due to digital advancements.

Part of this academic identity is knowing how to credit the ideas of others that you refer to as you communicate and learn about your subject, and another important element is learning how people within your discipline communicate – what academic language to use. Now we will return to ethical awareness and integrity and, especially regarding academic conduct, this includes providing guidelines so you avoid 'cheating' on your assignments. But they are more than this. It can sound clichéd, but they are there to help you think about how to conduct yourself in the academic community.

ACADEMIC CONDUCT

It's likely you will be given an academic contract or agreement at the start of your degree which you will be asked to sign. This will outline a code of conduct you are expected to follow as a student at that university. This agreement will provide you with the opportunity to learn the rules of your academic community, and an invitation for you to join this community by agreeing to these rules.

These rules will cover a number of areas of conduct. For example, there is much more training and a greater focus placed upon cheating at higher education level compared to what you would have been used to at school. This is because of the vast amount of autonomy and agency you have when studying at university. The majority of your work will be completed individually, without the aid of direct input from members of staff (other than lecture notes or tutorial material). Secondly, as we explored in Chapter 4, you'll be responsible for your own learning and how you engage with course information. You'll also be expected to conduct research in your field.

So, with this amount of agency and autonomy, academic misconduct becomes much more likely, either accidentally or on purpose. No one will be watching how you are studying, and you'll have a lot of decisions to make regarding your research. This can be daunting, firstly in terms of making sure that you are following the rules and, secondly, regarding concerns about how to manage your time and get everything done to the standard you would like.

This is when it's easy to make a mistake, to just guess a citation and reference to include in your work, to tweak your experimental results to show what you would like or, when you are desperate, to engage in some of the most serious misconduct such as the use of essay mills (companies who will charge you a fee to write your essay for you) or generative AI.

What is important to remember about academic misconduct is that it is your responsibility to know and follow the rules, as an autonomous student. Not being aware of a rule is not a defence for breaking it, and although it may be taken into consideration (as to whether you intended to cheat or not) you will still face penalties. The penalties can be severe. You could fail the assignment or module or, in serious cases, you could be dismissed from your degree and your university. Beyond the penalties, we can return to the idea of ethical awareness: when you don't follow good academic practice or you conduct your studies in a way that doesn't meet your university's standards, you are taking away from your community of learning, rather than adding to it. While there may seem to be a lot of rules, understanding them means that you can engage with this community, follow the rules and ensure that everyone is performing research to the same standard.

It's essential that you know your own university's guidelines, so ensure you check these. We can further explore the different areas of academic misconduct to help you understand what not to do.

PLAGIARISM

One of the most emphasised malpractices, which will be highlighted during your degree, is plagiarism. You will regularly be told to make sure that you reference correctly, so you don't plagiarise. Plagiarism covers a wide range of actions, from forgetting to include a reference to copy and pasting chunks of texts, to pretending someone else's work is yours. All these actions are various examples of plagiarism which, simply put, is the use of another person's ideas and claiming they are your own. The University of Oxford's guidance summarises this well:

> *Plagiarism is a breach of academic integrity. It is a principle of intellectual honesty that all members of the academic community should acknowledge their debt to the originators of the ideas, words, and data which form the basis for their own work. Passing off another's work as your own is not only poor scholarship, but also means that you have failed to complete the learning process. Plagiarism is unethical and can have serious consequences for your future career; it also undermines the standards of your institution and of the degrees it issues.*
>
> (University of Oxford, 2023)

You deliberately plagiarise when you intentionally represent someone else's research (including using generative AI) as your own. You can also plagiarise by accident; for example, this may happen when your writing does not clearly express what your own ideas are and what is already published. Therefore, it's important to both make good notes during lectures and reference clearly (as we explored in Chapter 7). This will be helpful in order for you to clearly highlight what has already been researched on the topic, what research you have conducted yourself and what your interpretations of the existing research are.

You need to set up good practice to ensure you don't plagiarise. Your university will use specialist software which scans your work to identify whether anything has previously been written in published material, on the web or submitted by other students. These practices are further important in making sure you are highlighting the great reading and research you have undertaken, and how you are joining the academic conversation and community.

REPEAT SUBMISSION/SELF-PLAGIARISM

Repeat or multiple submission is when you use the same piece of assessed work more than once. For example, you can't use the report you wrote for Assignment 1 in your module for Assignment 2 in that module. Nor can you use it for a different module. This rule can apply to previous degrees, and school or college work too, so make sure you check your university's rules, as each institution will differ.

CONTRACT CHEATING

This is one of the most serious types of misconduct and is where a student contracts or asks another person to complete an assignment for them. This could be a paid service, such as an essay mill, or it could be asking a friend to write the last bit of your report. Universities are very strict on contract cheating, especially as you can't do it by accident. Many of the essays these contract companies produce are actually given to multiple students and so are flagged by plagiarism detection software. Also, the person marking your assessment will know the usual approach of students on their module and what you have studied (they may even be familiar with the writing style of many of their students), so it's likely they will notice anything odd.

BREAKING EXAM RULES

This one you'll be familiar with from school. Some fairly obvious examples include sneaking answers into exam halls, going to the toilet to check answers on your phone or trying to copy someone else's answers. Depending on your university, exam rules may also include telling staff incorrect information (for example, that you have a medical condition meaning you need to keep leaving the exam hall when, in reality, you don't), leaving the exam room without authorisation, removing the exam questions, or lots of other things you may not consider. These rules are put in place to ensure an equal experience for everyone sitting the exam.

As the way we sit exams changes, especially with an increased number of open-book and online exams, it's important that you are aware of the rules. Make sure you check them well in advance of your exams, as looking at them right before you enter an exam room can cause more stress and you might not always remember everything. It is usual practice for invigilators to make students aware of the rules before each exam, so don't worry if you don't know all the rules before you go in.

AIDING AND ABETTING

Aiding and abetting is when you assist someone in committing academic misconduct. This means helping another student to break exam rules, plagiarise or commit any of the other malpractices outlined by your university. This could include obvious things like writing someone's paper for them, but also areas you may have not considered, such as sharing your work. As with other forms of misconduct, you face penalties whether you intentionally or unintentionally take part in it. For example, if you share your essay with a friend in class, perhaps so they can see an example of good structure, and they then submit your essay (or part of it) as their own, you would be liable. This is one of the main reasons why most universities discourage students from sharing work.

COERCION

Coercion, in an academic and assessment context, is when a student puts pressure on another student, or a staff member, in order to gain an academic advantage. This is probably the rarest of academic misconduct. An example would be trying to influence a staff member in order to receive a good grade or force another student to complete work for you.

FALSE CLAIMS AND CITATIONS

A false claim, also known as falsification or fabrication, is when you alter data or information. This could be a small change to a single data point in order for your graph to be clearer, manipulating results to meet a hypothesis, or it could involve changing details of an experiment or even making up the resultant data. Similarly, false citations arise when you incorrectly reference a text by attributing information to a source that doesn't actually contain that information or when you got the information from a different source. For example, you could reference a fact that you thought was from paper A but it was actually from paper B. You can imagine that, if you don't take careful notes, it could be easy to accidentally do this.

When we engage in any community we agree to the rules of that community, in order for us all to participate within it. Here, we have reflected on some of the rules of the academic community, thinking about how your ethical awareness and integrity will help you approach the significant issue of academic misconduct.

Having explored your agency in an academic community, we will now look at how you are an agent in other communities, considering your other communities at university, but also beyond this. We will especially look at how your agency can help you become a change-maker.

PRACTITIONER INSIGHT

Dr Joanna Thornborough, Senior Policy Adviser, the British Academy

Just by starting out, students are automatically a member of a community – their university. But universities are more complex institutions than that; they are communities within communities – whether that be a halls of residence, for example, a student's subject or department, or even teams or societies they may join. Universities are themselves part of wider communities as well, both in terms of a global community of higher education, but also within their region or their 'place' as well. Some universities will be more directly embedded within a town or city, others on more separate campuses, but students and staff live, shop, work and interact with their place too. It might be helpful to think of a university as part of a complex ecosystem, in which different communities coexist and which make each university a unique place and help to shape each student's individual experience of it.

10.4 RECOGNISING YOURSELF AS AN AGENT OF CHANGE

We have already discussed change a lot in this book in many different contexts, as it shapes every aspect of your university experience. As we are exploring agency and community in this chapter, in this section we are going to look at how you can be an agent of change. This is where you have the opportunity to contribute to your community or different communities to impact the lives of others and make a difference in the world. While this may seem daunting, you don't need to start an organisation or lead a movement to be an agent of change (although you might)! Instead it may entail smaller, yet impactful, actions, including challenging micro-aggressions or joining a society for a cause you are passionate about.

It can seem daunting to have another responsibility put upon you; university is already a time of trying to balance many areas, so you might be concerned that you now have to go and change the world (though your schedule doesn't look like it can accommodate that!). Instead, we are not giving you another responsibility, but highlighting an opportunity available to you when you commence your studies.

Students have had a history of being powerful change-makers, from the Rhodes Must Fall campaign we briefly looked into in Chapter 8, to climate change activists, to countless movements led across countries around the world.

For example, Vanessa Nakate is a climate change activist from Uganda: Vanessa was a First Fridays for Future (the school strike movement lead by Greta Thunberg) activist and founder of the Rise up Climate Movement, which highlights the great work of African activists. Her work includes campaigning to save the Democratic Republic of Congo's rainforest, and finding sustainable energy solutions for schools (United Nations, 2023). She shares her agent of change story in her book *A Bigger Picture: My Fight to Bring a New African Voice to the Climate Crisis.*

ACTIVITY 10.4

Agents of change

- Describe an agent of change you admire (they don't have to be a student). This could be someone known globally, or someone you personally know.
- Why do you find them inspirational?

Being an agent of change involves having a goal and putting that goal into action. This will call upon many of the aspects of skills we have explored in the book, from setting goals to improving your confidence and managing your time.

The goal may be providing more opportunities for you and your family or leading and contributing to social movements. You can effect change within yourself, in your social groups or in your communities. It could be your immediate community, the ones who you see every day, be it in the street, village or hall of residence that you live in. It could be a wider community, such as the community of your university. Or even wider, your city, your country or even the planet.

Agents of change become catalysts in these communities, acting as a positive force that not only generates positive outcomes, but inspires others to do the same. Here, an agent of change does not only think about creating good, but puts their goals into action by aligning their desired outcomes with their intentions.

When becoming a change-maker, it is essential that you are authentic and follow your passions.

It is especially important, if your change is advocating for others, that you ensure you are an ally rather than a saviour. As explored in Chapter 8, this means using your own privilege to highlight challenges faced by others and amplify their voices rather than speaking for them. It also means exploring issues through an intersectional approach, understanding that various aspects of a person's identity will mean that they face challenges differently.

This intersectional approach is essential if, for example, you are challenging educational systems which are difficult for students with specific learning differences to navigate. It's essential to acknowledge that these challenges may be even more difficult for students with specific learning differences who are also students of colour and/or who come from a working-class background. This is because the vast majority of research and policies in this area have focused on white students from middle-class backgrounds (Brissett-Bailey, 2023, p 21).

While it can seem daunting to become agents of change, university provides a fantastic opportunity to undertake these activities. You will have the infrastructure in place to support making change, from libraries and subject matter experts to societies and global networks. University is an excellent place to find likeminded students who have similar passions. These may be your biggest and most useful resource in becoming a change-maker!

In order to be an effective agent of change, you may want to think about the following elements.

- Passion: At the heart of being a change-maker is passion. In order to instigate change, you must have a strong desire for change and commitment to implement action; you will need to be enthusiastic and have dedication to your cause. Without genuine passion it's likely that your change will be superficial or short-lived.

- Research and evidence: Building upon this passion, it's important to research your topic so that you gain a good understanding of the subject area. If you know what the issues are and who they are affecting, you can create appropriate goals. You will also need to have evidence to highlight to others why your goals are important. Furthermore, within this research you can explore what approaches have already been undertaken; perhaps there is an organisation you can join or partner with?
- Resources and logistics: An agent of change will look into making action happen. Part of this is to look at what resources are available to you (this may only be time and skills), and what resources you will need to make change happen from a practical point of view. The logistics of implementing change can be daunting, and sometimes it's best to start smaller and build on your success gradually.
- Confidence: In order to be a change-maker, you have to believe you are one! This sounds slightly clichéd, but it is true. If you don't feel like you can contribute, that you can implement change, then you won't. That is why confidence is an essential part of our agent of change framework.

CHAPTER SUMMARY

In this chapter we explored two interlinking factors: agency and community. These factors will greatly impact your degree, shaping how you engage with your subject, how you navigate your learning and your sense of belonging at university. This chapter explored agency and community in three parts, firstly looking at their foundations, including how ethical awareness and integrity impact them. Secondly, it looked at agency in academic communities, reflecting on discipline identity and how to engage with this community, with a particular focus on exploring referencing and academic conduct. The final part of this chapter explored agency and community outside of your studies, looking at other aspects of your university life and wider society that you could impact, focusing on how you can be an agent of change.

As an engaged learner with a sense of agency, you are well placed to move on to Part 3 of the book, where we will look at how you can recognise and make connections between your skills and, crucially, articulate your skills to others.

TOP TIPS AND NEXT STEPS

- Actively engage in your community in order to have a strong sense of belonging at your university.
- Ensure your note-taking system is clear and well-organised in order to avoid plagiarism.
- Review your university's academic misconduct policy and ensure you understand the different types of misconduct.
- Reflect on what change you would like to see in the world. How can you make this happen?

PART 3

What next?

CHAPTER 11

CONNECTING AND ARTICULATING YOUR SKILLS

CHALLENGES WE EXPLORE IN THIS CHAPTER

In Part 1 of this book, we looked at where you are right now. In Part 2, we asked the question, '*Where are you going and how will you get there?*' and we focused on building yourself as a learner, setting goals, and the important elements of self-leadership, diversity, research mindset, connectivity, and agency and community. Hopefully, as you reflected on Part 2 you thought about the skills you have and those you would like to develop. Part 3 is all about looking forward, thinking about what strengths you are building, making connections between them and thinking about how you can articulate them to others.

Students tend to be busy doing things – you will likely be involved in your academic subject learning, plus some co-curricular and extra-curricular activities too. A challenge that we often see students struggle with is being able to connect what they do with the skills they have developed. This can be especially obvious when students are asked to talk about their skills, for example in interviews and application forms. To help you with this, in this chapter we think about how you can make connections across the skills wheel, reflect on the value of being self-aware and the strengths your combinations of skills give you, practise making connections between your activities and skills, and think about how you can map your activities to skills. We then think about situations where you might need to talk about your skills and examine some ways in which you might effectively do this.

INTENDED LEARNING OUTCOMES

By the end of this chapter, you should be able to:

- practise making connections between the categories of the skills wheel;
- reflect on the strength your own combination of skills gives you and appreciate the value of growing your self-awareness;

→

- practise making connections between activities that you undertake in curricular, co-curricular and extra-curricular settings, and the skills you develop as a result;
- explore the likely scenarios in which you might need to talk about your skills, verbally or in writing;
- understand the importance of being able to illustrate your skills with examples of where you have developed them and how you use them.

FIGURE 11.1: The *University and You* skills wheel

11.1 MAKING CORE CONNECTIONS ACROSS THE SKILLS WHEEL

Let's revisit our skills wheel in Figure 11.1. Throughout Part 2 of the book, we became familiar with the five categories and 20 skills within.

Now let's begin to think about the connections between the skills categories. Instead of just considering how you talk about your skills, let's also think about how your skills talk to *each other*. In other words, how does developing one skill category impact another? How can strengthening skills in one part of the skills wheel boost your development in another part? One thing to recognise in your learning and development journey is that so much is interconnected. For example, exchanging ideas in your tutorial may develop your skills in valuing diversity, but the different perspectives you encounter might also help you to think about the issues you discuss on a global scale. When we dig deeper and look at the specific skills involved, perhaps it was practising your ability to influence and negotiate (connectivity) that simultaneously caused you to develop your cultural appreciation (diversity).

Let's take another example from an academic setting; perhaps dealing with problems you encounter in a research project also develops your ability to stay calm and look for solutions when you're leading others in a group assignment. Here your research skills are strengthening your leadership skills, and the converse can also be true.

An example from an extracurricular setting could be working in a part-time job and choosing to embody the values and follow the workplace policies of the employer – in other words, behaving with integrity – allows you to become better at building networks as others can see that you behave honestly and are trustworthy. Here your agency and community skills are boosting your connectivity skills.

We can move around the skills wheel and make connections between different categories. Figures 11.2–11.4 are diagrams showing overlaps between three category combinations, each giving an example of where skills in one category can help grow skills in another. There are many more than three combinations in total, however! You might want to think of others.

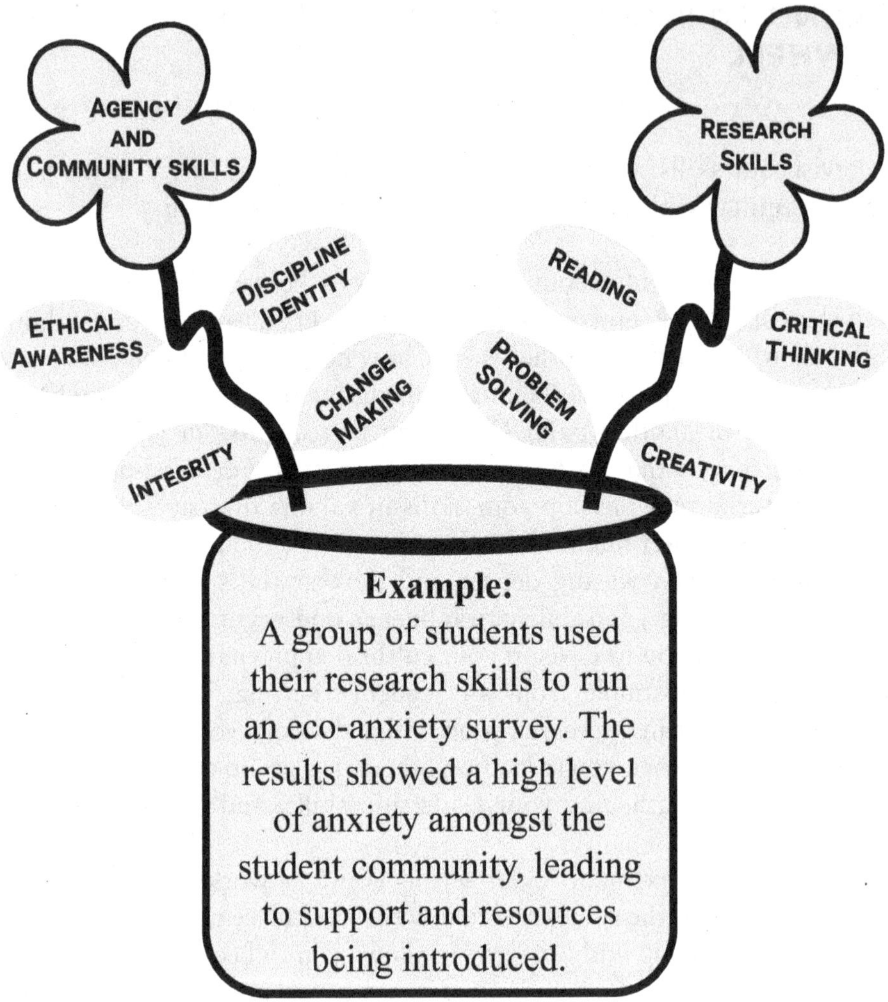

FIGURE 11.2: The overlap of agency and community and research skills

This is an example of how research skills can help a community. Think of an example of when agency and community skills might help develop research skills.

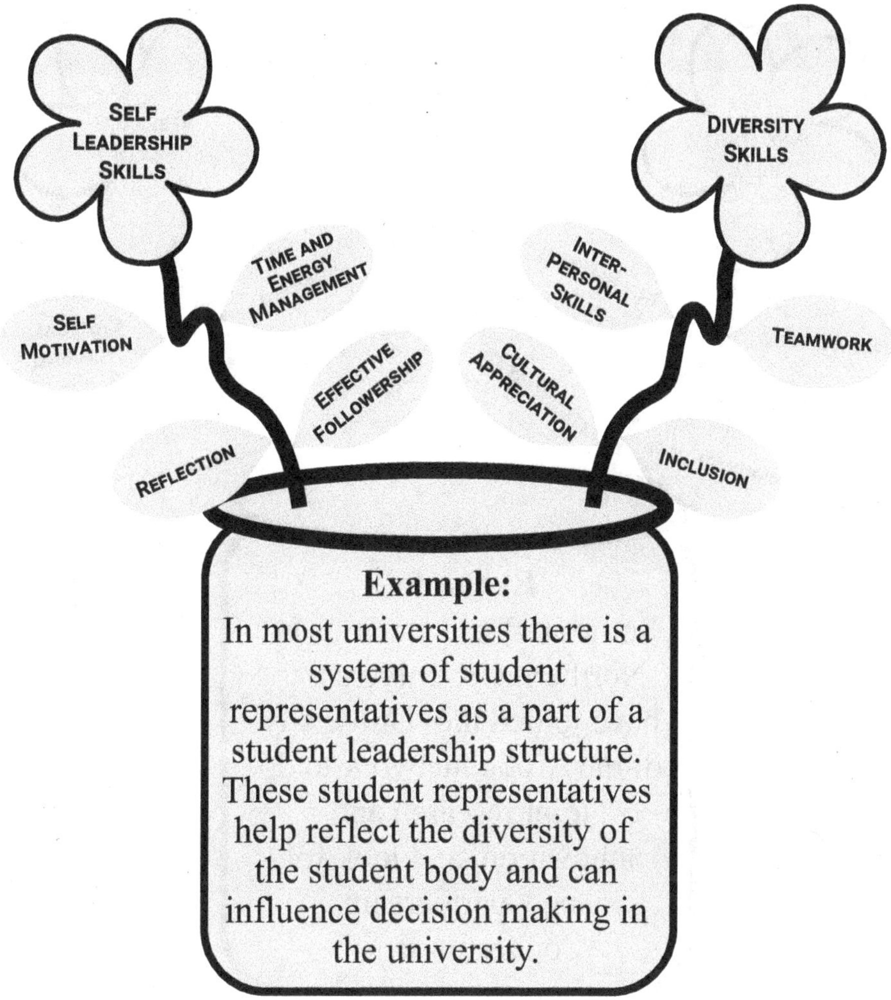

FIGURE 11.3: The overlap of self-leadership and diversity skills

This is an example of how students with leadership skills can help develop diversity skills in themselves and others. Think of an example of when diversity skills might help with leadership skills.

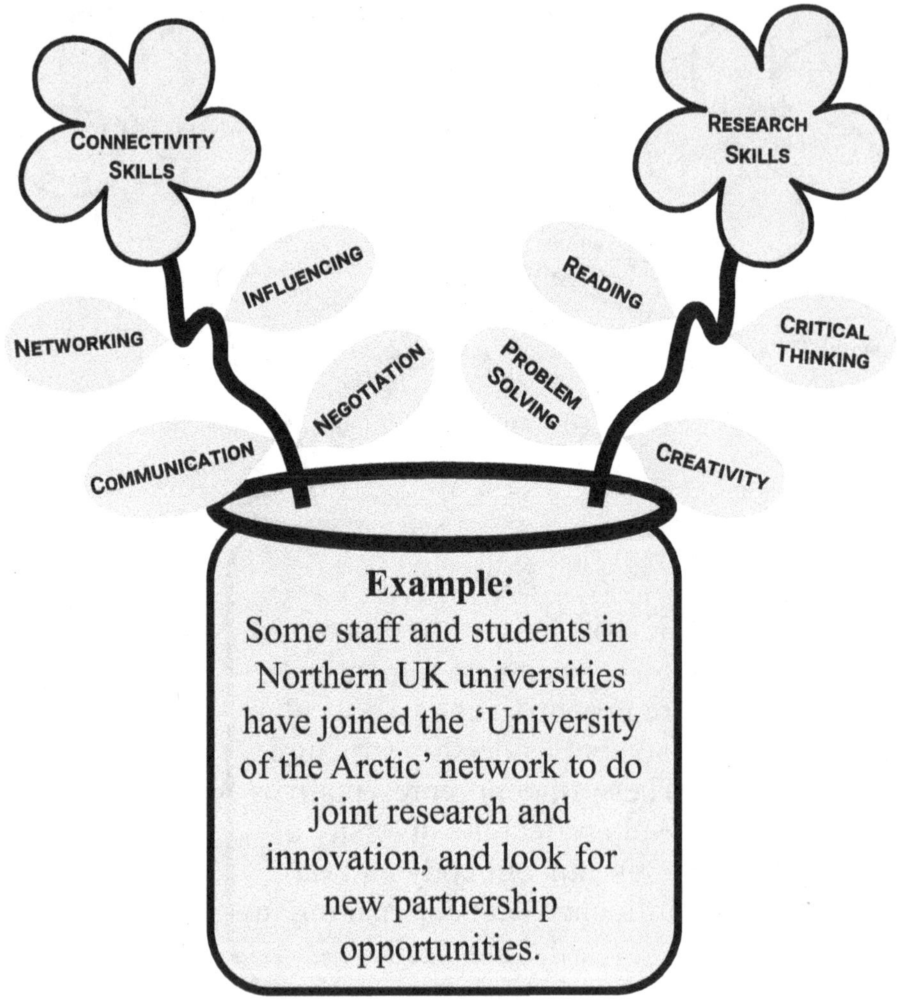

FIGURE 11.4: The overlap of connectivity and research skills

This is an example of how students and staff can use their connectivity skills to develop research skills in themselves and others. Think of an example of when research skills might help develop connectivity skills

It's your turn now! Complete Activity 11.1 to generate one more skills category combination.

ACTIVITY 11.1

Overlapping skills categories

- Complete the blank diagram below by choosing any two of the five skills categories and thinking about how they might relate to each other. Think of some examples to demonstrate this in practice.

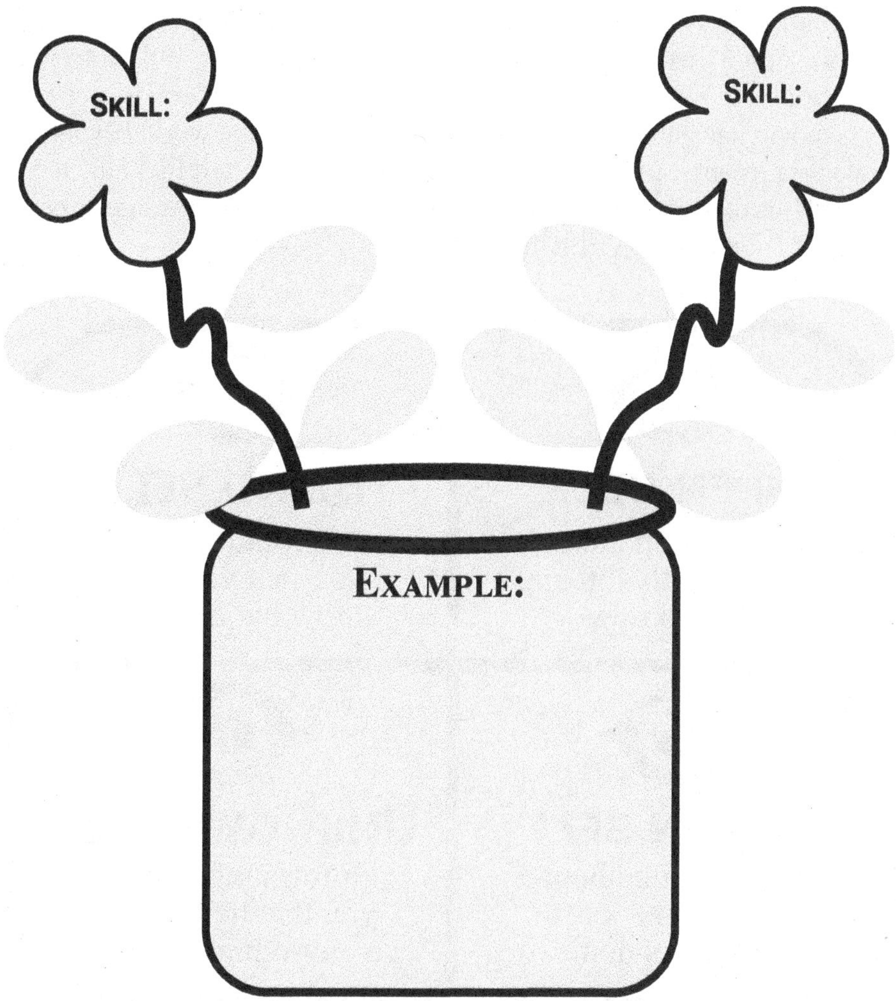

While we've thought about combining and connecting skills categories in general terms, let's now focus in on your awareness of your own combinations of skills and the strengths these present to you.

11.2 THE VALUE OF BEING SELF-AWARE: THE STRENGTH OF YOUR OWN COMBINATIONS

A great place to start is to appreciate the value of being self-aware. Self-awareness allows us to know what we're good at, what we enjoy and what we're comfortable at. It also shows us where we're lacking, what we're afraid of and what we dislike. Self-awareness can tell us where we need to put our resources of time, energy and effort. It can help us seek feedback in the right areas or set goals that will help us move forward. It can help us know what we're looking for in teammates to complement our skill set or allow us to lead with a style that is authentic and motivational to others. Knowing yourself – who you are and what you stand for – is a brilliant gift that will help you navigate through your studies and into the world beyond.

Psychologists Joseph Luft and Harrington Ingham (Luft and Ingham, 1955) were also interested in the value of being self-aware and produced a framework, as seen in Figure 11.5, called the **Johari window**.

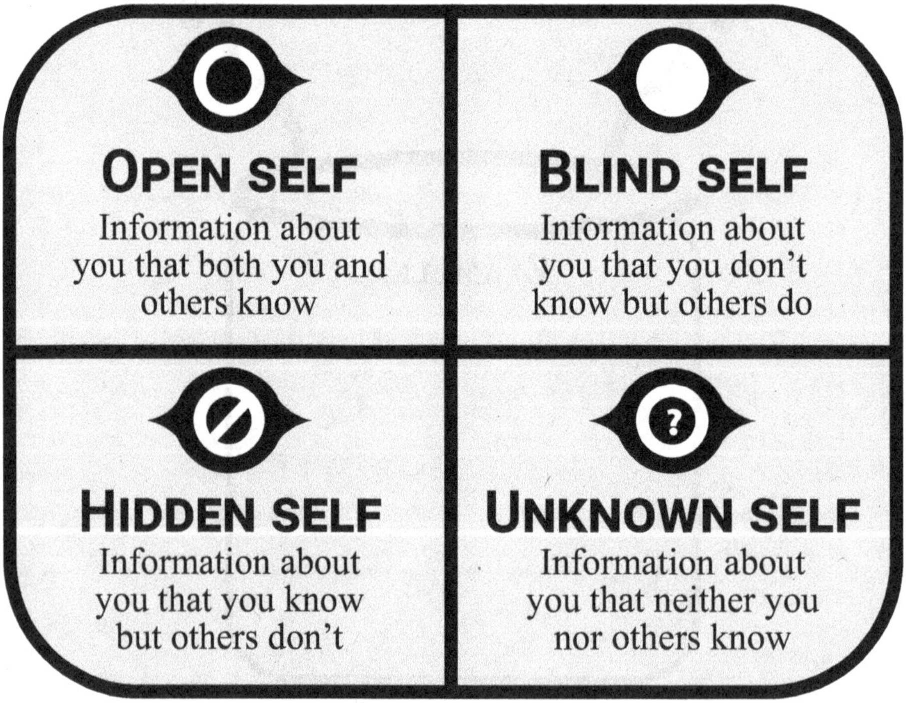

FIGURE 11.5: The Johari window

The Johari window is a four-box framework focused on what is known to self and what is known to others. In the top left, you have 'open self', a box of information about you that is known to both yourself and others. Effectively, this information is in the public domain. For example, you know that Cat works at a university and that she has written a book. Both of these facts belong in this open box. Underneath this is the 'hidden self' box. This is information that she knows about herself, but that you don't. For example, you probably didn't know that she failed her first ever university exam or gets nervous before giving a presentation – that's private, but now that we've told you it's hopped over from the hidden box to the open box. Next to the hidden box is the 'unknown' box. This is information she don't know about herself but nor does anyone else. She likes to think this is where her untapped talents are. Perhaps she is an excellent accordion player, only she's never picked one up in her life. This box is ripe for exploration. Lastly, there is a really interesting box called the 'blind' box. In this box there is information that you don't know about yourself, but that other people know about you. For example, perhaps you have picked up that Cat uses the word 'great' too much – until someone told her, she was completely oblivious.

Jo and Harri wanted us to make our open box bigger. Imagine adjusting the inner frame of the diagram as you see it in front of you now. What would happen? To make the open box bigger you would have to shrink the blind and hidden boxes to compensate. To do this you would have to disclose more information about yourself, and have other people share their observations of you. You might also want to shrink the unknown box – to find out more about yourself through having new experiences.

Therefore, in order to grow our self-awareness we have to try new things and seek feedback from others. Both of those things can be a bit scary, but hold great (argh, said it again!) rewards. Think about how you can take opportunities at university to help you learn about yourself, and think about how you can get some feedback from others. You will certainly get feedback on your academic work, but you can ask your friends and peers for feedback about other aspects of yourself too: What was their first impression of you? What words would they use to describe you? What do they think are your best attributes? Which areas do they think you lack confidence in?

As you become more self-aware, you'll also become more familiar with the bits of yourself that you might not like so much. Your shortcomings, your weaknesses, the aspects of your character you might not be proud of. That's okay. Everyone has elements that they are not happy with. Sometimes these weaknesses are the flip sides of our strengths – we can't have the strength without the weakness. Maybe you have an excellent ability of being organised all the time? It might mean you have a built-in weakness of not being spontaneous and following opportunities. Your strength of being a good listener? It could mean that you can be very quiet and are rarely the first to speak. Your weakness of sometimes being unfocused? It means that you might be able to make unexpected connections and be fruitfully creative. See? You often can't have strengths without weaknesses and vice versa.

Our diversity of strengths and weaknesses will be impacted by neurodiversity too. You might be aware that you process information and learn differently to others. There are an increasing number of students who are aware that they are neurodiverse and perhaps are studying with conditions such as ADHD, autism, dyslexia, and others. Like any diverse characteristic, this will give you strengths and weaknesses for you to be aware of. Perhaps you find your ADHD provides you with bursts of energy, spontaneity and hyperfocus, which can either be a strength or a challenge depending on the context. Perhaps your dyslexia results in you being able to think in an unorthodox way and generate imaginative solutions to problems, but also brings challenges around reading, writing and spelling. It might be that your autism allows you to possess a very high level of attention to detail and ability to retain facts, but makes understanding some social interactions trickier. Your neurodiversity will be uniquely yours, and the more you learn about yourself and understand your behaviour, the stronger your self-awareness becomes.

You can work on linking your self-awareness with self-acceptance and self-compassion: accepting that you have flaws, accepting that you're a work in progress and will make mistakes, and cutting yourself some slack. Being kind to yourself, as we saw in Chapter 3 on resilience, is something to practise regularly.

THE STRENGTH OF YOUR OWN COMBINATIONS

At the start of this chapter we looked at three combinations of skills categories, and you added a fourth in Activity 11.1, but there are several others we haven't looked at in depth. Re-imagine the skills wheel as being like the famous London tube map, where the categories are different coloured train lines (Figure 11.6). In a number of places the lines cross over, with stations at the intersections. You can combine any categories you like and think about the relationship between them. Each of these crossover points provides some fertile soil where skills can grow, intertwine and benefit each other.

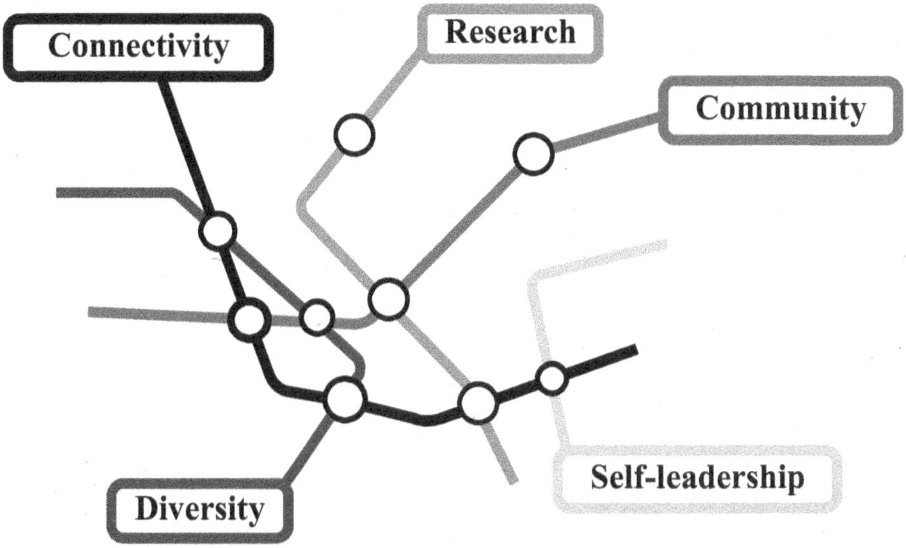

FIGURE 11.6: A 'tube map' example of skills categories intersecting

When you completed your skills wheel at the end of Chapter 5, you were left with your very own shape, we called it a 'splodge', which laid out where you rated your skills currently and where you wanted to develop them in the current year. Look back at that picture: what were the two categories that you were most developed in overall? Perhaps it was a combination that has already featured in this chapter, but it might well be different.

ACTIVITY 11.2

Your own skills category combination

- Write down the two categories you feel you are most developed in. How does each of the categories benefit the other? What does this combination give you? Write your reflections in this box.

We've been focused on the category level, but what about if we think about different combinations of skills *within* the categories? How about we look at our list of 20 skills, and pair some up. Have a go – pick any two at random. We could go for problem-solving and networking, or integrity and creativity, or reflection and teamworking, or any other of 187 combinations. Each pair of skills that you connect might spark something that makes you appreciate the combination. One might help you develop the other in a deeper or more valuable way. Take the pairings we just listed.

- Problem-solving and networking: Building a network might help you solve problems – think of the power of crowdsourcing – or being curious about solving problems might help you build a network. This pairing helps each other.
- Integrity and creativity: Having integrity will help you use your creativity for good, rather than finding creative ways to bend the rules, for example! Having creativity may allow you to take a fresh approach and find new ways to think about the relevance and importance of having integrity. This pairing helps each other.
- Reflection and teamworking: Being good at reflection will help you become better at working in teams as you learn from each experience. Being good at team working will give you plenty of examples to reflect on and develop your ability to learn from failure. This pairing helps each other.

No matter which combination you chose, look for the way in which the pair of skills can help each other. Now, instead of picking random combinations, look again at your skills analysis to give you some context. What happens when you pair a skill you're stronger in with a skill you're weaker in? Can you see ways in which your weaker skill could benefit and develop? You are on your way to being a master of skills development. When you start to be able to make connections between your skills with ease, and can see how they begin to support and develop each other, you are becoming very attuned to your holistic skills development, with the potential to be a better learner and get the most from your university education. And if you can articulate these connections too... Well, our work is done.

11.3 PRACTISING CONNECTING ACTIVITIES AND SKILLS

Self-awareness is largely about making connections. You connect experiences you have, things you are told or discoveries you make with your learning. To become good at talking about your skills, you need to become practised at knowing what your skills are and where they have come from. Skills rarely just emerge. They are built and developed and honed over time. Yes, you might have natural talent, but that doesn't always mean that you are naturally skilled. The skilled part takes time and practice.

A good habit to get into is to be alert to the skills you are developing when you take on a new activity. Activities can be big, such as part-time employment, learning how to code or enrolling in a development programme run by your university, or they can be small, such as working on a single assignment, doing some fieldwork as part of your studies or taking a daytrip to a new city by yourself. Being mindful of your ongoing skills development feeds into your self-awareness.

It can be very helpful to keep a record of the skills you are developing. You could keep a notes file on your phone or computer, buy a notebook and keep a list, or take a picture of activities you're involved in and keep a private Instagram account, hash-tagging your skills in each photo. It's up to you! It's really hard to track your skills development in your head, so getting it down into some sort of record that you can review and reflect on regularly is definitely recommended. You can refer back to Chapter 6 for some information about how to practise reflection.

When you are reflecting on activities and thinking of examples of the activities you do, you might find you have a natural tendency to focus on activities that you would consider positive experiences. However, it can often be the activities that we find hard or that don't go smoothly that actually help develop our skills the most. Something you can do to help you reflect on an activity that hasn't gone so well is to borrow from something called **critical incident technique**. This is when you reflect and analyse an incident that has gone very well or very badly and extract some learning from it. Below are some examples of the types of questions you can ask. They won't all be appropriate in all cases, but you might find some that help unlock an 'a-ha moment' for you.

- Were you prepared for it?
- What was your attitude towards it at the beginning?
- Did you do anything differently to how you've behaved in similar experiences in the past?
- Did communication play a factor?
- Was there enough resources/support?
- Is there a trend here?
- How did you prepare?
- When did you realise it was going well/badly?
- What problems did you encounter along the way?
- What was your reaction when things started to go well/badly?
- Were you pro-active in making things better? How?

- What would you do differently in future?
- What was it that was ultimately good/bad?

An activity you can do right now to help understand the connections between your activities and how they caused you to develop is to create a skills map.

ACTIVITY 11.3

Mapping your skills

All you need for this is a large piece of paper (A3 or bigger) or a whiteboard or an online tool that works for you.

- Fold your paper length-ways, or draw a line down your whiteboard, then draw some circles on the left-hand half of the paper/board.
- Without thinking too much about it, try to fill every circle with an activity that you do. If you have a big activity, like a part-time job, you can break it down into smaller components: for example, 'barista at a coffee shop' might become 'serving customers', 'managing stock' and 'training others'. Your activities can be anything – you can draw on examples related to your education, hobbies, work experience, etc. They can be current activities or ones from the recent past.
- Once you feel like you've captured all your recent activities, focus on the second half of the paper/whiteboard. In this section, you're going to draw lots of circles and fill them with skills. These could be skills that an employer is looking for, or you could use our list of skills from our skills wheel. There are 20 of these, introduced in Chapter 5, if you want to use them all!

integrity	team working
change making	interpersonal skills
ethical awareness	influencing and negotiation
discipline-specific identity	communication
time and energy management	networking
effective followership	problem solving
leading others	academic argumentation
self-motivation	creativity
reflection	critical thinking
cultural appreciation	reading and note taking

- Now, begin drawing lines from your activity circles to your skill circles. Draw a line from the activity to the skills you think that activity has helped strengthen. There might be multiple lines from one activity to several skills. You might end up with a very busy map with lines going all over. Step back and take it in.

This activity will hopefully help show you the value of the activities you do, and give you a feel for where your skills are being built. There might be skills that don't have any activity lines attached. That's okay. This will change as your university journey continues or you might want to look out for opportunities to take on activities that will help you in this area. Don't worry though. It would be unusual to have all 20 skills developed at the start of your university journey.

Now that you have mapped your activities to your skills, you have completed an exercise that you can do regularly while you go through university. It can be valuable to do it at the end of each term or year and see those new connections forming! You can take a picture of your map each time you do it to track your progress. Your activities will change over time. That activity you did last year which you might not do any more still helped develop a skill, and you can still use it as evidence in job applications and interviews. It's in the bank and still has value.

You can also do this activity in reverse. Instead of starting with your activities and thinking about which skills have developed as a result, you can start with a list of skills and then map them back to activities you do. This way around can be helpful if, say, you have a list of skills you want to develop or have been given a list of skills it would be useful to have, such as a job description for a role you want! This way round, you'll be creating a bank of examples you can call on to evidence your skills development – exactly what you need to do in an interview or application form.

11.4 WHEN YOU MIGHT NEED TO TALK ABOUT SKILLS

As a student there will be plenty of times when you might need to talk about the skills you have developed. Indeed, you won't have been awarded a place at university without already having had to do this in your personal statement, so you can think of yourself as already having some ability in this area!

JOB APPLICATIONS

The most obvious occasion when you might need to talk about your skills is when you have put yourself forward for a job and want to demonstrate why you are well qualified for the post. As a student you might want to apply for a part-time role alongside your studies, or you might be looking for summer work experience, a placement or internship. Alternatively, you might be applying for a voluntary role in a club or society, or as a student representative. Towards the end of your degree, you might be looking for graduate employment and your first post-university job, or perhaps getting ready for an interview for a higher degree and further study. Whatever the context, the basic requirement of articulating your skills remains. Let's take a more in-depth look at job applications and interviews.

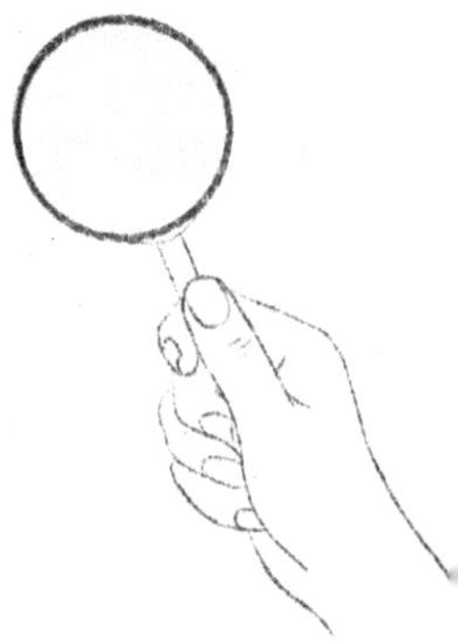

We'll start by switching seats and not thinking as a candidate but as a *selector*. What is the selector, the person (or in some cases, artificial intelligence reader) reading your application or asking you questions in an interview, trying to do? Essentially, they are trying to sift through a pool of applicants and find the candidate who is the best match against the list of skills and competencies that they have identified as being important to be able to do the role. Ideally, they are wanting to go about this process as objectively as possible – not using subjective measures like first impressions or gut feel, but by amassing factual evidence about whether you are well-suited to the role. One of the best ways to amass this factual evidence is to find out about what you've done in the past. If you ever train to become a recruiter, one of the things you might learn is '*the best predictor of how someone will behave in the future is how they've behaved in the past*'. This isn't 100 per cent accurate of course, but selectors will tend towards asking questions about what you've done in the past in certain situations, rather than hypothetical questions about what you might do in the future. So, you can think of your selector as a detective hunting for evidence of your skills, and it's your job to provide that evidence. You have a bright torch that you can shine in exactly the right place for them so they can say, '*Yes! Here it is. This is exactly what I was looking for!*'

Now, this all sounds very easy, doesn't it? The selectors are usually very helpful because they tell you exactly what skills they are looking for (in the advert, job description or in the 'person specification' where they list the skills they are looking for, often in categories of 'essential' or 'desirable' skills), and then you simply show them that you have the skills they are looking for by providing evidence and examples. Yet this is something that even the best and brightest students do not always find easy. Instead of shining their bright torch right at these desired skills, they tuck the skills away in hard-to-find places or disguise the skills by calling them something else, or forget about a requested skill entirely.

So, if we had to summarise a good approach to talking about your skills in an application form or interview, we would say the following.

- Figure out what skills they are looking for ahead of time. A good advert or job description should list them in an obvious way.

- Undertake a skills mapping exercise like the one you did earlier in this chapter to link your activities to the requested skills. Dig deep to try and provide evidence for all the skills they have set out, especially any that are indicated as 'essential'. If you truly don't have any evidence for a certain skill, don't panic. You could state how you intend to develop this in the near future as an alternative.
- List your evidence/examples in a clear way on your application form or cover letter to make it easy for the selector to spot them. A bullet-pointed list might work well. Call your skills by the same name as the advert.
- Predict and practise what the interview questions and answers might be: it's likely that some of the questions in a job interview will be directly asking you for evidence on the desired skills laid out in the advert or job description. So if the advert says that they are '*looking for strong team-workers with good people skills who can work in a busy environment*', you can likely assume that you might be asked for evidence about a time when you worked well in a team, an example of when you have displayed good interpersonal skills and evidence of when you've remained calm under pressure. If you know these questions might be coming, you can have your activity examples to hand and can have rehearsed your answer. This will definitely put you at an advantage.

In undertaking this activity, you will see that giving evidence about your skills isn't the only thing that selectors are looking for. Some recruiters will also assess your skills through using situational judgment tests. These tests will outline a situation you might typically be faced with in the role and ask you to choose the most effective response from a multiple choice selection. Although you won't need to specifically talk about your own skills or activities here, your prior reflection and experience will be helpful in choosing the most appropriate answer. Selectors might also be looking to find out more about your motivation, values and strengths. Why this particular role? Why this particular club, project or organisation? As well as being able to provide evidence about your skills, you also need to be able to explain why your own values are a good match to those of the organisation, what motivates you and why that's a good match for this role, and what strengths you will bring. Reviewing Chapter 6 on self-leadership might be useful here to remind you of these areas.

A useful exercise to undertake before you have an interview is to ask yourself these four questions in relation to the role:

1. What do you do well? (give evidence of skills)
2. What are your greatest strengths? (where are you confident?)
3. What would you like to do in this role and career area? (what are your goals?)
4. Why do you want this role? (where does your motivation come from?)

Before you get invited to an interview, at a much earlier stage of a selection process, it's likely that one of the first ways you will talk about your skills is in writing via a CV; you can find information about writing your CV in Chapter 12.

REFLECTIVE WRITING

Aside from job applications, there are other times in your university experience when you might be called upon to talk about your skills development. For example, when writing reflective reports as part of your academic studies, you might talk about how your experiences have developed your skills, or what skills you needed to use in different situations. A sort of reflective writing you might have to do beyond university is CPD or '**continuing professional development**'. Many careers require people to regularly reflect and document how they are performing and developing in the role, and here too you will need to be able to articulate your skills development. Finally, if you are teaching or coaching, you might have to encourage others to reflect on and articulate their skills development, meaning you must also be able to do this.

Overall, you can begin to see the importance of being ready and able to draw connections between what you do, the skills you use and how they develop. This is an excellent ability to have as a student and into the workplace beyond. When you can easily make connections between activity and expertise, a love of learning follows.

11.5 BACKING UP YOUR SKILLS WITH EXAMPLES

We have already looked at the value of connecting activities with skills development, and vice versa, and thought about when you might be called upon to communicate your skills to others. We have specifically looked at the importance of being able to identify clear examples to evidence your skills development – this is what employers tend to look for.

NEGATIVE AS WELL AS POSITIVE

When talking about our skills, for example as part of a recruitment process, we tend to want to impress, so it's natural to spotlight things that went well for us. However, quite often our skills can be developed to the greatest degree when things don't quite go as we had hoped. It can be useful, then, to think of 'negative' as well as positive experiences when talking about your skills development. In some job interviews you might even find that the selector flips a question to focus on exactly that; it tends to be that candidates will be less rehearsed in this area and give more honest and revealing answers. For example, instead of asking '*Tell me about a time you worked well in a team*', the question might be '*Tell me about a time when you were in a team that* didn't *work well?*' The selector is still looking for evidence about your team-working ability, but they are extracting it in a less obvious way! Here, it's important to focus on why it didn't go well and what you would do differently in the future.

SHOWCASE A RANGE

Another aspect to consider is whether you have a range of examples to demonstrate your skill set. It can be very tempting to use the same example to evidence a range of skills – perhaps you don't feel you have a wide range of activities to draw upon yet, or perhaps this one example is very significant and lends itself to several skills, for example being director of a play, or team leader in a previous job. However, if you can, try to think of a selection of examples to demonstrate the robustness of the skills you have. A skill is likely to be better developed if it's been honed in multiple ways from a variety of experiences.

FRESH AND RELEVANT

Allied to this is thinking about whether your examples are recent and relevant. For example, you might have done a range of activities at school, but if you were still talking about them towards the end of your university degree they would likely hold less weight. It's better if you can draw on examples from the last couple of years – they will have a freshness and relevance that shows that your skill is in good shape. You can think of an analogy of maintaining fitness. It's more advantageous if you can say you did a 5k run last month than talk about a half-marathon you ran three years ago.

DON'T LIE!

You might well be thinking, '*So I need a* range *of examples from a* recent *time period to demonstrate* multiple *skills – I just don't have them!*' That's okay, if so. It would be very unusual if you had quality examples for every single skill you wanted to evidence, and in a recruitment situation it would be normal for candidates to not tick every box of the desired criteria – often employers don't expect candidates to be able to do this. Focus on the skills essential to do the job if you can, and if you find you are missing evidence for one of these, the best thing to do is to explain why you think you would be capable of demonstrating the skill. Let's say the essential skill is leading others but you have not had any experience of being in a leadership position. In this situation you should be honest and say you don't have direct experience (it's never a good idea to lie!) but that you anticipate you have strong leadership skills because you think the elements required for good leadership are strong communication skills, being good with people and resilience, and here are some examples you have of those things. In other words, you could try to break the required skill down into related skills and talk about those instead.

WHAT MADE YOU DEVELOP?

Finally, when you're backing up your skills with examples, don't forget to say how the example grew the skill. It wouldn't be enough to say '*I was a team leader in my previous job, so I have excellent leadership skills*', you need to say *how* being a team leader helped grow these skills. What specifically happened, and what did you learn? The next section will look at how you can do this.

Collecting experiences and developing skills will set you up for whatever comes after your degree. A study by the Department for Education (2019) demonstrated that students who had graduated three years ago thought that the skills they had acquired at university were more important than their degree subject, demonstrating the importance of these transferable skills. In fact, many graduate roles don't ask for a specific degree subject.

PRACTITIONER INSIGHT

Louise Poole, Group People Director, Cala Group Ltd

The specialist skills and knowledge you will gain from your degree are important, but as the world and workplace continue to change through advances in technology and AI, it's more important than ever to focus on the transferable skills you can gain.

The most successful people that I see aren't those with a long list of academic qualifications but those that have honed their transferable skills, particularly interpersonal skills such as being emotionally intelligent, showing strong leadership and being an excellent communicator. I believe I was put in the role I am in not because of my 'technical' skills or academic qualifications, but because of the relationships I had built with the various people around the business. Building those relationships relied on me being able to ask good questions, have good listening skills and communicate effectively. These are skills that you can also build and, more importantly, can take with you in any job that you go to.

The future of work remains uncertain, and we don't know what jobs will exist in the future. You will need to be able to see things at a big picture level while also being on top of the detail. Having a combination of both specialist skills and transferable ones, such as problem-solving, critical thinking and creativity, will help give you the best chance to succeed in your chosen path.

TALKING LIKE A STAR

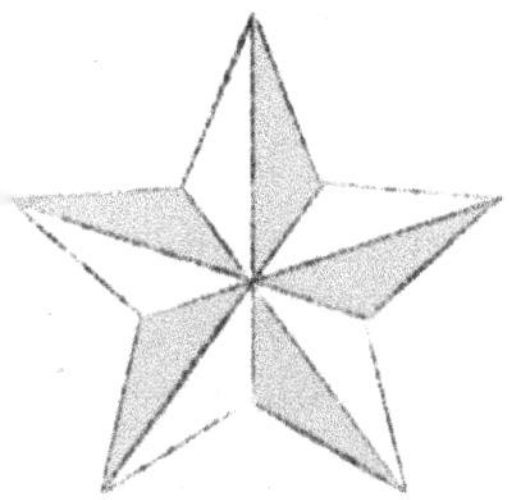

A really good way to talk clearly about your skills is to remember a simple acronym: STAR. This can help you structure a solid answer in an application form or interview, or reflecting on your continuing professional development, or when coaching or teaching others. It's versatile and easy to remember!

- **S** = situation: This is when you give some background about the overall situation. Set the scene, and give some context.
- **T** = task: What was the specific task or tasks that you identified that needed to be done within the situation? Be clear about why this was important.
- **A** = action: Now you talk about what specifically you did to complete the task. You are drilling down into some detail here. At this stage be careful of if and when you are using 'I' or 'we'. It can make a difference if you were the one doing it, or if you were part of a team, or if someone else was doing it and you were just in the vicinity. If you always say 'we' it can sound like you didn't have any individual responsibility – take ownership and use 'I' if you did!
- **R** = result: This is the slam-dunk. What was the outcome? Did you deliver the task successfully? Was there a quantifiable difference at the end of all those actions? What did you learn? What would you do differently next time? This is the section that we find students tend to forget about, but it's the one that can leave the biggest impact.

Let's look at a worked example of the STAR technique. In this scenario the question is '*Can you give me an example of when you have been an effective team worker?*' and the student is reflecting on a time they were working as a group on a university assignment.

SITUATION

....

As part of a university module I was allocated to a six-person team. The team was asked to research a topic and prepare a report and presentation to summarise our findings, and the project was assessed as part of our overall module grade.

TASK

....

We needed to self-manage as a team and allocate the work between us, deciding who would take on which parts of the research and presentations. We were working to a deadline so we needed to manage our time well and create an agreed plan of what would be done when.

ACTION

....

My role was to contribute a section to both the report and presentation. The group experienced some conflict due to differing leadership styles and levels of contribution so I took the approach of staying focused, making the best contribution I could to the task and also providing constructive feedback to a team member about their leadership style.

RESULT

....

The outcome was that we delivered the required outputs on time and that my fellow team member thanked me for the useful feedback. We received positive comments on our work from our lecturer and I became even more effective as a team worker because I used my communication and interpersonal skills productively.

ACTIVITY 11.4

Being a STAR

Now it's your turn. Choose from one of the questions below (or use your own if you like) and practise writing a STAR response.

- Tell me about a time when you worked well under pressure...
- Tell me about a time you demonstrated resilience...
- Tell me about a time you used creativity to solve a problem...
- Tell me about a time you exhibited leadership....
- Tell me about a time you demonstrated integrity...
- Tell me about a time you worked with a diverse range of people...

BLENDING CURRICULAR, CO-CURRICULAR AND EXTRA-CURRICULAR ACTIVITIES

Your co-curricular and extra-curricular efforts are just as important as all your academic work in terms of equipping you with the skill set you will take as a graduate into whatever comes next. Just as pairings of skills can give you more than a single skill alone, so too can the combination of curricular, co-curricular and extra-curricular activities give you more than operating in a single sphere. For example, the time management you develop for getting through your reading list before the next class also benefits the time management you require to make it to sports practice at the weekend. The creativity you use in your hobby art class also feeds the creativity you exhibit in the argument you put forward in your seminar. It's all connected.

If you think of a single skill – pick any of the 20 – consider how you might develop it in all three of the areas – curricular, co-curricular and extra-curricular. There's no expectation that you will, of course. Developing 20 different skills simultaneously in three different ways is a bit much for anyone. But think of how a single skill can be reinforced and strengthened in these different arenas. You can think of it like eating potatoes. Hopefully you like potatoes, but if you don't just imagine for the next 30 seconds you do. Mashed potatoes might be your favourite, but if mash was the only kind of potato you ever had you might get a bit bored of it, or not appreciate it in quite the same way. How about if you got mash one day, and boiled potatoes the next, and then chips at the weekend! They're all the same vegetable and they fill you up in the same way, but they taste, look and feel different. This can be true of developing a single skill in different domains – curricular, co-curricular and extra-curricular. Variety is a good thing.

ACTIVITY 11.5

Developing attributes in multiple ways

- Choose three or four attributes and enter them in the first column of Table 11.1. Now take some time to think about how a student might be able to develop this skill through curricular, co-curricular and extra-curricular activities. The first row is completed as an example.

TABLE 11.1: Listing multiple ways to develop a single attribute

Attribute	Curricular	Co-curricular	Extra-curricular
Oral communication	*Opting to do a presentation as a piece of assessed coursework.*	*Attending a skills workshop run by your careers centre on practising interview skills.*	*Volunteering to give a talk about your subject to a group of prospective students on a visiting day.*

STUDENT INSIGHT

Clara Forbes, sustainable development and geography, second year

The most useful skill that I have developed throughout my time at university is interdisciplinary thinking. As a sustainable development and geography student, our coursework draws on everything from calculating carbon sequestration capacity to evaluating the economic consequences of ageing populations. By learning theoretical methods and practical applications of interdisciplinary thinking, connecting typically distinct fields of study has become second nature in my learning process. Outside of the classroom, I am a member of the 'fashion team' as part of a student-run charity fashion show. My role necessitates a simultaneous awareness of each garment's historical context, environmental implications and physical construction. Both my studies and my experience with the show have fostered real-time critical thinking spanning disparate spheres of knowledge. I believe that developing my interdisciplinary thinking skills will be infinitely useful in both my career and my personal life long after graduating university.

We are nearing the end of our journey through skills development, but we're not quite ready to go yet. There is one final important thing to think about – it's '*what do you do now?*' You know how much we love goal setting and planning! We want to leave you in the best possible shape – ready to get out there and get the absolute most from your university experience.

CHAPTER SUMMARY

This chapter looked at the challenge of being able to recognise how your activities and skills relate. We looked at some intersections of different skills categories and encouraged you to think about if and how combining skills generates additional value. We specifically looked at examples in three combinations (agency/research, leadership/diversity, connectivity/research) but there are others too. We also looked at the importance of being self-aware, and explored how you can widen the 'public' box in the Johari window to help with this. You were invited to reflect on your own skills combinations and think about what strengths these combinations give you. We thought about how you can use your self-awareness to make connections between the activities you undertake and the skills you develop, and you created your personal skills map to demonstrate this. We then looked at when you might need to articulate the skills you develop in applications and continuing professional development, using the STAR framework to help you provide examples. Finally, we thought about the multiple ways you can develop a single skill, and examined the different environments of curricular, co-curricular and extra-curricular as a way to develop a skill through multiple different activities.

TOP TIPS AND NEXT STEPS

- Stay open to opportunities to develop skills through a mixture of curricular, co-curricular and extra-curricular activities.
- Be open to asking for and receiving feedback from others.
- Look out for projects and opportunities you could get involved in that use and develop combinations of skills.
- Reflect on combinations of skills you feel strong in, and think about what value this gives you.
- Map your activities against your skills periodically to keep track as to how they are developing.
- Practise talking about the evidence that demonstrates your skills.

CHAPTER 12

WHAT DO YOU DO NOW?

CHALLENGES WE EXPLORE IN THIS CHAPTER

When you read a book such as this one, which aims to help you reflect on how you approach your university experience, the challenge is how to make your insights and learning stick and how the book can keep helping you after you finish the last page. This final chapter draws on the learning you have taken from the book so far and reflects on how you can best implement your new knowledge. We explore the key elements you need to consider to advance the plans and goals you have set in this book. Specifically, we examine the importance of perspective, self-awareness and confidence, before looking at how you can best implement your plans with optimal support in place for success. Finally, we reflect on the progress you have made so far over the course of working through this book.

INTENDED LEARNING OUTCOMES

By the end of this chapter, you should be able to:

- instil a sense of perspective on where you are in your development journey;
- recognise the value of being self-aware in terms of developing skills;
- value confidence in your own skill set;
- be aware of the importance of self-compassion and maintaining mental and physical well-being while at university;
- check that you have an achievable development plan in place, with identified first steps;
- articulate your skills in CVs and applications;
- be aware of additional sources of support as you develop your skills;
- appreciate the progress you have already made in terms of developing your skills.

12.1 TAKE A STEP BACK

Well, how do you feel? You don't have many pages left to get through. We've been on a journey together. You might have read this book in a single sitting, or you might have taken many days, weeks or even months to make it to Chapter 12. Perhaps you have dipped in and out of the chapters that interested you. Whichever route you took, we have all made it here to the end anyway. See, it's a bit like skills development – there are many ways to get to where you are.

So, since we're all here, this feels like a good opportunity to catch our breath and take stock, to think about how to make the very best of your university experience. An opportunity to think about what the most important messages are that you can take from this book, and to be confident that you know what the next steps are and that you are capable of nailing them. Whether or not you believe it just yet, you have amazing potential.

The first step in this last chapter is to get some perspective on where you are going now. Quite often, when you're in the middle of something, it can be hard to see the bigger picture. In a sense, you can't see the forest for the trees. It might be that this book has put you slap-bang in the middle of lots of trees. We have looked at lots of individual skills – 20 in fact – and now it is time to zoom out a bit.

Our first bit of perspective is to zoom out to place our 20 skills back into their five categories: diversity, self-leadership, connectivity, research, and agency and community. Hopefully, these categories now seem familiar to you from Part 2 of the book, and you can think and talk about how you relate to them. As you move onwards through university and beyond, these categories will evolve and move with you. Perhaps some will become more or less important than others; perhaps you will want to swap one of the categories out for a new one you come across on your journey. Nothing stays the same forever, so it's right to treat the skills and categories we've looked at as those that might be useful to you right here, right now, but to build in a bit of flexibility for later.

If we zoom out from our skills to categories and then out again, what might we be looking at now? We might be looking at you as a student, at the time and place you find yourself in. Perhaps you're right at the start of your university journey, or only a little way through it, and are trying to best equip yourself for what's to come. It might be that you've come to this book mid-way through your degree or even nearing the end of your university studies. That's fine too – hopefully you've been able to extract something that is helpful for whatever your next step might be, be that further study, entering or returning to the job market, taking some time out, volunteering or starting a business. Whichever the scenario, you are still part of a community within a university, with classes to attend, things to learn, and demands on you to produce outputs that reflect your knowledge and skills.

But what if we zoom out again? Beyond skills and categories and being a student. Here we might be looking at you as a human within a changing world. Someone who is grappling with all the bigger questions of life and trying to envision and build a future that you want to live in. The world is changing quickly in some ways, and slowly in other ways, and there will likely be aspects of this that you are anxious and upset about, and other aspects that bring you hope and optimism that a better, more just world is possible. You are an individual who is changing in a world that is changing, and that gives plenty of uncertainty and potential at the same time.

What if we try to zoom out even further, beyond you as a changing human in a changing world? Here we might find the unchanging core of you – the parts of you that stay constant over time. Those founding experiences that will be part of you throughout life, the personality traits and characteristics that make you *you*, and perhaps those key values that will influence your outlook and direction in life. If you have a sense of who you are at this zoomed-out level, that is great! Good for you. All those skills that we have been talking about in this book won't affect who you are at this macro level, but they may well help you navigate through your life experiences and get the most from them.

FIGURE 12.1: Zooming out from your skills to being a human in a changing world

It can be useful zooming out from time to time, especially if it's very busy and stressful in the forest, surrounded by all the trees. If you're feeling a sense of urgency or that you have somehow fallen behind on your journey to fulfil your potential at university, please try not to worry. Being able to step back and look beyond can be very helpful in providing a sense of calm and perspective.

ACTIVITY 12.1

Zooming out

Try and zoom out into the 'you as a student' zone. Think about how you have developed and grown since starting university. Here are three questions to help you to reflect.

- What are the main ways you think you've changed in the past year?
- What skill/s do you see the biggest development in, and what helped with this?
- What advice would you give to someone who is 12 months behind you in your timeline of starting university?

12.2 RECOGNISE YOUR INCREASED SELF-AWARENESS

As well as putting some things into perspective, now is also a good time to recognise that you likely have a little bit more self-awareness at the end of this book than you did at the beginning. This book asked you questions, invited you to complete activities, and gave you tools to try things in maybe a slightly different way to what you had done before.

You will likely have a *bit* more self-awareness because, let's be honest, you might have skipped some of the activities, or given some sections more attention than others; it's perfectly normal to not give all of yourself all of the time. That said, hopefully over the course of the book you were able to do some really valuable thinking – about who you are, where you're going and how to get there, as well as thinking about thinking and the importance of reflecting regularly. You can dip back into Chapter 6 if you need a framework for how to do this. Being able to reflect well, and use the learning you derive from it, is one of the secret weapons of being an effective student, and of being a human in a changing world.

One of the only constants of your future will be change, and how you deal with that will be improved by the ability to reflect well as you experience that change. It will help you keep up with things as they shift around you. The activity we have done in this book – comparing where you are now with where you want to get to – is one that you will likely do many times over in the course of your career and wider life because you will often want to get to somewhere new, somewhere there will be no handbook for.

So, as you can see, this reflective process of asking '*where am I going?*' is an iterative one. The skills you need when you get to where you want to be will vary, and you will also need to reflect on what skills you have and which you might have to develop. Being self-aware about your current and required levels of skills is also a good life-habit to get in to. You might have finished this book and done all of the activities and feel pretty confident about the level of some of your skills, but you'll never get to say 'done' and tick a skill off and forget about it. Your self-awareness will be required to keep maintaining and developing them as needed.

STUDENT INSIGHT

Rose Overton, medicine, second year

The most important skills strength I have is communication. Your communication abilities influence so much of your life and student experiences, from discussions with friends to emailing your lecturers and, particularly as a medical student, understanding non-verbal cues. For many students like me, university is the first time we've lived independently and

→

away from home, and being able to develop good communication skills is critical to being able to create your own support network and express how you are feeling.

Living independently and recognising when you may need this help requires another important skill: reflection. As a student, it's important to check in with yourself and question whether your experience is truly what you want to get from your time at university, as reflecting on your behaviour, feelings and goals helps you recognise whether you need support or if you can change anything yourself to enhance your experience. I consider my ability to reflect one of my strengths, and use it to help me maintain a work–life balance, and I've also used our school's support team for advice during exam season when I noticed I was struggling with my mental health.

12.3 BE CONFIDENT IN YOUR SKILLS STRENGTHS

Hopefully one of the outcomes of having increased self-awareness is that you now know what your strongest skills are and have a sense of your own skills profile. We want you to be confident in your skills strengths.

We will hazard a guess that your combination of skills is really interesting. You have developed them over time in a range of different ways and you use them in different activities for different ends. Collectively, they help describe you. Hopefully, you appreciate the uniqueness your own combination brings. Quite a lot of students we speak to feel that they are in competition with other students – for grades, opportunities, postgraduate options or jobs. Sometimes this perception is accurate, and sometimes not so much. We hope understanding your skills profile helps with that a bit because it gives you variety, meaning that your profile can set you apart from others. There's no 'right' skills profile to have as you go through university, so in that regard there is no competition around developing yours.

Some of the confidence in your skills strengths comes from being able to articulate them to others, and you can revisit Chapter 11 if you need to remind yourself about this. Hopefully, this book has given you the confidence to back yourself – the experiences you have had are valuable, and now you know how to extract that value and tell it to others.

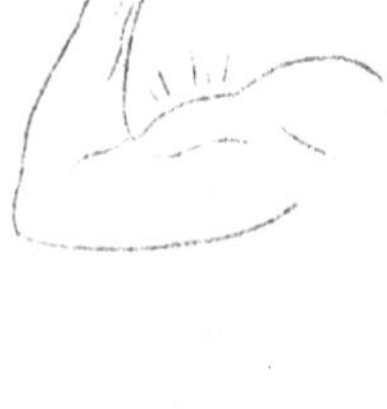

Take stock of the skills you have practised and are strongest in. You won't have become strong in a particular skill without having had a range of experiences in which you used and practised that skill. No one else had all those exact same experiences. No one else processed and interpreted those experiences in the exact way you did. The relationship you have to your skill is unique! This is something to derive confidence from and feel good about as you move through the world.

12.4 BE KIND TO YOURSELF

Having confidence and feeling good about yourself can be hard to maintain all the time. Like everyone, students can struggle with their mental health, and the rate of students reporting mental health issues has never been higher (UCAS, 2021). Part of this tells a good story – students are more comfortable than ever talking about their mental health and seeking help and support at an early stage, but part of this reflects the fact that university comes with challenges and struggle built into it, and it won't always be smooth sailing.

When setbacks come – and they will – you can choose to interpret them as experiences which help to grow your skill set. When things are hard, as you move through them your resilience and problem-solving ability grows. Perhaps so too does your communication (as you tell a friend) or your networking (as you explore the support services your university offers) or your energy management (as you navigate through the situation) or your reflection (as you take learning from experience).

If you are able to adopt and practise a growth mindset as you encounter difficulties, so much the better. This growth mindset will hold, especially when you encounter failure. Have we already mentioned that Cat failed her very first exam at university? At the time she felt terrible. She had a fixed mindset about it. She thought it meant that she wasn't intelligent enough to be at university and felt ashamed to tell people. This was not the case. She failed her first exam because she didn't put enough effort into learning the course materials and revising properly. But here's where she has to be kind to herself. She didn't put enough effort in because she was a bit overwhelmed by being away from home for the first time and not being used to learning in a different way from school and not knowing what help and support was available. Looking back now, she'd quite like to tell herself that lots of people haven't got it all figured out in their first year at university, and here is a book that will help you with revision, and you're going to do absolutely fine in the re-sit.

And of course, it's not just mental health; physical health is also something you need to be mindful of, and kind to yourself about, at university. Your body and physique might undergo change as you experience student life, and you should look for ways to treat your body kindly and give it the rest, nutrients and hydration it needs. Time and time again at university, you will get metaphorically bumped and bruised as setbacks occur, confusion surrounds and failure happens.

Having perspective when failures occur can be helpful. Building on the perspective we gained at the start of this chapter, it can be useful to zoom out when failure happens. A good technique is to think 10×10×10×10. Ask yourself: will this be important to me in 10 minutes? 10 weeks? 10 months? 10 years? In the case of Cat's exam failure, it definitely seemed like it would be important in 10 minutes and

10 weeks, but she could see that in 10 months' time it would be behind her, and a new university year would have started, and in 10 years' time it wouldn't matter at all.

So a single failure is rarely a disaster that can't be recovered from, and the better able you are to cut yourself some slack and move on, the better you will be at taking what value you can from failure (in some cases, this is lots) and using it to make you a better student. Some of the students we work with have a very high bar for what constitutes 'failure'. For some individuals, anything less than a first-class grade will be perceived as such. They are driven by extrinsic motivation – the grade someone else will give them. If you think this might be a pattern you follow too, perhaps have a think about taking a wider perspective. Personally, we'd rather students not have a first-class degree and be able to have a wide range of skills they can articulate well than have a first-class degree and not much else to speak of.

Skills development won't go in a straight line – there will be steps forward and missteps; you will try things that will backfire; you will think you're an expert in something and then find out you have a way to go. This is all quite normal and part of navigating changing you in a changing world.

PRACTITIONER INSIGHT

Jill Stevenson, Director of Student Life, Robert Gordon University and Chair, Association of Managers of Student Services in Higher Education (AMOSSHE)

I would encourage all students to take care of their health – mental and physical – so that they are in the best possible position to enjoy life in all its wonderful variety! We don't tend to have the same energy or enthusiasm to live life to the fullest and grab opportunities for growth, development and fun if we are not feeling at our best, so we owe it to ourselves to look after our bodies and minds.

There are some basics that I would recommend to all students; firstly, make sure you get enough sleep. I can't over-state the importance of sleep for positive mood and energy. Try to get outside and enjoy nature as much as you can. Spend time connecting with friends or with animals. A walk with a dog and a friend is always such a tonic to me! Little steps and changes make all the difference. You don't need to train for a marathon … sometimes just 20 minutes walking in the park is enough to lift mood massively. Finally, if you're not feeling great, speak to someone about it. I can guarantee that people care about you and want to help, so never be afraid to ask for help.

12.5 PLAN YOUR SKILLS DEVELOPMENT OVER THE NEXT MONTH, TERM, YEAR

We've just spoken about being kind to yourself when failure inevitably happens, but that is different from setting yourself up for failure and welcoming it in! It is good to be as pro-active as you can and put plans in place to set yourself up for success. It's best not to leave things to chance and think it will all fall into place. It will fall into some kind of place, but not the best place you could have prepared for.

So, planning is good, and you learnt all about how to do this well in Chapter 5. In fact, you might already have a set of SMART short-, medium- and long-term goals ready to go. If not, now is still a good time to set some goals as to how you want to develop your skills from here. You can use your skills analysis from the end of Chapter 5 to help you prioritise the skills you want to develop. You may have identified activities and opportunities you want to get involved with that will help you develop your chosen skills over the coming term and year.

A plan isn't the same as a goal: a goal is the end point, but a plan helps explain how you are going to get there. For each of the skills you want to develop, you can think about *how* you might be able to do that, what the individual tasks and steps might be, and do a bit of sequencing and scheduling in the creation of your plan.

Once your plan is in place, don't forget to review your progress against it regularly. If you are able to build in review points at the end of each term and year, then that can be a very rewarding process. You can see the areas in which you've grown and developed, and if there are areas where your development hasn't been as much as you had hoped, then it simply gives you a chance to re-set, tweak your goal (perhaps the R in SMART for 'realistic' wasn't quite right), and go again.

There are few things more satisfying than being conscious of your own skill level improving. To get to a review point and be confident that you have a set of academic, professional, digital or even entrepreneurial skills that have developed over the preceding weeks and months can be very motivating. This experience of hitting the goals you set for yourself (even partially) should be celebrated. You can then use that motivation and confidence to set new goals, and so the positive cycle continues.

Now that you have your plan, we want it to have the best chance of happening. We've already mentioned using SMART to make sure that your goals are as specific, measurable, achievable, realistic and time bound as they can be, which hopefully means that your plan is built on some strong foundations. However, there are other things you can think about and put in place to give it that extra little boost towards success.

One thing is to loop back to our change equation that we first met in Chapter 5: $D \times V \times FS > R$ (dissatisfaction multiplied by vision multiplied by first steps must be greater than the natural resistance against the change). Do you remember how we can use it to form a really clear vision of where we want to get to, and also have clarity around why we don't want to stay exactly as we are? Having this in place can give your plan some motivation and momentum, but it is the third element of the change equation that might really help us with making our plan more likely to happen – first steps.

Having a first step to get your plan up and running is really important. We have seen lots of excellent plans (including some of ours) never make it out of the starting gate because they seemed too daunting, or because it felt like they could be started tomorrow or next week. There wasn't a tantalising, easy, first step just waiting there, asking to be taken.

Think about your own personal plan for your skills development. Is there a first step identified that is easy and immediate, and will make you feel good about completing it? If so, yes! We're excited for you. If not, why not put one in place right now? Let's say, for example, that one of the goals you've identified is to develop your communication skills, and part of your plan is to take a workshop in how to give a good presentation later this term. You know that this is something the Careers Centre at your university delivers. So far, so good, but there isn't really an easy first step here. We can envision a situation where this plan sits, unstarted, because signing up for a presentation workshop is something that can be done next week or next month, and next week or next month never comes because there's always too much to be getting on with today. How about you identify your easy first step as being '*google when the next presentation skills workshop is running and sign up for it*'. That will take you five minutes, max. You could be completing the sign-up form in less time than it takes to read this paragraph ... you get the idea.

ACTIVITY 12.2

First steps

- In Table 12.1, identify a possible first step to start your plan/s for skills development. The final column should have a time commitment in it no later than one week from today!

TABLE 12.1: Identifying first steps to get your plan started

My plan relates to the skill of ...	The first step I have identified is ...	The time I estimate it will take is ...	I will do this ...
Communication	*Google and sign up for presentation skills workshops*	*<5 minutes*	*Now!*

Another strategy you can employ to make your plan more likely to happen is to build in some external accountability. Suddenly a well-intentioned plan floating around the back of your brain can become much more front and centre if you have told someone else what you are doing and by when. Having someone who you are committed to reporting back to, who you don't want to have to go back to with an excuse, can give you that extra motivation you've been looking for.

You can also take steps to hold yourself accountable – an easy step is to have your goal or your first step visible – somewhere where you see it regularly. This could be a sticky note on the fridge, or a note that you have in your phone, or even an email that you send to yourself so that it's in your inbox every time you go in there. In fact, there's a nice website called 'future me' that lets you send emails to your future self. This can be great for giving yourself a nudge towards your goals: www.futureme.org.

Once you've made yourself as accountable as possible, it's time to reach out and think about external accountability on top. If your development plan concerns an academic skill, perhaps you can let a tutor or lecturer know, and commit to checking back in with them at the end of term to let them know how you've developed. Perhaps you have a course-mate or flat-mate that you can make an arrangement with to act as each other's Plan Accountability Officers. Perhaps there's a friend or family member who can take on the role of chief nudger? Whatever works for you, it's a great idea to put this in place and increase the likelihood of your plan happening.

Lastly, as your first step has been taken and your external accountability person is helping you progress your plan towards your goal, don't forget that there will be bumps and wobbles along the way. This isn't a reason to quit on your plan, but simply to tweak and readjust it and keep going. In the midst of the bumping and wobbling there might well be a tendency to employ some faulty thinking – you might catastrophise or do some 'all or nothing' thinking, for example. Your increased self-awareness should allow you to catch yourself doing this, and the ABCD model in Chapter 3 gives you a framework for pushing back against and dispelling some of these unhelpful thoughts.

You have the tools now to devise a good plan, make it happen and stay on course when things might not be going entirely smoothly. It's over to you now. You can do this.

12.6 SPOTLIGHT YOUR SKILLS: CREATE A GOOD CV

Now that you have a skills development plan, and have increased the likelihood of making it happen, it's also important that you are ready to talk about the skills you develop. We saw in Chapter 11 when you might be called on to articulate your skills in interviews and reflective writing. Having a good CV is a shop window for you to display who you are and what skills you have.

You don't have much space – ideally just one page, no more than two – and you have to get the most relevant information across concisely. You should aim to have a 'default CV' that you edit for each role you go for – adding and highlighting the information most appropriate for the role. This could be adding a skills section aligned to the skills required for that specific role, or showing that your values and interests are matched to the organisation.

Your university Careers Centre will likely have guidance about how best to write a CV, as well as templates you can look at, or even a CV-checking service where you can take your CV along and get some advice. You can also find some nice templates for CVs online or use free software such as Canva, and AI tools are becoming increasingly common for creating a basic CV for a particular post that you can then edit. It's not too early to create your default CV at the start of your university journey, and this is something you can do right now.

Most CV layouts will have a 'skills' section, where you can list the specific skills you have which are relevant to the job you're applying for, with some brief detail about how you acquired each skill. There are also other sections in a CV where you will show where you developed your skills. For example, there could be an education section where you can list your modules or qualifications, and a 'Work experience' or 'Volunteering' section where you can list any employment experience or volunteering you've undertaken and positions of responsibility you've held. You might also choose to list some of your hobbies and extra-curricular activities in a separate 'Interests' section.

Think back to when you undertook the skills mapping activity in Chapter 11. There you started with activities and mapped them across to skills. When writing a CV, you can now do the opposite – you are starting with the skills that you know are important for the role, and here you can provide the evidence through listing the sorts of activities that have developed these skills in you. As we've already discussed in this book, you will have developed your skills through curricular, co-curricular and extra-curricular activities so it is likely that you will list a mixture of these in your CV too. Employers in particular are often keen to see what students have done outside of the classroom, so those co- and extra-curricular activities are worth showcasing.

The best thing to do is to have a look at some of the resources provided by your own university's Careers Service, and have a go at creating or refining your CV. You can do this as part of Activity 12.3.

12.7 INVESTIGATE ADDITIONAL RESOURCES

It's not just me who wants you to succeed at university and in your skills development journey. Your university wants this too. Let's say this one more time just so there's not even a tiny bit of doubt about it: your university wants you to succeed. And they will have so much in place to help you with this. For starters, they might have their own set of graduate attributes or skills in place that they will want to help you develop, which may or may not be similar to the ones in this book. They will most likely also have their own set of online resources, workshops and opportunities that you can explore to help you develop them.

Your university will also have its very own teams of people whose job it is to help you develop your career or support you through your studies. These are people who are highly trained and experienced in working with students, and who want to help you. It's quite surprising then that there seem to be lots of students who don't access the help that's available and waiting for them, or they do but not until things have become overwhelming and they're facing something of a crisis situation. Because you have made it all the way to Chapter 12, we suspect that you are a more pro-active sort who isn't bad at taking responsibility for your own development. When it comes to your employability or making sure your well-being is in a good place, sooner tends to be better, so do reach out and avail yourself of the services offered or at the very least be aware of what they are.

ACTIVITY 12.3

Student and career support

- Take half an hour to explore the support your university has in place for you. Learn about the Careers Centre at your university, and the resources and services in place for supporting your well-being and studies. This can sometimes be called Student Services or Student Life, and should be linked to from your university's student homepage.

In terms of support for your skills development journey, we can even go wider than your own university. Other universities tend to be quite good at sharing, and often post resources and information online without password protection. You can use your research skills, developed in Chapter 7, to see what other universities can offer in relation to skills development. You can use your networks, outlined in Chapter 9, to tap into resources and opportunities that might develop your skills. Additionally, there are professional bodies related to your subject area or possible career sector that often have 'resources', 'events' or 'opportunities' sections on their websites.

Similarly, lots of graduate employers are so keen to help you develop your skills (particularly ones that they would like you to use in their organisation) that they have resources and even online workshops that they offer for free in particular skills. There is also a range of government initiatives that might be worth exploring or researching further. Here's a starting point: www.gov.uk/career-skills-and-training.

Finally, the people who went before you – the alumni from your university – are often kind enough to want to give back to the generation of students who follow them, and so you might be able to connect with them on LinkedIn or through organised schemes your university might run. The people around you on your course – other students and staff members – are also invested in you and want you to do well. In sum, there are so many people who want you to reach your potential in developing your skills that you always have someone you can turn to for advice and guidance.

12.8 THE GOOD NEWS IS YOU'VE ALREADY STARTED

We have some good news for you: you have already started on your skills development journey. With some incredible efficiency, you have read this book and if you've done the activities as you went along then you have already made a tremendous start. By virtue of the fact you have read this book, it shows that you are interested, that you want to do well at university, that you are willing to invest time in yourself, and that you know you are worth spending time on. These are all excellent positive indicators.

If you've taken the time to do the activities and reflect on your skills as you go, then an even more powerful amount of work has been done. You have a skills analysis, set of goals and a plan, and the knowledge of how to develop these skills. You know how you can articulate these skills and how you can think about skills in conjunction with one another. You are a skills wizard! All you need to do now is keep going.

ACTIVITY 12.4

Summary of learning

- In this final activity, write down one thing you've taken away from each of the preceding 11 chapters.

Chapter 1: You as you are: becoming the student you want to be

Chapter 2: You as you change

Chapter 3: You in a changing world

Chapter 4: You as a student: how to build a learner

Chapter 5: Your skills and attributes

Chapter 6: Your self-leadership

Chapter 7: Your research mindset

Chapter 8: You and diverse universities

Chapter 9: Your connectivity

Chapter 10: You, agency and community

Chapter 11: Connecting and articulating your skills

CHAPTER SUMMARY

This chapter built on your previous learning throughout the book. It aimed to help with the challenge of how you can continue to develop your skills into the future. It revisited some of the important elements of building sound plans, and encouraged you to have a development plan in place to implement after you finish the book. We particularly looked at the need for clear first steps to help get plans up and running, and the helpfulness of tracking plans and building in accountability. We also looked at the importance of keeping perspective, getting back on track when plans derail, and utilising the additional resources and support we have open to us. Finally, we completed one last reflective activity to revisit each chapter in the book to collect the points you found most salient. We reminded you that your skills development journey is well underway, by virtue of you reading this book at all. There are lots of other resources that can help you with what we've covered in this chapter: for CV writing the Prospects website is a good place to start, there are apps that can help you set and track goals (eg accomplishapp.com), and podcasts, books and presentations about the value of learning from failure (the How to Fail podcast, for example).

TOP TIPS AND NEXT STEPS

- Expect setbacks and failures as you develop your skills.
- Having a SMART plan in place to develop your skills over the short, medium and long term can really help you work towards your development goals.
- Develop your knowledge about the sources of support available to you, and draw on them when you need them.
- Teaching some of your skills in which you feel confident to others can help strengthen them even more.
- Think about how this book has changed you, even in a small way.
- Practise reflection regularly to continue to develop a strong self-awareness.
- Put down this book and enact a first step to continue your skills development journey.

GLOSSARY OF KEY TERMS

TERM	DEFINITION
Academic misconduct	Intentionally or unintentionally breaking rules to gain an unfair academic advantage.
Academic skills	A range of skills that are required for being effective at studying an academic discipline.
Active attention	Focusing on something in a deliberate or conscious way.
Active listening	Consciously paying attention to the person who is speaking to you and showing them you are listening.
Adaptable	Being able to deal with new situations.
Agency	A person's capacity to formulate preferences and develop strategies to realise those preferences.
Analyse (analysing)	Methodically examining, dissecting, and scrutinising a topic to interpret it and create new conclusions.
Argumentation	A reasoned claim made using evidence.
Attention residue	When part of your attention is still on the task you were doing previously instead of the one you are doing currently.
Authentic leadership	To adopt a leadership style that projects your true self.
Autonomous	Being accountable to yourself and taking responsibility for your actions.
Bloom's Taxonomy of Learning	A model that sets out six different levels for learning: remembering, understanding, applying, analysing, evaluating and creating.
Challenge zone	When you undertake activities that are beyond your comfort zone and push you to learn new things.
Coaching	A form of development that helps you achieve goals by reflecting on specific options and identifying actions.
Co-curricular	Related to what you learn alongside your academic studies but which isn't part of your credit-bearing course.

→

TERM	DEFINITION
Cognitive science	The study of how the brain processes information, solves problems and learns.
Cognitive switching penalty	When the brain uses effort to process moving between tasks, resulting in lost efficiency.
Comfort zone	Includes activities that you feel at ease completing. These are individual to each person.
Community	A group of people who are linked together by having things in common such as location, characteristics or values.
Conference	An event where a group of people gather to discuss and learn about a topic they have a shared interest in.
Connectivity	The capacity for making connections.
Contingency time	An additional block of time added into a project plan to provide for any unforeseen slippages.
Continuing professional development (CPD)	Ongoing learning that you undertake as part of your professional development.
Core concerns	A framework of five identified emotional dimensions that may be salient in a negotiation situation.
Critical incident technique	A process for reviewing significant events to extract information and learning.
Curricular	Related to what you learn in your academic studies.
Danger zone	When you feel so overwhelmed you struggle to undertake activities.
Deep learning	Absorbing information as connected facts and analysing it to create new meaning.
DiSC profile	A framework that lays out four distinct workplace styles of behaviour: dominance, influence, steadiness and conscientiousness.
Discipline identity	A set of associations that make you feel part of your academic subject.
Diversity	Recognising and understanding the ways in which people are different.
Emergent leadership	When environmental conditions promote a particular person taking a leadership role.

GLOSSARY OF KEY TERMS

TERM	DEFINITION
Emotional intelligence	The ability to read and be aware of your own emotions and the emotions of others.
Evidence	Facts, data or information (which are reliable), used to prove or verify a claim.
Extracting learning	Drawing understanding from an experience that will help you in a similar situation in the future.
Extra-curricular	Related to what you learn outside of your studies.
Extrinsic motivation	Deriving motivation from external factors such as a fixed deadline that must be met.
Fixed mindset	The notion that your success or failure is pre-determined.
Flexibility	The ability to modify plans in order to meet a goal or overcome change.
Gantt chart	A tool for helping map out which tasks in a project happen when.
Gibbs' reflective cycle	A framework to help people reflect on a past experience or event, comprising descriptions, feeling, evaluation analysis, conclusion and action planning.
Global mindset	Having a thinking style that is conscious of the interconnectedness of the world.
Global network	A collection of connected people around the world who have a shared interest.
Graduate attributes	A set of skills that students have the opportunity to develop while at university.
Grit	Perseverance towards a long-term goal.
Growth mindset	The belief that, with hard work and effort, abilities can be developed.
High-impact breaks	A purposeful break between activities that you gain enjoyment from.
Hypothesis	A proposed theory or claim used to explain a problem or answer a question.
Imposter syndrome	A belief, due to a lack of confidence, that you're a 'fraud' and not good enough.
Inequalities	The unfair treatment or circumstance of an individual or group.

→

TERM	DEFINITION
Intersectionality	The framework which highlights multiple strands of prejudice or privilege faced by individuals. It looks at the multifaceted factors that make up identities, which cut across gender, national identity, class, sexuality and race and the privilege in certain identities.
Intrinsic motivation	Deriving motivation from internal factors such as the joy of overcoming a challenge.
Inverted pyramid	A way to structure a piece of writing, with the most important information first.
Johari window	A framework to conceptualise open, blind, hidden and unknown elements of yourself.
LinkedIn profile	Your individual profile outlining your professional experiences on a global networking site.
Metacognition	Thinking about thinking, reflecting on the process you undertake and having a critical awareness of your learning.
Mindset	A series of beliefs or thoughts held by an individual or group that impacts behaviour.
Motivation	Your drive and reasons to achieve goals.
Negotiation	A conversation in which there is a difference of opinion that is aimed at reaching an agreement.
Neurodiversity	Differences between people with regard to how their brain functions.
Outcome goals	Goals focused on achieving a particular result or outcome.
Overconfidence	Overestimating your abilities.
Passive attention	Focusing on something in an involuntary or reactive way.
Peer reviewed	Evaluation of work undertaken by those working in the same field to check its quality.
Perfectionism	The feeling that your work, or sadly sometimes you, will never be good enough, as you are aiming for everything to be exact.
Performance effort	The energy you invest in doing the skill when it is needed.
Performance goals	Goals focused on achieving a particular level of performance.
Plagiarism	Presenting someone else's work or ideas as your own.

TERM	DEFINITION
Pomodoro technique	A technique to block time into manageable chunks when doing an activity.
Prioritisation	Deciding what is the most important thing to focus on at a particular time.
Process goals	Goals focused on achieving a well-executed process.
Procrastination	The active avoidance of doing a particular task.
Professional skills	A range of skills that are required for being effective in a professional setting such as a workplace.
Referencing	Acknowledging the source you found your information from. There are many different types of academic referencing styles such as Harvard, APA and MLA.
Reflection	The act of reviewing a past experience or event with the aim of deriving learning from it.
Research	Systematically investigating a topic.
Research mindset	Having a thinking style that applies research skills, such as spotting opportunities and applying creativity to new scenarios.
Resilience	The ability to respond in a positive way to adversity.
Scheduling	Putting a timeline against a sequence of steps or tasks in a project plan.
Self-confidence	A belief in yourself. Thinking about your own ability, predicting your future performance and reflecting on your past tasks.
Self-leadership	The ability to self-organise and lead yourself by influencing your own thoughts and behaviours.
Semester	A period of the academic year, usually when teaching takes place. For example, semester one at university may run from September to December. Also known as 'terms'.
Sequencing	Putting the steps required for a successful task or project in the most sensible order.
Shared leadership	The act of leadership being shared between team members, each person taking responsibility for their own part in achieving the team goal.
Skills	An ability, or knowledge to undertake a task.
Skills framework	A model which lays out a suggested range of skills that you might find useful to develop.

⟶

TERM	DEFINITION
SMART acronym	A framework for helping set achievable goals: specific, measurable, achievable, realistic, time-bound.
Society	A group of students who share a specific interest, formalised through a university club.
Surface learning	Absorbing information as stand-alone facts.
Time management	The ability to prioritise tasks and plan and allocate your effort and time appropriately.
Transferrable skills	An ability that can be used in multiple situations.
Unconscious bias	An unintentional judgement towards an individual or group of people that affects our decision making.
Values	A set of underlying factors that you place high importance on which influence your attitudes and behaviours.
Working memory	Our short-term memory, which has limited capacity to hold information.

REFERENCES

CHAPTER 1

Bhopal, K (2020) Confronting White Privilege: The Importance of Intersectionality in the Sociology of Education. *British Journal of Sociology of Education*, 41(6): 807–16.

Locke, E A and Schattke, K (2019) Intrinsic and Extrinsic Motivation: Time for Expansion and Clarification. *Motivation Science*, 5: 277–90.

Robbins, M (2017) *The 5 Second Rule: The Surprisingly Simple Way to Live, Love, and Speak with Courage: Transform Your Life, Work, and Confidence with Everyday Courage*. New York: Post Hill Press.

Young, V (2011) *The Secret Thoughts of Successful Women: Why Capable People Suffer from the Impostor Syndrome and How to Thrive in Spite of It.* New York: Crown Publishing Group.

CHAPTER 2

Dweck, C (2017) *Mindset – Updated Edition: Changing the Way You Think to Fulfil Your Potential.* London: Robinson.

NHS (2024) Every Mind Matters Mental Wellbeing Tips. [online] Available at www.nhs.uk/every-mind-matters/mental-wellbeing-tips/self-help-cbt-techniques/tackling-your-worries (accessed 20 May 2024).

Pink, D H (2010) Drive. *The Surprising Truth About What Motivates Us.* Edinburgh: Canongate.

CHAPTER 3

Beylier, P and Molinari, V (2022) COVID-19 in Europe and North America. In Molinari, V and Beylier, P (eds) *COVID-19 in Europe and North America: Policy Responses and Multi-Level Governance* (pp 1–25). Berlin: De Gruyter Oldenbourg.

Dehaene, S (2020) How We Learn. *The New Science of Education and the Brain.* London: Allen Lane.

Ellis, A (1991) The Revised ABC's of Rational-Emotive Therapy (RET). *Journal of Rational-Emotive and Cognitive-Behaviour Therapy*, 9: 139–72.

Epstein, D (2020) *Range: How Generalists Triumph in A Specialized World.* London: Macmillan.

Hickman, C, Marks, E, Pihkala, P, Clayton, S, Lewandowski, E, Mayall, E, Wray, B, Mellor, C and van Susteren, L (2021) Climate Anxiety in Children and Young People and Their Beliefs About Government Responses to Climate Change: A Global Survey. *Lancet Planetary Health*, 5: 863–73.

CHAPTER 4

Koriat, A and Bjork, R A (2005) Illusions of Competence in Monitoring One's Knowledge During Study. *Journal of Experimental Psychology: Learning, Memory, & Cognition*, 31: 187–94.

Office for Students (2024) National Student Survey 2023. [online] Available at www.officeforstudents.org.uk/advice-and-guidance/student-information-and-data/national-student-survey-nss (accessed 20 May 2024).

Roediger III, H, McDaniel, M A and Brown, P C (2014) *Make It Stick*. Cambridge: Harvard University Press.

Weinstein, Y, Sumeracki, M and Caviglioli, O (2018) *Understanding How We Learn: A Visual Guide.* London: Routledge.

CHAPTER 5

Beckhard, R and Harris, R T (1977) *Organizational Transitions: Managing Complex Change.* Reading, MA: Addison-Wesley.

Bloom, B S (1956) *Taxonomy of Educational Objectives Handbook 1.* New York: Longman.

Curry, O S, Mullins, D A and Whitehouse, H (2019) Is It Good to Cooperate? Testing the Theory of Morality-as-Cooperation in 60 Societies. *Current Anthropology*, 60(1): 47–69.

DiSalvo, D (2020) Why we Fail to Reach Goals: Our Brains Begin with One Focus, but Closing the Deal Requires Another, Study Suggests. [online] Available at www.forbes.com/sites/daviddisalvo/2020/02/24/why-we-fail-to-reach-goals-our-brains-begin-with-one-focus-but-closing-the-deal-requires-another-study-suggests (accessed 26 May 2024).

Doran, G T (1981) There's a Smart Way to Write Management's Goals and Objectives. *Management Review*, 70(11): 35–6.

Feverbee (2022) A Community Consultancy. [online] Available at www.feverbee.com (accessed 26 May 2024).

Fogg, B J (2019) *Tiny Habits: The Small Changes That Change Everything.* Boston, MA: Houghton Mifflin Harcourt.

Guest, D (1991) The Hunt Is on for the Renaissance Man of Computing. *The Independent*, 17 September.

Petrova, M (2018) We Traced What It Takes to Make an iPhone, from Its Initial Design to the Components and Raw Materials Needed to Make It a Reality. [online] Available at: www.cnbc.com/2018/12/13/inside-apple-iphone-where-parts-and-materials-come-from.html (accessed 26 May 2024).

CHAPTER 6

Covey, S (2020) *The 7 Habits of Highly Effective People.* London: Simon and Schuster.

Duckworth, A (2013) Grit: The Power of Passion and Perseverance. TED. [online] Available at: https://www.ted.com/talks/angela_lee_duckworth_grit_the_power_of_passion_and_perseverance?subtitle=en (accessed 22 August 2024).

Duckworth, A (2016) *Grit: The Power of Passion and Perseverance.* New York: Scribner.

Dunn, L B, Iglewicz, A and Moutier, C (2008) A Conceptual Model of Medical Student Well-Being: Promoting Resilience and Preventing Burnout. *Academic Psychiatry*, 32(1): 44–53.

George, W (2003) *Authentic Leadership: Rediscovering the Secrets to Creating Lasting Value*. San Francisco, CA: Jossey-Bass.

Gibbs, G (1988) *Learning by Doing: A Guide to Teaching and Learning Methods*. Oxford: Oxford Brookes University.

Goleman, D (1995) *Emotional Intelligence: Why It Can Matter More Than IQ*. New York: Bantam Books.

Kelley, R (1988) In Praise of Followers. *Harvard Business Review*, 66: 142–8.

Kouzes, J and Posner, B (2023) *The Leadership Challenge: How to Make Extraordinary Things Happen in Organizations*. 7th ed. San Francisco, CA: Jossey-Bass.

Marston, W M (1928) *Emotions of Normal People*. New York: Harcourt, Brace.

Newport, C (2018) *So Good They Can't Ignore You: Why Skills Trump Passion in The Quest for Work You Love*. London: Piatkus.

CHAPTER 7

Krathwohl, D (2002) A Revision of Bloom's Taxonomy an Overview. *Theory Into Practice*, 41(4): 212–18.

Li, L (2022) Reskilling and Upskilling the Future-Ready Workforce for Industry 4.0 and Beyond. *Information Systems Frontiers*. https://doi.org/10.1007/s10796-022-10308-y

World Economic Forum (2020) The Future of Jobs Report 2020. [online] Available at: www3.weforum.org/docs/WEF_Future_of_Jobs_2020.pdf (accessed 20 May 2024).

CHAPTER 8

The Access Project (2023) About Us. [online] Available at: www.theaccessproject.org.uk/about-us (accessed 20 May 2024).

REFERENCES

Agarwal, P (2020) *Sway: Unravelling Unconscious Bias.* London: Bloomsbury Sigma.

Bhambra, G K, Gebrial, D and Nicole, K (2018) Introduction: Decolonising the University? In Bhambra, G K, Gebrial, D and Nişancıoğlu, K (eds) *Decolonising the University* (pp 1–18). London: Pluto Press.

Boring, A, Ottoboni, K and Stark, P B (2016) Student Evaluations of Teaching (Mostly) Do Not Measure Teaching Effectiveness. *ScienceOpen Research*: 1–11.

British Council (2013) Culture at Work. [online] Available at: www.britishcouncil.org/research-policy-insight/policy-reports/culture-work-intercultural-skills-workplace (accessed 20 May 2024).

Byrne, E and Clarke, C (2020) *The University Challenge.* London: Pearson Education Limited.

Carter, P (2018) The First Women at University: Remembering 'the London Nine'. *Times Higher Education*, 28 January. [online]. Available at: www.timeshighereducation.com/blog/first-women-university-remembering-london-nine (accessed 20 May 2024).

Centre for Intersectional Justice (2023) What Is Intersectionality. [online] Available at: www.intersectionaljustice.org/what-is-intersectionality (accessed 1 August 2024).

Combahee River Collective (1977) Combahee River Collective Statement. [online] Available at: www.blackpast.org/african-american-history/combahee-river-collective-statement-1977 (accessed 20 May 2024).

Connell, R (2019) *The Good University: What Universities Actually Do and Why It's Time for Radical Change.* London: Bloomsbury Academic.

Crenshaw, K (2022) *On Intersectionality: Essential Writings.* New York: The New Press.

Goleman, D (2020) *Emotional Intelligence: Why It Can Matter More Than IQ.* 25th Anniversary Edition. London: Bloomsbury Publishing.

Hartley, P and Dawson, M (2010) *Success in Groupwork.* London: Palgrave Macmillan.

Hofstede, G (2022) Why Is Culture So Important? [online] Available at https://geerthofstede.com (accessed 1 August 2024).

Meyer, E (2014) *The Culture Map*. New York: Public Affairs.

Mitchell, K and Martin, J (2018) Gender Bias in Student Evaluations. *PS: Political Science & Politics*, 51: 648–52.

O'Connor, A and Robbins, E (2024) *Colonised Minds: Narratives That Shape Psychology*. London: Sage

Office for National Statistics (2023) Gender Pay Gap in the UK: 2022. [online] Available at: www.ons.gov.uk/employmentandlabourmarket/peopleinwork/earningsandworkinghours/bulletins/genderpaygapintheuk/2022 (accessed 20 May 2024).

Reynolds, A and Lewis, D (2017) *Teams Solve Problems Faster When They're More Cognitively Diverse*. Harvard Business Review [online]. Available at: https://hbr.org/2017/03/teams-solve-problems-faster-when-theyre-more-cognitively-diverse (accessed 20 May 2024).

Rhodes Must Fall, Oxford (2018) *Rhodes Must Fall*. London: Zed Books.

Seethamraju, R and Borma, M (2009) Influence of Group Formation Choices on Academic Performance. *Assessment and Evaluation in Higher Education*, 34: 31–40.

Smith, J, Robinson, S and Khan, R (2022) Transgender and Non-Binary Students' Experiences at UK Universities: A Rapid Evidence Assessment. *Equity in Education & Society*, 1: 18–31.

Sutton Trust (2023) Our Priorities. [online]. Available at: www.suttontrust.com/our-priorities (accessed 20 May 2024).

Tomlinson, S (2019) *Education and Race from Empire to Brexit*. Policy Press Scholarship Online.

Universities UK (2019) Black, Asian and Minority Ethnic Student Attainment at UK Universities: #ClosingTheGap. [online]. Available at: www.universitiesuk.ac.uk/sites/default/files/field/downloads/2021-07/bame-student-attainment.pdf (accessed 20 May 2024).

University of Kent (2023) Effective Allyship. [online]. Available at: www.kent.ac.uk/equality-diversity-inclusivity/effective-allyship (accessed 20 May 2024).

Willets, D (2017) *A University Education*. Oxford: Oxford University Press.

CHAPTER 9

Crompton, C J, Ropar, D, Evans-Williams, C V, Flynn, E G and Fletcher-Watson, S (2020) Autistic Peer-to-Peer Information Transfer Is Highly Effective. *Autism*, 24(7): 1704–12.

Duarte, N (2012) The Secret Structure of Great Talks. TED. [online] Available at: www.ted.com/talks/nancy_duarte_the_secret_structure_of_great_talks (accessed 26 May 2024).

Duhigg, C (2024) *Supercommunicators*. New York: Penguin Random House.

Fisher, R and Shapiro, D (2005) *Beyond Reason: Using Emotions as You Negotiate*. New York: Penguin Books.

Shannon, C E and Weaver, W (1949) *The Mathematical Theory of Communication*. Urbana, IL: University of Illinois Press.

Spiceworks Ziff Davis (2022) Workplace Communications in 2022 and Beyond. [online] Available at: https://swzd.com/resources/workplace-communications-in-2022-and-beyond (accessed 26 May 2024).

CHAPTER 10

Brissett-Bailey, M (2023) *Black, Brilliant and Dyslexic: Neurodivergent Heroes Tell Their Stories*. London: Jessica Kingsley Publishers.

Hack, K and Knight, C (2023) Higher Education in the Era of AI. *Advance HE*, 9 February. [online] Available at www.advance-he.ac.uk/news-and-views/higher-education-era-ai (accessed 20 May 2024).

Larsen-Freeman, D, Driver, P, Gao, X and Mercer, S (2021) Learner Agency: Maximizing Learner Potential. [online] Available at www.oup.com/elt/expert (accessed 20 May 2024).

Pedler, M L, Willis, R and Nieuwoudt, J E (2022) A Sense of Belonging at University: Student Retention, Motivation and Enjoyment. *Journal of Further and Higher Education*, 46: 397–408.

Smyth, L, Mavor, K I and Gray, L (2019) Not Just Who You Are, but Who You Were Before: Social Identification, Identity Incompatibility and

Performance-Undermining Learning Behaviour in Higher Education. *Journal of Community and Applied Social Psychology*, 29: 474–91.

Smyth, L, Mavor, K, Platow, M, Grace, D and Reynolds, K (2015) Discipline Social Identification, Study Norms and Learning Approach in University Students. *Educational Psychology*, 35: 53–72.

United Nations (2023) Vanessa Nakate. *Office of the Secretary-General's Envoy on Youth*. [online] Available at: www.un.org/youthenvoy/vanessa-nakate/ (accessed 20 May 2024).

University of Oxford (2023) Plagiarism. [online] Available at: www.ox.ac.uk/students/academic/guidance/skills/plagiarism (accessed 26 May 2024).

Waldman, L, Sharp, J and Woods, J (2019) Disciplinary Identities and Other Barriers to Advancing Interdisciplinary Working. *PLOS*, 4 June. [online] Available at: https://everyone.plos.org/2019/06/04/interdisciplinary_authorship (accessed 23 June 2022).

CHAPTER 11

Department for Education (2019) Graduate Choices in Post-Education Jobs and Careers. [online] Available at: www.gov.uk/government/publications/graduate-choices-in-post-education-jobs-and-careers (accessed 26 May 2024).

Luft, J and Ingham, H (1955) The Johari Window: A Graphic Model of Interpersonal Awareness. *Proceedings of the Western Training Laboratory in Group Development*. Los Angeles, CA: University of California, Los Angeles.

CHAPTER 12

UCAS (2021) Starting the Conversation: UCAS Report on Student Mental Health. [online] Available at: www.ucas.com/file/513961/download?token=wAaKRniC (accessed 26 May 2024).

INDEX

INDEX

INDEX

INDEX

INDEX

INDEX

INDEX